SINGING'S GONE GLOBAL

EXPLORING CHRISTIAN SONGS

Steve H Hakes

Books by this author:
Vampire Redemption
Vampire Extraction
Vampire Count
Vampire Grail
Vampire Shadows
Israel's Gone Global
Prayer's Gone Global
Singing's Gone Global
The Word's Gone Global
Revelation's Gone Global
Revisiting The Pilgrim's Progress
Revisiting The Challenging Counterfeit
Salvation Now and Life Beyond

Singing's Gone Global

Exploring Christian Songs

~

Steve H Hakes

Copyright © 2016 by Dr. Steve H Hakes

All rights reserved. No part of this publication may be reproduced, stored in a retrieval system, or transmitted in any form or by any means—for example, electronic, photocopy, recording—without the prior permission in writing from the copyright owner. The only exception is brief quotations in printed reviews. All lyrics are property and copyright of their owners, and those provided here are for educational purposes only.

Paperback ISBN: 978-0-9957013-1-1
Hardback ISBN: 979-8-4490512-8-8
Kindle ISBN: 978-0-9957013-0-4
V251128113159

Scripture quotations marked...
CEB are taken from the Common English Bible®, CEB® Copyright © 2010, 2011 by Common English Bible.™ Used by permission. All rights reserved worldwide.
CEV are from the Contemporary English Version. Copyright © 1991, 1992, 1995 by American Bible Society, Used by permission.
ESV are taken from The Holy Bible, English Standard Version. Copyright © 2001 by Crossway Bibles, a division of Good News Publishers. Used by permission.
NCV are taken from the New Century Version®. Copyright © 2005 by Thomas Nelson, Inc. Used by permission.
NET are taken from the NET Bible®. Copyright ©1996-2016 by Biblical Studies Press, L.L.C. Used by permission.
NIV are taken from the Holy Bible, New International Version® NIV®. Copyright © 1973, 1978, 1984, 2011 by Biblica, Inc.® Used by permission of Biblica, Inc.® All rights reserved worldwide.
NKJV are taken from the New King James Version®. Copyright © 1982 by Thomas Nelson, Inc. Used by permission.
NLT are taken from the Holy Bible, New Living Translation. Copyright © 1996, 2004. Used by permission of Tyndale House Publishers, Inc., Wheaton, Illinois 60189. All rights reserved.
NRSV are taken from The New Revised Standard Version Bible: Anglicised Edition. Copyright © 1989, 1995 the Division of Christian Education of the National Council of the Churches of Christ in the United States of America. Used by permission. All rights reserved.
Phillips are taken from The New Testament in Modern English by J B Phillips. Copyright © 1960, 1972 J B Phillips. Administered by The Archbishops' Council of the Church of England. Used by permission.

Thanks...
- to Anne, my wife, for her love.
- to those I have talked songs with over the decades.
- to those who have led songs of pain—annoyance evokes analysis.
- to those especially who have led me in pleasurable songs of praise—such inspire the life of worship; such point to deity.
- to abba—thank you for the music...I'm a fan within family.

True life is a life of gratitude.

Contents

Part 1	**Power and Christian Songs**	**10**
	Chapter 1 Israel-Church Songs	10
	Are Songs Worship?	25
	Chapter 2 The Impact of Songs	32
	The Demonic Level	32
	The Deific Level	33
	The Human Level	34
	Attack of the Mûmakil	44
Part 2	**Prayer and Christian Songs**	**47**
	Chapter 3 The Trinity and You	47
	From QuadCap to OneCap	47
	Chapter 4 The Holy Spirit and You	53
	Reflections on Prayer	53
	Quasi-Requests	55
	Whom Should You Ask?	56
	Father, Lord, or Spirit?	58
	Adding Back the Spirit	60
	Trinitarian Fellowship	62
	Father First	63
	Chapter 5 Praying to the Spirit	**65**
	Request	65
	Gratitude	68
	Praise	70
	Worship	71
	Adoration	71
	Dedication	72
	Apology	73
	Chat and Complaint	76
Part 3	**Problems and Christian Songs**	**78**
	Chapter 6 Grammatical Problems	**84**
	Ø: Mixed Themes	84
	A: Incompletism	86
	B: Archaism	88
	Chapter 7 Theological Problems	**98**

	C: Blessing God	98
	D: Buddy, Boyfriend, and Baby	99
	E: Polytheism	106
	F: Voxdeism	110
	G: Unitarianism	112
	Chapter 8 Proseuchological Problems	**114**
	H: Misdirection	114
	I: Misvisualisation (prayer)	115
	Chapter 9 Miscellaneous Problems	**129**
	J: Boasting	129
	K: Decontextualising	136
	L: Hermit's Harakiri	138
Part 4	<u>**Particulars and Christian Songs**</u>	**144**
	Chapter 10 Selected Song Books	**144**
	Chapter 11 Selected Songs	**151**
	We Declare Your Majesty: Malcolm Du Plessis	153
	Will You Come And Follow Me?: John Bell and Graham Maule	154
	The Lord's My Shepherd: Stuart Townend	155
	Holy Spirit, Rain Down: Russell Fragar	156
	Chapter 12 Selected Carols	**159**
	Hark! The Herald Angels Sing	160
	Joy to the World	162
	Oh Come All Ye Faithful	164
	O Come, O Come, Emmanuel	167
	Oh Holy Night	170
	Oh Little Town of Bethlehem	173
	Silent Night	176

Biblical Abbreviations

Ac. *Acts*	Is. *Isaiah*	Nb. *Numbers*
Am. *Amos*	Jas. *James*	Neh. *Nehemiah*
Chr. *Chronicles*	Jg. *Judges*	Ob. *Obadiah*
Col. *Colossians*	Jhn. *John*	Phm. *Philemon*
Cor. *Corinthians*	Jl. *Joel*	Php. *Philippians*
Dan. *Daniel*	Jnh. *Jonah*	Pr. *Proverbs*
Dt. *Deuteronomy*	Job *Job*	Ps(s). *Psalm(s)*
Ec. *Ecclesiastes*	Jos. *Joshua*	Pt. *Peter*
Eph. *Ephesians*	Jr. *Jeremiah*	Rm. *Romans*
Est. *Esther*	Jude *Jude*	Ruth *Ruth*
Ex. *Exodus*	Kg. *Kings*	Rv. *Revelation*
Ezk. *Ezekiel*	Lk. *Luke*	Sam. *Samuel*
Ezr. *Ezra*	Lm. *Lamentations*	Sg. *Song of Songs*
Gal. *Galatians*	Lv. *Leviticus*	Ths. *Thessalonians*
Gen. *Genesis*	Mic. *Micah*	Tm. *Timothy*
Hab. *Habakkuk*	Mk. *Mark*	Tts. *Titus*
Heb. *Hebrews*	Ml. *Malachi*	Zc. *Zechariah*
Hg. *Haggai*	Mt. *Matthew*	Zp. *Zephaniah*
Hos. *Hosea*	Nah. *Nahum*	

Grades[1]

Percent	100-95	94-90	89-85	84-80	79-75	74-70	69-65	
Letter	A+	A	A-	B+	B	B-	C+	
Point	4.3	4	3.7	3.3	3	2.7	2.3	
Percent	64-60	59-55	54-50	49-45	44-40	39-27	26-14	13-00
Letter	C	C-	D+	D	D-	U+	U	U-
Point	2	1.7	1.3	1	0.7	0	0	0

---

[1] For handier sorting in tables, I advise using A1/A2/A3 and B1/B2/B3, etc, for grade letters. I have put these here in the more familiar forms of, eg, A+/A/A- and B+/B/B-. For grade points, I round final totals to the nearest 0.5 points.

Preface

In Jane Austen's *Pride and Prejudice*. Lizzy's performance was pleasing, though by no means capital. After a song or two, and before she could reply to the entreaties of several that she should sing again, she was eagerly succeeded at the instrument by her more proficient sister, Mary, but in song Elizabeth Bennet rose above the humdrum, and she was the more pleasing singer. But pleasing or not, in songs we—excepting fatuous Collinses and attention seeking Marys—can all fly. I celebrate song as offering blessing, life enrichment, a focus on God. I sadden over writers who know more of cents than sensibility.

I believe that when it comes to good Christian songs, the best on show are the best songs in the world, since the most meaningful. As icons of glory, they offer times of deep awe, a weight of tangible glory. In fact it's because of the type of person I am, and because I wish to love every Christian song, that too often my hidden tears are of the disenchanted, rather than the enchanted, sort. Had I kept my guitar, it would weep buckets. In this book I wish us to weep together, and to rejoice together. When (more likely than *if*) I'll disillusion, it is because I wish you—my brothers and sisters—as singers to demand more from song suppliers, and that you songsmiths, smithy better songs. Healthy Christians make for more healthy churches, which will best grow in size, too. I wish to demolish the substandard and the unsafe, both for safety and to free up space for better builds. Did I just say *smithy*? Perhaps like Norway's Sigurd, we have to break some swords, before the smith—in our case a songsmith, not a blacksmith—will make us one that cuts through anvil and wool to slay the dragon. Mine is not a lone voice, though we are a minority voice. When it comes to instrumental music, although long ago I used to blow a borrowed cornet, I have never blown my own trumpet. So I may quiver, but I shall not quaver. But I do love good singing.

For Bible texts, my main English versions (MEVV) are the CEB/CEV/ERV/LEB/NABRE/NCV/NIV/NKJV/NLT/NRSV. For grading, the best will be A+, and the worst D-: none shall fail. In quotes, I often amend [the LORD] to [Yahweh], and remove false capitals from nouns and pronouns. I sometimes take liberties when quoting generally: for example, updating gender style, adjusting tenses, standardising abbreviations, and simplifying bibliographies intext.

Steve H Hakes: mallon.detc@gmail.com

Part 1   Power and Christian Songs
Chapter 1   Israel-Church Songs

Out of the Silent Planet is a fine title for a book, but in one sense our planet is not so silent—we sing. Christian songs have a powerful history. They came out of deep heaven, not out of thin air, though many have mixed provenance and cold be our warmest thoughts. Christian songs "may not be in [the] theological front line, but for many Christians [they are] a significant part of their spirituality, fill a major segment of their 'worship,' and eat voraciously into their budget for tapes, CDs, musical instruments, copying, and sundry kinds of software" (Chris Idle: Reform).[2] As a Christian teen I enjoyed much CCM. And most of my few close friends in those days, ie JB and KS (two out of three), did gigs at my local church using their own lyrics. I still remember them singing an eschatological song to Steeleye Span's *All Around My Hat* (1975) tune, and a song about Green Shield Stamps. Hats off to good old songs that still stick!

Of course, way before my time, significant songs were being enjoyed. Each generation has them. "To know nothing of what happened before you were born," observed Cicero over 2,000 years ago, "is to forever remain a child." From what some would say was pre-Adamic man, a five-holed vulture bone flute, discovered in a German cave (Hohle Fels), has been dated as being over 30,000 years old. Some think we have found a 40,000-year-old flute in Slovenia (Divje Babe). Some reckon that dating is fundamentally flawed, deny that Earth is that old, and simply say that such instruments date subsequent to a M5 BC Adam, and might even have been poorly made even in their time.

For a balanced review of arguments for and against such dates, see Kevin Logan's, *Responding to the Challenge of Evolution*. I think that neither side should claim the scientific high ground, without first considering the other's evidence and methodology. One that does that keeps the best and drops the worst from both Random Evolutionism and Intelligent Design, effectively espousing a new position, Intelligent Evolution: Perry Marshall's *Evolution 2.0* argues scientifically that intelligence is frontloaded, not drip fed. But, certain

---

[2]   www.reform.org.uk (2013). Idle wrote as a lyricist.

presuppositions aside, it's fascinating to speculate about how music (a term I shall limit to instrumental) and singing developed and varied within humanity. *The Silmarillion* began with the music of the Ainur!

It is said that music is a bridge between Earth and Heaven. If we look back to *Genesis*, as we often should, we can speak of Jabal as the *father* (pattern) of nomads, and Jubal as *typical* (father) of stringed/wind musicians (Gen.4:20-1). I don't believe that we must take these texts as saying that they were the first of their kind. Likewise, biblically 'father Abraham' meant the outstanding 'pattern/paradigm/model' of connection to God. There were earlier examples of faith-fathers, but Abraham was the ideal example for the primitive church in Rome, especially as being a link between ethnic Israel and the Gentile world.

That church ethnically contained ethnic-Jews and ethnic-Gentiles, yet both ethnic sides could see that they had equal spiritual and covenant claim to Abraham, and to the new covenant—they stood together as one. Jubal was an outstanding musician, possibly in sacred music: *Genesis* appreciated good songs. Jubal's sister Lamaah married into the line of Seth (from which would come Abraham), and indeed her first son followed the patrilineal custom of being named similar to or exactly as her father, thus another Lamech was born. But her brother was of Cain's line. *Genesis* commended the musical talent in the non-covenant line of Cain.

By common consent, Israel's deliverance song (Ex.15:1-18), *The Song of the Sea*, is dated at least as old as the C12 BC, a probable date of the exodus. That, and Jg.5, "are part of a whole genre of such compositions, triumph hymns to celebrate victory or dominion, attested from the later third millennium and best known from the second half of the second" (Kitchen 218). Incidentally, even in the Ancient Near East, poetic licence existed, giving basic, not necessarily precise, details. Likewise, here the prose accounts of Israel's deliverance are more precise, historically speaking, than her poetical accounts, such as in *Psalms*.

On coming out from slavery, the people sang of Yah's victory over their enemy's army; Miriam followed this in dance. It then moved to what Yahweh was to his people (2), his strength (3-6), his majestic greatness (7-12), his covenant dedication (13-7), and his eternal kingdom (18). Abel Ndjerareou sadly noted that "the singers did not know that their own failings would mean that they would end up wandering in the desert for forty years" (Adeyemo 105). Woe to us if we have the best songs, but have not holiness! As an aside, so-called Liberation Theology often treats the story of Israel's exodus as if it were a pattern for all the downtrodden.[3] At its best, Social Liberationism is a biblical ethic, but it is not a theology. Nor was a particular event in salvation history intended as a paradigm for social reconstruction as such. *Liberation Theology* tends to rob humanity of the ultimate eternal, in order to pay for short-term social gain.

Ethnic Israel has had a lot of singing. Even as a precarious fiddler on the roof, it still sings. Its great dynastic king, David, sang while still a shepherd boy. A good number of his songs made the official Hymn Book, *Psalms*. In fact, so many were written by or about him, that some today often relate all of *Psalms*, to David, whatever the captions say or contents imply. What a difference a song makes. "God was not marginal but a vital reality of Israel's life. The [OT] does not contain lengthy philosophical or theoretical essays about God. We hear about... God not from the essayist but from the worshipper. A [reminder] of his attributes...was always in the context of prayer or praise" (Martens 171).

We could look at the Pentateuchal structure, the divisions of Yahwistic and Elohistic psalms, the types of parallelism the songsmiths delighted in, and the acrostic psalms. I bet some took days, perhaps weeks, to write. We could see what care and skill was put into constructing these songs, some good for individual singing, some better for community song. The New Testament (NT) is full of citations from the psalms. For instance, Beale and Carson's

---

[3] "God is especially close to the oppressed; God hears their cry and resolves to set them free (Ex.3:7-8). God is father of all, but most particularly father and defender of those who are oppressed and treated unjustly. Out of love for them, God takes sides, takes their side against the repressive measures of the pharaohs" (Boff & Boff 51). No Boffs, the god of biases is not God: God has no bias towards those we call oppressed (though *we* should) and he calls all humanity oppressed. Note the Boffs' jump from a historical particular of releasing his chosen people for salvation history, to asserting a principle that he released them not as *chosen* people but as *oppressed* people. Talented and commendable Garth Hewitt, sadly fallen into 'Liberation Theology,' confused it with Negro Spirituals: "if you look at negro spirituals, as they used to be called, they are really liberation theology in code".

Commentary of the NT use of the OT, 2009:1176-82, shows that, excepting Ps.150, there are mentions, at least allusions, to every psalm in *Psalms*. This shows just how integral *Psalms*, the hymn book of the second temple, is to the new covenant, with its traces of suffering and prophecy. *Psalms* are earthy songs with a prophetic edge.

Although Ethnic Israel was alone in covenant with God, nevertheless at times she wished her joy to go viral. God was transnational, and the non-covenant nations should see that and sing for joy. One has only to read the Egyptian hymn to the god Aton, to catch a glimpse of a certain joy in God beyond Israel's borders. But such knowledge was very limited, both as regards who had it, and to its depth. It fell below the Yahweh standard of Israel. Yet even to see God's hand in delivering Israel, could help the nations to sing for joy. All peoples did, or would, worship Yahweh (Ps.66:4). They could all rejoice in his justice (67:4). They were encouraged to sing, probably along with music, to God as lord (68:32). Even the dark side of God's light was still the light of joy, but the true light did not go global until the messianic age dawned. Compared to the true light, even the light in Sinaitic Israel shone dim.

The primitive church too, was encouraged to rejoice among themselves, using *psalmois* and *hymnois* and *ōdais pneumatikais* (Eph.5:19; Col.3:16), three forms of singing. That is, ways to spiritually mull truths over, as the community shaped itself in love (Eph.4:15). Paul's exact meaning of *psalms/hymns/songs* is lost to us, partly because he didn't major on them. Perhaps Paul's message to us is, "use your culture, use your songs." Gordon Fee concluded from the preceding encouragement of Eph.5:18 that "however we are to understand the adjective 'Spiritual' in relation to the various expressions of song, Spirit songs are at least one expression of the Spirit's presence, whose 'fullness' will guide and inspire all of the worship in its several expressions" (Fee 102).[4]

---

[4] I think Fee further argued that here *pneumatikos* has Paul's usual meaning (ie directly or indirectly about the spirit), like a charismatic hymnody in accord with 1 Cor.14:15,16,26, modifying not *psalms, hymns, & songs,* but only *songs.* Further, that it is nonglossolalic prophetic enhancement to others (1 Cor.14:3).

Eph.5:18-9 contrasts inebriated boozy singing with ultimate meaning (spiritual) songs. Yes, even boozy *psalms* existed (Ps.69:12—*psalmos*)! Today many mean by *hymns* the multi-stanza poetry that C18 Christians wrote, and by *psalms* whatever we see in *Psalms*. Paul's original audience would probably have chuckled. Coming from a range of peoples—Ephesus was a Roman capital city—they probably had a number of ideas associated with each word, not least the odes of Greek bards, and psalms of ancient Israel. Perhaps Paul simply wished to kick off ideas by using a spread of terms, already faded with use. In principle, it's good to listen to Christian songs, and to sing them. But Paul did not guarantee that every song written by Christians, would be good to sing. Indeed, to whom much is given, much is expected, and those dealing in spiritual songs need the greater care to ensure that the songs are spiritually good for us, free from toxins. Heresies and other nonsense can come through spiritual songs. Many of Paul's letters to Christians, some of whom probably wrote songs, underlined mistaken ideas they had. Paul didn't want them in circulation.

Analysing Israelite and Jewish psalms is interesting. Hermann Gunkel helped to group the psalms into distinct literary patterns (genres). We can now say that the main types of psalm express Greatness (for example creation, cultus, city), Groans[5] (and thus pleas for help), and Gratitude. The many laments show that life wasn't unalloyed bliss. Yet "the lament psalms suggest that Israel, whether [communally] or as individuals, experienced God as one who was involved in life with them.... The confidence statements are a study in intimacy, for they consist of confessional statements about God and testimonies to past experiences with him. Perhaps the most striking fact of all is that while one third of the psalms are in lament form, all but [Ps.88] end in praise" (Martens 167). Ps.88 remains the benchmark of prayerful hopelessness.

Together, these three types of psalms formed a rich tapestry of inspired songs and covered a range of human situations, emotions, and meditations. As a pattern, Ethnic Israel was the church (qāhāl) of

---

[5] Pentecostals are not the only Christians who, by shying away from songs of lament, "end up living in a state of dualism" between experience and worship (Warrington 197).

the OT. I make the argument in my book, *Israel's Gone Global*, that the messianic church does not continue it,[6] arguing that prior to the cross, none were spiritually born, none indwelt by God's spirit. However, both sides of the cross, the churches have sung.

Jesus and his disciples, following Jewish tradition, "sang a [Passover] hymn."[7] As said, the terms *psalm*, and *hymn*, can interchange. Mk.14:26 has *hymnos*, and refers to the practice of singing praise/gratitude psalms, possibly Ps.113-8. The Geneva Bible translated *hymnos* as "a psalm" (functional equivalence) and in fact it was probably the closing psalm. The primitive church, initially an ethno-Jewish thing, was quite familiar with the psalms. Even as she outreached to other ethnicities, the psalms were cherished, since her founder had extensively shown them to be relevant to his nature and mission.

This is not to say that all the psalmic material is as meaningful in today's church, as it was to Ethnic Israel. This is something that Isaac Watts picked up on—he Christianised what he could and dropped the rest. For instance, on the one hand it valued meeting in the temple and animal sacrifices. On the other hand, Christians are God's temple, and the true sacrifice has been made: animals need not apply. We should be aware of, and beware of, anachronistic theology, lest we await what has come, and visualise a temple of lifeless, rather than living, stones. We must factor in the new creation.

Jesus' brother James, too, encouraged fellow believers to sing (Jas.5:13): presumably he enjoyed singing. Besides the obvious songs in *Revelation*, the NT letters might also have extracts from primitive Christian songs (Php.2:6-11; Col.1:15-20; 1 Tm.3:16). We might suspect—since that well before Johnny Cash prison singer Paul enjoyed the best of songs in the worst of times (Ac.16:25)—that Paul wrote songs he later reworked into his letters. They may at least indicate the kind of songs he preferred. "Singing was especially important to worship, in both Old and New Testaments" (Grudem 1012), and continued to be so in the messianic community.

---

[6] Many themes fulfilled by Jesus were, so to speak, beta tested by Ethnic Israel, such as *vine, temple, church*.

[7] There were various commemorative drink stages in Passover, linked to Ethnic Israel's history. The last drink was linked to a set psalm, or medley of psalms.

Power and Christian Songs

Moving on a generation or so, we can probably see a hostile witness of Pliny about Christian songs. Aged 18, Gaius Plinius Caecilius Secundus (a.k.a. Pliny the Younger) witnessed the eruption of Vesuvius, which claimed the life of his uncle, Pliny the Elder. Talented in administration and law, about 30 years later this tactful social climber was working in Bithynia as trouble-shooter for the emperor Trajan. His job description included executing Christians simply *because they were Christians*. Politically correct, he assumed Christianity to be a harmful superstition. After all, Christians rejected the gods in favour of one god—some even called them atheists. He condemned more and more Christians from all walks of life, until his conscience forced him to reconsider his liberal bigotry. He investigated what Christians said they believed and did.[8]

In the end he concluded that Christianity was a harmless superstition —other than it claiming that an unauthorised (*illicita*), apparently nonthreatening god, had greater authority than Rome. In seeking clarification about judging and punishing Christians, he reported to the emperor, Trajan in AD c.111, that "...their habit on a fixed day [is] to assemble before daylight and recite by turns a form of words to Christ as a god..." (Stevenson and Frend 19). Pliny's mention of Christ as *a god*, possibly squeezed Christian theology into pagan terms.[9] His words *carmen* (a form of words?)... *dicere* (spoken?) might have borne the sense of *singing*, not of *saying*.

Ralph Martin noted that Pliny's use is chronologically between Horace's use of *dicere carmen* for singing/chanting to the gods, and Tertullian's comment that Pliny talked about Christians singing to Christ. Pliny's *carmen* might well have meant for him what the Greek *hymnos* meant.[10] Pliny had probably discovered that the early church

---

[8] Some Christians probably renounced their faith under torture, but Pliny got the idea from those who didn't, that deniers had been false Christians. Pliny even discovered that women slaves could be in Christian leadership.

[9] Though unlikely, Pliny might have understood and recorded what these Christians really believed about Christ's deificity. Even today some Christians seem to believe that Jesus is a god, or even alone God, an idea popularised by Pentecostal Oneness.

[10] www.biblicalstudies.org.uk/pdf/vox/vol03/footnote_martin.pdf (2010)

Israel-Church Songs

loved to sing, fitting in worship and affirming allegiance (*sacramentum*) to deity, before getting down to their Sunday jobs.

Moving on a bit, here's part of a very ancient song by Clement of Alexandria (C2-3), translated into rhyme: *Bridle of colts untamed / Over our wills presiding / Wing of unwandering birds / Our flight securely guiding / Rudder of youth unbending / Firm against adverse shock / Shepherd with wisdom tending / Lambs of the royal flock / Thy simple children bring / In one, that they may sing / In solemn lays / Their hymns of praise / With guileless lips to Christ their king.*[11] Whatever imperfections might be in this, such as asking *Jesus* about his *children*, it is interesting both in being a sample of early church hymnology, and showing a range of biblical and extrabiblical imagery. Among other ancient songs is the *Phōs Hilaron* (Cheerful Light), the earliest hymn extant to reflect the persecuted church's early trend of facing east to the sun, symbolic to them of Radiant Justice (Mal.4:2). One Elim chorus (181) speaks of the morning we shall meet inside the Eastern Gate.

In a C4 pagan bounce back, Emperor Julian urged pagan priests to out-sing the Christians (Frend 165). Soon, after Julian died in 363, Ambrose of Milan was urging congregational singing in churches (Frend 179). Augustine of Hippo recalled that the Milan church sought comfort and spiritual strength through introducing the Eastern example of singing hymns and psalms. "Ever since then the custom has been retained, and the example of Milan has been followed in...almost every church in the [Empire]" (Pine-Coffin 9.7.191).

Moving two centuries forward, we could also look at Gregorian chants, such as *O Come O Come Emmanuel*, a style made famous by C6 Pope Gregory the Great.[12] Page 10 notes that creative songs became

---

[11] http://en.wikisource.org/wiki/Ante-Nicene_Fathers/Volume_II/Clement_Of_Alexandria/The_Instructor/Book_III/Chapter_XII

[12] Gregory was, quite simply, great. He is named one of the original four academic doctors *par excellence*, of the Roman Network, along with Ambrose, Jerome, and Augustine of Hippo; the Eastern Orthodox network has its four champions, as well, in Athanasius, Gregory of Nazianzen, Basil the Great, and John Chrysostom. The numbers have now risen, by such as Thomas Aquinas, Anselm, Leo 1, St. Cyril of Alexandria, St. Cyril of Jerusalem, and Bede, being

controversial within Roman Catholicism from the C5. Some feared that subcanonical songs, if heretical, would contaminate the canon (Scripture). True, some Christian songs are heretical, but singing Scripture can be, too. For example, what if we sing an OT prophecy of the incarnation as if it is still to come, or sing stipulations specific to the Sinaitic Covenant as if still valid? My own little number, which I have tenderly called, *My Circumcised Son* (© Steve H Hakes (2016)), begins like this: Stanza 1: *A snip in time / before day nine; Will link you in / yet do not sin; If you eat ham / we will you ban; But kosher meat / is juicy sweet*. Ask your song leaders to sing it! Or if you prefer pure Scripture, why not give Gen.17:12 a whirl?

Physical circumcision made good singing for the heretical C1 Circumcision Party (Gal.5:12). Even songs about going into deity's *temple* can revert to a time before individuals became deity's temples. I say again that singing the psalms isn't as theologically safe as it might first seem.[13] Within this debate, unofficially Roman Christians enjoyed more freedom than officially allowed. And singing became more interesting when rhyme came to dine. "Latin poetry did not rhyme, but rhyme began to be used in the C10. People found rhyming hymns easier to remember and sing" (Chadwick 211). Rhyme extended into the wider arena of poetry. Christian songs developed. Page sketched the idea of rhyme and metre (Page 117-8).

---

added by Rome, and a few women including Teresa of Avila, and Hildegard of Bingen. But even to be in a top-40 global list, is exceptional honour. As to Great popes, the only other pope suffixed as Great, was Leo 1. Yet some prefer the term, *Roman chants*, partly because it sounds wider within the Roman Catholic network, and also because the extent of Gregory's influence to these chants, is now being downgraded. To hear some online, goto http://inchoro.net. Another term, *plainchant*, is also used, which highlights the simplicity of the lilting songs. They are purely vocals, melodies without harmonies, and melodies some would call eerie, not punchy.

[13] "It is not enough that our songs use scriptural phrases or simply sound like the Bible; so do some Birthday Card verses and the Book of Mormon". Page came across this same, "ah, but it's in the Bible", naivety (Page 87). I once had a lyricist, with a satisfied smile, tell me that her song, which I'd inadvertently commented on, was OT text—ouch!

Israel-Church Songs

If you imagine that musical instruments were always alive and well within the church, think again. The ancient records suggest that there was an almost total ban on such, with a slight breaking of ranks by Titus Flavius Clemens (a.k.a. Clement of Alexandria). Why, when the old Israel was replete with instruments for song, did the new Israel have such a down? Some say it was to distance the church from the synagogue, perhaps because the further from the synagogue, the better. Or, that in the dark days before messiah, Yahweh gave his immature people some slack, but with the dawning of the new age, using lifeless instruments had become passé.[14] A bit like Ac.17:30, God now called for a change of heart and mind, even though it does seem that he had encouraged temple musicians.

Actually, and especially since unlike the temple the synagogue did not use musical instruments, it seems better to follow the documentary trail. Then we will say that on the one hand the church was born in synagogue style, and on the other hand didn't take kindly to the pagan style where musical instruments played a big part in sexual immorality and pagan rites, as the philosopher Aristotle had noted. This connection was so bad that some Christians even believed that musicians were banned from heaven, or at least from the church. The church remained happily synagogal, with a synagogal attitude to musical instruments.

In fact, it didn't even start theologising opposition to instruments until the C3-4. But it had always seen that wild music is a form of drunkenness, as Clement himself said about public rave parties. The Salvation Army came down strong on strong drink, lest those converted from the sodden world should be tempted to stumble back into it. Likewise, perhaps, the church had felt that there was no safe scope for encouraging music from the musically sexualised world, and soon felt that musical instruments needed to be actively

---

[14] "The Church Fathers constantly commented upon the Old Testament which was for them the inspired word of God, and thus were forced to reconcile their own antagonism toward instruments with the embarrassing fact that God allowed instruments in the worship of the Temple" (James McKinnon). C4-5 Niceta of Remesiana reckoned that dropping the Sinaitic sabbath was like dropping temple instruments. See www.catholicculture.org/culture/library/view.cfm?recnum=9134.

discouraged. The devil had all the good instruments, and was welcome to them. Keep clear, keep safe, keep singing.

Later there were sparks of musical interest, such as what's become known as Moravianism, initially better called *Unitas Fratrium*, effectively meaning United Family/Friends [in Christ]. It was based on the platforms of John Wycliffe and Jan Hus. In 1501, this proto-protestant fellowship produced its own book of 89 hymns in local language for local people. It was a pattern for such as the Wesleys to follow. Their singing gave comfort in their long night of suffering, rather like Paul and Silas' singing (Ac.16:25). But the position of the early church fathers cast a long shadow over medieval times, yet in that era, musical instruments became accepted in church services. So much so that Erasmus even complained that instrumental music was getting as bad in church as it was in the theatres.

Erasmus was one who encouraged, however unintentionally, the Reformation. And the Reformation required a new batch of songs, especially of songs in local languages, though some of the older Latin songs were translated into metre or rhyme. It revived singing in church, though the big three Reformists didn't agree about whether it was a blessing or a curse. The German, Martin Luther, believed that hymns were a powerful godsend, serving both biblical teaching and devotion within church. The Swizz, Ulrich Zwingli, agreed that they were powerful. In fact, too powerful, he said. Since they could very easily take our minds off God and Scripture, the lyricists becoming the new preachers and idols, they should be banned. Similarly, some folk, rejecting set-prayers, "went even further and objected to singing as another 'form' of prayer, where people might sing what they did not actually believe or think about" (Cox 320). The Frenchman, John Calvin, chose to stand somewhere in between. Church songs were a potential blessing, if biblical, he said, putting a big emphasis on singing the psalms, presumably as good emotion and good theology. But he ditched musical instruments and choirs, to both dampen excessive emotion, and to fully involve congregations.

In Germany, Philip Spener was a founder of Protestant Pietism,[15] a movement of reflection and devotion to deity. If Luther was about

---

[15] A form of inner life devotion and holiness with happy gains and sad losses.

Israel-Church Songs

getting on the Christian train, Spener was about enjoying the trip: Zinzendorf made this concern more central to the interdenominational church. After all, it was a reformation worth singing about. For the actual model of *hymn* writing, C17-8 Isaac Watts probably takes the credit (Page 12). He forced himself to write in popular style, rather than poetical and scholarly. However his hymns—perhaps too popularly phrased rather like Kenneth Taylor's *The Living Bible*—have dated more quickly than have the Wesleys'. The Wesley brothers (Anglicanism to Methodism) were outstanding in their blend of propositional and pietistic songs. Their throughput of about 7,000 songs through evangelicalism, was "a major factor in the success of congregational singing" (Page 11).

With *Hymns Ancient and Modern* (1861), Anglicanism had moved from Zwingli to Luther. In the USA, Moody and Sankey designed songs for evangelism. In the UK, William Booth, founder of The Salvation Army, used common images and popular music hall tunes. Why, he asked, should the devil have all the good music? And Christian music marched onward as to war. By the end of the C19, about 400,000 church songs were in circulation. Only a few hundred have survived—a high mortality rate. If hymn books were to sell, they had to contain only well written songs, acceptable to a wide target audience. Big might not be better, but big names sold better so probably many fine songs died through under circulation. Sing we must, for as Cliff Barrows put it, the Christian faith is a singing faith: *I sing because I'm happy, I sing because I'm free.*

Freedom! was the cry of *Braveheart*. Not all are free, however freedom is defined. Jesus distinguished between two forms of freedom (Jhn.8:33-4). Others exist. Freedom from water is not good for fish, nor necessarily for a spouse from marriage, nor a leader from their *noblesse oblige.* Some bonding is good, and when spiritually freed by God's spirit we are meant to remain in that freedom (Gal.5:1), bound to the New Jerusalem. But social oppression is not right, and is a part of man's inhumanity against man. One of the great songwriters produced *Amazing Grace.* He had served in the overseas slave trade, and, becoming a Christian, he initially kept in the trade, feeling that Christians could best transport slaves with the consideration of fellow human beings.

Power and Christian Songs

Later he helped Wilberforce to pester parliament into abolition. Among downtrodden African slaves, the Negro Spiritual arose. These were often laments of their plight, yet as exodus songs on their long walk to social freedom, nurtured their spirits. A C16 pattern developed in freeform of a leader singing a few lines, then the illiterate congregation singing them back: they who suffered together sang together. For example, **Leader**: de talles' tree in Paradise, de Christian call de tree of life. **Chorus**: And I hope dat trump might blow me home, to de new Jerusalem. Blow your trumpet, Gabriel, blow louder, louder. And I hope dat trump might blow me home, to de new Jerusalem. **Leader**: Paul and Silas, bound in jail, sing God's praise both night and day. **Chorus**: And I hope... (Chadwick 243).

We jump forward again. In the mid C20, hymns were going out of fashion and hackles were raised against folk music, rock music, and charismaticism. Songs became shorter: new language and musical styles required another Wesley—perhaps none was found.[16] The pattern changed from fitting music to words, to fitting words to music. "In a world where words don't matter much, composers are much more likely to write their own lyrics", even when lacking the talent (Page 40). Objective words took second place to an emphasis on personal feeling, and objective meaning became the victim. With extended

---

[16] R T Kendall suggested Graham Kendrick, even though Kendrick had had "no formal theological training and depended on the critique given by qualified friends" (Kendall 7), such as Clive Calver's tip on *Servant King* that changed "clothed in humanity" to "kneels in humility". As Clive said, *clothed* could suggest the ancient heresy of docetism—that Jesus appeared to be human but wasn't. Kendrick himself rightly felt Kendall's praise overgenerous.

Rather uncritically Kendall's book used Kendrick's lines as launch pads to indepth teaching. For example, "the man who is God" inviting the question of whether a limited man can be unlimited God. "Deific man" would better indicate the person who entered our world with dual citizenship, an interface, shifting the focus from a mortal who happened to have an extra dimension, or vice versa. Even "is Jesus our lord", would improve.

Similarly, "this is your god" (and "this is our god" = Jesus) in *Servant King*), tends towards Jesusism. Kendall bypassed this and, in polytheistic language, ended by saying that the kind of god we have is one we call *father* (ie *not* Jesus) (Kendall 224). "He shows us God" might improve: having sung the deity of God's son, why limit deity to him in this line?

Israel-Church Songs

families going out of fashion, we became Relative. There are numerous voices protesting that Christian songs have become far too self-centred, focusing on our feelings.

And another type of spiritual singing had already awoken in some circles—what Paul had called singing with the spirit (1 Cor.14:15), a.k.a. glossolalia.[17] This too is controversial. Paul contrasted public glossolalia to public local language, and basically suggested that, whether sung or spoken, glossolalia should be confined to private times, unless in a Christian forum where interpretation of meaning could be normally given. Lewis 1981:124-5 made some comparisons between glossolalia and church singing. Grudem made the point that no matter how nice even group singing in/with the spirit could be in believer groups (1 Cor.14:4), it was not a good idea in potential evangelistic settings, even if at times it has challenged unbelievers to conversion (Grudem 1074).[18] Again the rider: unless interpretation could be naturally expected.[19] More could be said about experimenting with various musical styles, tempos, and moods, for glossolalic singing.

However, I have mentioned this kind of singing for depth, not for didactic, and this book will confine itself to singing "with the [human] mind." Frankly, I cannot see how one can critique a song sung in a language outside of one's scope, though it would be fascinating to see one which was spontaneously sung in English, the foreign singer not even knowing what language they had sung in. If from God (and the

---

[17] Some think Paul contrasted human emotion to divine knowledge, rather than divine knowledge to human understanding (for example, Idle 4).

[18] Probably non-Christians only came into church if invited by Christians. In this evangelistic opportunity, Paul feared distractive glossolalia, unless it was interpreted. If whispered too quietly to be overheard, Grudem argued, it would have been OK to Paul and was OK to him! Arguably, if the only non-Christians present are known to be OK with glossolalia, glossolalia won't undermine evangelism, especially if the non-Christians know the glossolalists to be sane.

[19] 1 Cor.14:27-8 implies it is easier to release speech in the spirit than to tune in to his wavelength. Unless those emotivated to speak congregationally think they are ready and able to interpret at a pinch, they should keep a discreet silence unless aware of someone present who has shown the ability to interpret.

psychic can lurk for sub-pneumatic simpletons) we might be the challenged and the critiqued. Would we hate them without just cause?

Some songs can trigger more rage than Luther's red rag to the Roman bull! Susan Wise Bauer was unwise when within a 'conservative' circle, she suggesting singing a popular number from her former 'liberal' circles. It was Alfred Ackley's 1933 number, Christ "lives within my heart" (Mouw and Noll 2353 of 3791). Personally, I think Ackley's number is factually true, but apologetically weak. Since Ackley's subjective "within my heart" cannot be verified or falsified by surgery, he answered only to himself. If Christ lives, it's primarily transcendent of our hearts. How do *I* know he lives? Firstly, I must validate knowledge of his transcendent life, before claiming that immanently he is integral to my life. Likewise, if I claim that Plato lives within my heart, I should show that he lives independently from my heart, unless my claim simply bears the liberal ethico-romantic sense that Plato's message is precious to me.

Kant said that we can never be logically as sure about what we cannot see (the noumenal) as about what we can see (the phenomenal)—even the latter requires trust. Am I alone, or is there a phenomenal world? I believe there is, and believe I have good reason to believe and to trust reason. Faith is logical. Reason advises me to trust the anaesthetist, not irrational doubt. Of course, Ackley used Schleiermacher's idea of responding to a feeling of absolute dependence on the concept, *God*. But how we feel, and how we interpret feeling, does not validate the external reality we nominate as responsible. In *Great Expectations*, Pip's rich benefactor was not whom he thought, upper class Miss Havisham, but whom he despised, working class ex-con Abel Magwitch. Similarly true psychics feel that they are tapped into neutral or good power, though it's demonic.

Postmodern expressions such as 'true for you', 'my truth', 'their truth', often mean no more than feelings of meaning, of certitude, in a belief system that discounts the absolute. "If a witch says, 'It feels right' or 'it feels true,' we must respond, 'How do you know you can trust your feelings'…. The experiential, existential epistemology of witches, emphasizing emotions, feelings, and intuition, is insufficient to discern truth" (Hawkins 149). Duck the PhD in apologetics if you like, but not the fundamental question of why we know Jesus lives—a little

Israel-Church Songs

history, logic, and philosophy, goes a long way. Even a little study can prevent building on the sand of feelings.

I'd certainly reword Ackley a little bit—including the idea that Jesus lives *to* impart salvation (say rather that his life does impart salvation).[20] But he made a lot of good points: that Jesus is saviour, risen from death, lives (by the spirit) in Christians, is always near (though it's the spirit rather than Jesus who walks and talks with us), will return, the storms of life are not the last word, and we should rejoice, O Christian. What Susan flagged up was a fear lest the church overlook the objective in favour of the subjective reality beloved by pietism. Yet what some call pushing God into the background, can in fact be seeing God within the foreground of our personal lives.[21] God should be in both background (systematic) and foreground (narrative), since he is both transcendent and immanent. Let's move a little more into biblical theology.

Are Songs Worship?

One may rightly speak of *sung* worship—a division of sung-prayer—and worship *songs*, but song leaders as such are not, in a biblical sense, worship leaders, even if they help focus worship. "The idea that 'worship' is something that only takes place in a church or a conference—and then only in a 'time of worship' is profoundly unbiblical" (Page 24). Indeed, it can foster the idea that once we give deity his weekly shot in the arm and/or get our fix, our duty's over for another week, while we get on with real life. It is more biblical to say that 24/7 church pastors as such, are the worship leaders, encouraging believers to "give [their entire self] to God because of all he has done for [them. To be as] living and holy sacrifices—the kind he...finds acceptable, [which] is truly the way to worship him" (NLT: Rm.12:1). Paul linked in with the Levitical *hôlâ* offering (Lv.1), that total transfer into the domain of heaven.

At the end of the day, talking about times of worship is like talking about having times of breathing, or times of being ourselves. Songs

---

20 I don't live *to* please my wife, but living pleases her, or so I hope.

21 Susan well says that "Liberal Protestantism..both celebrates and trusts experience (unless of course, such experience might affirm a moral code that rates others' experiences as unhealthy or untrustworthy)" (Mouw & Noll 2376-7 of 3791). It is at best a deficient form (or residue) of Christianity.

are not worship, but can encourage expressions of worship and the vision to live as worship. I love my wife; at times I do loving things. I worship God; at times I do worship things. Both love and worship should be 24/7, even if they slumber in focus. Residual, background. For us, there can be times when the glory of God is so felt, that we metaphorically or literally bow done in worship, and I've even done some holy rolling. Such times can come through biblical revelation, through prayer (2 Chr.7:1), the grandeur of the mountains, the brilliance of the stars, in healing services, and triggered by song (2 Chr.5:13-4). Thank God they come, but songs are not key.

So, how should songs fit into church? Planning can be good. Some churches have spontaneous song selections from the congregation, but where there is a set menu, it can make sense if the speaker is at least consulted, both to coordinate singing to speech (Prime and Begg 207), and to avoid song vs speaker. Imagine, say, following a hearty Hillsong singsong with a talk on trinitarianism. If for no other reason than to save embarrassment, it's worth checking beforehand.

When it comes to the song menu, Chris Idle argued that music leaders have hijacked the idea of worship, and often fail to redeem the time that should have been given to other aspects of corporate service, such as preaching, teaching, quiet reflection. This is not to say that the corrective is to condemn corporate singing, as if it steals away the best, but that we should think in terms of balance. Fit it around church, not church around it.

Ritual can be good, without us becoming ritualistic. In the OT there were worship leaders, in the sense of Levites getting the people to bow down in ritual, which for the faithful reflected their inner obedience. There was the sense of doing worship, but not of being worship. It helps to see that there were three kinds of Sinai-Israelite. ① Those who neither loved Yahweh nor the ritual: they had leave to depart—non-Yahwists dead to Yahweh and to Sinai. ② Those who didn't love Yahweh but were content with ritual: they were free to remain—nominal Yahwists dead to Yahweh but alive to Sinai. ③ Those who loved Yahweh and the ritual: they were spiritually blessed—true Yahwists alive to Yahweh and to Sinai, people after God's own heart. Sinai was far from perfect, though its ritual helped preach that Yahwism was for everyday life.

After 25 years, through the daily rituals of marriage Tevye and Golde had converted to mutual love. Conversion can come through ritual, familiarisation, acclimatisation, the periphery of the divine, which is something that Paul hinted at (1 Cor.7:14).[22] Singing is a good part of ritual. Quite possibly Sinai folk often sang their own songs, but the noticeable singing was that of the temple. Many psalms involved a director, a cantor. They would sing the lead parts, with the people at large responding with their own set lines.

In some Christian circles, a church-priest will sing or chant a line, followed by a sung or chanted response from the congregation. Martin Smith's, *Shout to the North* (1995), has a stanza for women to sing to the men, and one for the men to sing to the women. In the OT, 2 Chr.7:2-3 reflects the lay part, though perhaps they didn't need a cantor to set them off that awesome day. Indeed, only as the weight of glory dimmed, could the official worship begin with the musicians in place (6). Likewise, Ps.136, the Great Hallel (Extreme Praise), shows lines by the Levites, followed by lay response. Song leaders seem to have been selected from Levites, who probably combined music with lines inviting bowing down, obedience, worship.

Let's get down to worship. *Leviticus* is chock full of once meaningful ritual. The five types of Levitical offering were the Total Commitment (Enslavement), the Loyalty (Passion), the Fellowship (Oneness), the Restoration (Normalisation), and the Restitution (Pay Back). They give insights into how worship went down, and what it symbolised. We could look at what some still call the Holiness Code, a C19 nickname[23] for a portion of *Leviticus* that some once thought was a document added to a document, to be precise, rules about ethico-dynamic holiness added to ritualistic rules of static ceremonial holiness: two lines of thinking by two sets of people.

Nobuyoshi Kiuchi (*Leviticus* (AOTC) 2007) scotched both that idea and the desacralising idea that formed it. Here I shall limit myself to a few

---

[22] He said that children and spouses of Christian had an advantage of proximity to eternal life, by virtue of being in a holy family, yet that living with a preach and receiving eternal life through the message preached, were two different things.

[23] A throwaway term by August Klostermann in 1877, to be thrown away.

Hebrew terms. The main one for *worship* (*shakah*, similarly *kâra'*) involved low bows, even nose and forehead to the ground, prostration before the object of worship. Some parts of the world still practice this posture in showing filial submission to their fathers. The main NT term for worship (*proskunēsis*) comes from a background idea of the obedient kiss of submission. This is probably because the Greek social custom of picturing worship, differed from the Hebrew. Jewish translators usually used *proskunēsis* to translate *kâra'* and *shakah*. Likewise, Est.3:2,5 employs both terms, *kneel* (*kâra'*) and reverential *bow* (*shakah*). The Greek *gonupetō* carries more the idea of bowing down. Mk.15:19 combines both words "with no real difference in meaning", in the mocking context of Roman soldiery (VanGemeren G1206 (gonupeteō)). Php.2:10 basically carries the *gonupetō* visual: every knee must one day bow to Jesus.[24]

Yet those who teach that true worship requires physical prostration and/or kissing, are high on literalism and low on meaning. 1 Sam.15:22 indicated that while meaningful ritual had been established, the true meaning of ritual was heart submission to Yahweh. According to Is.1:11-7, symbolic ritual might as well be discontinued as meaningless, unless people lived its meaning of neighbourly concern. Likewise, Mt.23:23 showed that while vassal tribute (tithing) should see out that covenant, unless Sinaitics reflected the heart of Sinai, namely God's concern for others, they literally strained out unkosher gnats but metaphorically swallowed unkosher camels (Lv.11), and were morally unclean. Peripherals can help, but it's the meaning they serve.

I think of Paul Stookey's *The Winner* (1977): *if you get the message, you might refuse it / but if you get the meaning / hey, don't ever lose it*. The meaning is where it's at. I'm not saying that there can never be times when physically bowing or kissing in worship, isn't highly meaningful whatever one's culture. What I'm saying is that inner submission, love, and real awareness of being inferior, are key. Without such,

---

[24] This is not Universalism. Universalism teaches that God's love will eventually win every human spirit (possibly every demon spirit) to himself, thus all shall be saved. Php.2:10 simply says that even those who reject Jesus will see that he is lord. Likewise, demons reject God yet acknowledge him.

Israel-Church Songs

ritual is merely going through the motions (Mk.7:6). Worship in church should be corporate submission and awe.

Worship is neither praise nor thanks. I can praise my wife as being a good cook, and thank her for her cooking, without worshipping her as cook. I am grateful for food (thanks), any food, but enjoy (praise) good food, and can honour (worship) the cook even if having none of their cooking. Worship is meaningful recognition of those who are in some or all good ways, greater than we. The bigger the perceived greaterness, then the bigger the worship, and the more the head is metaphorically down. Pliny the Younger noted that the early church had weekly times of corporate submission and respect to Jesus, perhaps followed by antiphonally chanting Christian realities, their obligations, and reaffirming their sacred vows (*sacramento*) to live as Christians in society.

Nor is worship meant to be only to deity. This is a concern that gets some uptight. They sometimes cite the unhappy case of Herod[25] lest we get praised instead of God. It is good, for the sake of the people, to get folk looking towards God rather than to our merits (Ac.14:13-8), though the latter can help the former (Mt.5:16). But it remains a fact that literally Lot worshipped angels (Gen.19:1), Abigail worshipped David (1 Sam.25:23), Ruth worshipped Boaz (*Ruth 2:10*), Jacob worshipped Esau (Gen.33:3), and Nebuchadnezzar worshipped Daniel (Dan.2:46). Tell me they were wrong. Of course, they would not have said it was on par with worshipping Yahweh, and Bible translations are right to choose alternative words in line with the range of meaning of *kara'/shakah*.[26]

In Mt.4:10/Lk.4:8, it refers to a context of God vs *spirits*, and in *this* sense Israel's worship was limited by covenant to God: covertly Satan

---

[25] This was Herod Agrippa 1 of Judea, grandson of King Herod the Great.

[26] See Terence E Fretheim: VanGemeren 2001: H2556 (*chavah*). Similarly, the NT says that for us there is only one lord (1 Cor.8:6), yet commends Sarah for calling her husband *lord* (1 Pt.3:6). Paul & Silas were called *lords* (Ac.16:30). Again, semantic range was in play. *Kurios* (lord) sometimes simply meant on a social level, *sir*, a common level of courtesy, but at its highest level the NT says that it excludes any rivals to deity and even transcends Jesus. Worship words had a meaning range: the English word *worship* likewise has a word range.

was claiming worship as if God.[27] The Israelites were fine to worship in lower senses, so long as the lower did not dismiss the higher. In Rv.19:10, the context of being beyond the human arena, made it appropriate for an angel to say "worship [only?] God": focus on the Author, not the postie. In fact, in that context it would seem to mean the father, not the son, nor the spirit, though it seems appropriate to take the angelic words as a basic contrast between created and creator. When the creator is in view, reverence and obedience to any creature, seems feeble by contrast.

Thus, biblically, the overall idea is not that only deity is to be worshipped, but that supreme worship is only appropriate to him. Somewhat akin, we may say that while worship—as obedience and respect—is proper to human levels of authority, it is not due when the authority clashes with deity's authority (Ac.4:19; 5:29).

In short, the biblical idea of supreme worship is yielding 24/7 to deity, in awe of him who transcends his universe[28] yet indwells it. As said, *proskunō* conveys the idea of bowing down, a kiss of obedience, orientation of the mind. Related terms are *sebazomai* (a feeling and yielding in service to awe: the numinous theme of Rudolf Otto) and *latreia* (sacred service). Tabernacle/Temple paradigms in the OT have been transferred to the NT church, both corporately and individually. That is, Global Israel over the millennia is deity's holy place, likewise any local congregation serves as an inner sanctum to him, and so does each Christian. Each format of sacred space, besides being separated by him to him, is to be ultimately and effectively submitted to him. Every aspect of our lives, for example family, workplace, marriage, finances, emotions, all are to bow to him. This is in line with OT awareness that the Sinaitic Covenant was partly intended to show the limitations of what deity can do, short of inner change at the

---

[27] Biblically we should jettison the ideas of Satan as a horned beast in a red suit making a pitch, in favour of a fallen photosomatic being with some authority over lesser evil spirits, all using deception and psychic power against humanity and strongly involved in politics.

[28] Antony Flew's *There is a God*, 2007:120-1, well noted that atheism's creative invention of a multiverse, besides lacking science, only escapes having to explain the laws of nature by having to explain the imagined superlaw of natures. Scientifically, creation appears limited to one universe.

Israel-Church Songs

individual level (Jr.31:31-4; Ezk.36:24-7). True love and true insight is the worship the father seeks for our wellbeing and our wholeness.

Corporate singing can focus on reverence themes, as well as on gratitude and praise themes. Themes such as deity's transcendence, his love to us, redemption, and our covenant relationship with him and with each other. It can be a manifestation of our corporate life. Few songs survive from before the C18, and the few C18 songs that survive have not necessarily done so because of biblicality. Old, does not mean, right. However, in days before discrimination became a criminal offence—yes, discrimination was once believed a virtue—probably many bad songs got killed off without having done much harm, and the better ones, at least ones by better known writers, have had more chance of making it through into our days. A natural weeding process.

But even popular ones weren't necessarily biblical: nor are today's popular numbers necessarily biblical. It's simply that they should be. Popularity should sometimes sound alarm bells (Lk.6:26—which The Message paraphrases well). Songs can be nice; they can even be true. But no matter how popular, we should still engage brain before opening mouth. When *Lord of the Rings'* author, J R R Tolkien, wrote the ultimate beginning, he pictured Ilúvatar (the One) teaching creative wisdom through song. Later, the One's greatest created power, Melkor, introduced his own darkening thoughts into the Creation Song, and having moved into discord was cut off from Ilúvatar, becoming Morgoth, whose second in command was Sauron. Effectively Melkor was accursed because he sang a false gospel which he himself had invented. Tolkien well understood the impact of song (*The Silmarillion: Ainulindalë*). Tolkien's close friend, C S Lewis, also wrote about the creation song of Narnia (*The Magician's Nephew*).

Let us be in no doubt: songs are powerful, and popularity should not be the measurement of truth. For paraphrasing Paul, even heaven's most popular angel should be kicked out of heaven, if preaching against the true gospel (Gal.1:8).

Chapter 2   The Impact of Songs

Like talk, music and silence are potential blessings, unlike chaotic, choking, confusing, interference, noise. Lewis supposed a demon's perspective: "Music and silence—how I detest them both! How thankful we should be that ever since our Father entered Hell—though longer ago than humans, reckoning in light years, could express—no square inch of infernal space and no moment of infernal time has been surrendered to either of those abominable forces, but all has been occupied by Noise—Noise, the grand dynamism, the audible expression of all that is exultant, ruthless, and virile—Noise which alone defends us from silly qualms, despairing scruples, and impossible desires. We will make the whole universe a noise in the end. We have already made great strides in this direction as regards the Earth. The melodies and silences of Heaven will be shouted down in the end. But I admit we are not yet loud enough, or anything like it. Research is in progress. Meanwhile you, disgusting little—" (Lewis 1975:113-4). Meaningless TV can be noise, but songs can have spiritual impact.

The Demonic Level

"To presume that, because we are singing about spiritual warfare, we are actually engaged in it, is fallacious" (Warrington 197). Yet Graham Kendrick's, *I Will Build My Church* (1988), has us singing to the powers in the heavens [and] on the earth below, to bow down.[29] Perhaps he should have reworded it from command to statement, *so the powers of the heavens/earth bow down*. Are our songs strong to the pulling down of strongholds? Do exorcists work by song? I fancy that the effect of our songs on Satan, on the entire demonic, is simply indirect. That is, biblical songs help to spiritually mature and energise us (Jude 1:20), so we become the better for the spiritual warfare of challenging the devil and freeing his captives. Contrariwise, if unbiblical, songs may actually increase Satan's hold on us. In *Genesis*, Eve's unbiblical song, so to speak, led to her demise. The effect of spiritual songs on Satan is indirect to their effect on us. They focus our minds.

---

[29]   We even sing as if Jesus: *I will...* instead of *Christ will*, then switch to ourselves, singing lordship to the angels (whether unfallen or fallen) and to other powers (whether human or demonic). It mixes bits from Mt.16:18 and Php.2:10.

The Impact of Songs

The better Christians they help us become, the greater effect they have on the demonic. The more we bow in worship, as worship, the more like God's son we become—christification. The centre of spiritual warfare is inner discipleship, not delivering folk from demonisation. Primarily, spiritual warfare is engaged on the level of temptation and inner discipline (see John Bunyan's *The Holy War* (1672)). In this sense, singing about spiritual warfare—as discipleship—should be engaging in it, building ourselves up in our most holy faith. If I am right about Kendrick being wrong, then one effect of that song is to get us thinking that songs directly defeat demons. Shadow boxing can make us champions without the need to get into the ring. Popularity without power? I sing, therefore it is? Some, like Curdie in George MacDonald's *The Princess and the Goblins*, can even suffer from the idea that a new song even sung badly, is a better weapon than an old song sung well—demons prefer old songs?

The Deific Level

Here too, we do not need to spend much time. We can neither mislead nor misinform deity. The main ingredients are right relationship and faith (Heb.11:6; 1 Jhn.5:14-5; Jhn.15:14-5). Songs that to some extent reflect his will, are possible even if shoddy in the areas of grammar, logic, and theology. Shoddiness doesn't improve songs. I say "to some extent," because his definition of love includes our rationality (Mk.12:30).

Scripture puts much weight on pleasing deity: the spirit (Gal.6:8); the lord (2 Cor.5:9); and God (1 Tm.2:3).[30] What should be our supreme desire? To please ourselves? Surely not such egocentricity. To please others? If by that we mean to really please them by helping them know God, that's got more going for it. That would be anthropocentric. And 'doing God' could be a means to the supreme end of anthropocentricity. Yet is treating God as a means to an end, not a little dubious to say the least? Ought our supreme desire go no

---

[30] Some would restrict *pleasing* to deity, as they do *worship* and *meaning of life*. Scripture commends soldiers pleasing their superiors (2 Tm.2:4), spouses pleasing each other (1 Cor.7:34), children their parents (Col.3:20), etc. Songs ought to follow Scripture, for example not that we *only* love God or that God is *all we need*, but that he has the highest place and meets our deepest need.

higher than the human level, however worthy that desire be? Should it not rather be centred on the supremely worthy? If so, and if God is tripersonal, then to please the spirit would be to please the son, and to please the son would be to please the father. And getting there we might find that even the desire to please him pleases him, and that getting there we will see that his heart is towards humanity more than ours ever has been or could be. Then, looking so to speak from his throne, we are perhaps the more likely to engage in mission on earth, what some call the *missio dei*—God's own mission.

These are deep questions. They call for deep response. How do our songs figure in this enterprise? To ask if "the one thing which really does rejoice God's heart is a prolonged sing-song", is not simply an Idle question. But *do* our songs please him? Or, more to the point, can we please him through our songs? "We must beware of the naïve idea that our music can 'please' God as it would please a cultivated human hearer" (Lewis 1981:129). This applies somewhat to lyrics, too. While singing words of praise are good, substantially it is the likeness of Jesus that most pleases the father. Now if songs help us mature this likeness, *per force* the father is pleased. Indeed, the more like Jesus we become, the more our words of praise will really reflect inner insight. After all, who sees the praiseworthiness of the father so well as the son? So, in this area our songs can have a powerful effect on deity—pleasing him if developing family likeness. Though christification is 24/7, songs can play a useful part.

The Human Level

Before proceeding, let me say that each song is a narrative, and that personally I have a problem with processing one-to-one conversation, while a narrative is being loudly blasted out in the 'after-service' time when folk mill around perhaps to talk. This, on a personal note, has an adverse effect on me. And some songs being prayers inviting us to engage, increases the issues: should we ignore a call to prayer, in order to natter with friends?

But me aside, much more needs to be said here, because the human level is where it's happening. This is the stage of cause and effect. For instance, we should look at another type of 'spiritual warfare' in song, which is about taking the *nations* for Jesus, and claiming God's land, as if we only need sing the magic words. This is a happy theme of postmillennialism, and has been enjoyed even by those who would consciously reject its eschatology. It is buoyant, it is bullish. Unlike premillennialism (whether pre~ mid~ or post~trib), postmillennialism holds that Jesus will only return after the millennium (Rv.20:2). Unlike amillennialism, it does not insist that we are yet in the millennium, and prefers to think that all, or just about all, will be eschatological wheat before Jesus returns.[31] It has been held during momentous revivals. It is the mindset of a seemingly irresistible force. It might encourage evangelism more than does premillennialism, since expecting bigger results. Premillennialism is more likely to hold the fort awaiting rescue, though proclaiming the good news that those in God's fort won't be 'left behind'—a blessed hope.

Of course, we shouldn't choose our doctrines like we choose our soap. Doctrines should only be chosen because they convince us that they best fit the facts. It is safer if we bow to their power, rather than them bowing to our whims. Some "people [do] not tolerate sound teaching. They...collect teachers who say what they want to hear because they are self-centred" (CEB: 2 Tm.4:3). So beware lest it's merely the power of song that persuades. Our songs colour our thinking; our thinking colours our songs. These are virtuous or vicious spirals, making better or worse depending on whether the underlying doctrine (concept) is biblical or not. We must avoid the artificial colouring of a good and welcome tune. Eschatology is just one of many concepts. Eschatological songs affect those who sing them, and can increase evangelism. They are still subject to proper grounds for singing them—let's be conviction choirs. Silas sang; God gave the victory. But can we sing our way to victory?

---

[31] But see Mt.13:36-43. Some big names linked with this idea include Isaac Watts, Daniel Whitby, Jonathan Edwards, and John Wesley. The World Wars undermined postmillennialism, but it re-awoke as a positive reaction to premillennialism's alarmist anticipation of antichrist: "the dominion of the messiah will be exercised until the whole world acknowledges his lordship" (Chant & Pratney 225). I believe the biblical doctrine is of imminency (anytimeness), which could only coincide with postmillennialism in times of global revival. If postmillennialism is valid, then much of church history has known not to expect anytime return.

Songs can daily bless us. As bakers of the best kind, John and Charles Wesley provided much daily bread to the prayerful. Like daily bread, songs have enriched my life in many ways, nourishing and sustaining. We are partly what we eat, and songs are part of our weekly diet. Some radicalisation is wrong, some is right. Songs can radicalise us: the radix is the root, and that can be where we must let God work. A songfest can be as a memorable banquet which changes our eating habits for good.

For example, in my late teens I thought that the planet Vulcan was where it was at, and some still call me Mr Spock. I was well aware that to love is to be vulnerable. I was less aware that to fear vulnerability leads to dehumanising decay. Saint Augustine, a better man than me, Gunga Din, made the same mistake. My life took on the tones of Simon and Garfunkel's *I Am a Rock* (1965): It's laughter and it's loving I disdain...I am an island, and an island never cries, and a rock feels no pain. Well, one day some songwriter friends tested their new song on me, confident I wouldn't have heard the tune before. I had, and burst into chuckles over their surprise. I quickly stopped and apologised for emotional reaction. But asked why I had apologised, I was at a loss. Yes, why was laughter itself wrong? It hit me that being human (not Vulcan) was part of God's nature—humanity is after all in his likeness. Therefore laughter, even emotion, was fitting, even if not always appropriate. That song radicalised me, thank God.

Another radicalising song for me was *Silly Love Songs* (Paul and Linda McCartney). It asked, *What's wrong with that?* It opened me up to emotion. The Simon and Garfunkel song is still me, but I can still be gay at times, even in troubled waters, or when the Gorgorothian trolls reach down with clutching claws . I sing because I'm happy. I sing because I'm free. I sing because songs have impacted me. Songs aid victorious attitude (Is.52:1).

I have also sung my lungs out in congregational worship times, because they are memorable events. Good songs can be exhilarating, and leave a residual blessing too. For the record, one such time was at a convention where we sang Andraé Crouch's *Bless the LORD, O my Soul* (1973), over and over and over and over again. It was a glorious touching-heaven moment. Not all repetition is mere psychological intoxication. Yet today I'd avoid the term *bless*, when

The Impact of Songs

directed towards deity (Heb.7:7).[32] Back then, it captured me as I was, and the song, in its direction and gusto, enriched. Still, *Bless the LORD*,[33] reworded, would have blessed us more, had it been reinforced by a better biblical base.

If a thing's to be a blessing for the people, it's worth getting it right. Carson captured this principle: "public praying is a responsibility as well as a privilege. In the last century the great English preacher Charles Spurgeon did not mind sharing his pulpit: others sometimes preached in his home church even when he was present. But when it came to the 'pastoral prayer,' if he was present, he reserved that part of the service for himself. This decision did not arise out of any priestly conviction that his prayers were more efficacious than those of others. Rather, it arose from his love for his people, his high view of prayer, his conviction that public praying should not only intercede with God but also instruct and edify and encourage the saints" (Carson 1992:35). In lecture times I used to only allow one student, who had learnt how, to publicly pray, until students complained higher up that they felt out of the loop. Then only I prayed aloud. I still find prayer-meetings flinchy, and have a book on this subject. Presumably Spurgeon thought that since he better knew his congregation, and was competent in Scripture and prayer, he could best pray for them. He knew that a spiral effect is set up whenever we pray, sing, or speak, publicly. Let lyricists take note.

Songs impact our level of belief: I sing, therefore I believe, or I believe, therefore I sing? Once songs have left the lyricist, they can assume the level of creeds, for we are urged to make the same declarations in unison, to sing from the same hymn sheet, so to speak. 2 Cor.4:13 is applicable: we should sing only what we believe. Lyricists aren't God, and might know the Bible far less than your local pastor(s). But would your pastor(s) dare speak up? Would copyright allow them to tweak?

---

[32] Its basic meaning is 'enrich': the one who has can enrich the one who hasn't; we can't enrich God.

[33] Andraé Crouch (1973): quadcaps, since Ps.103:1's about Yahweh, not Jesus.

Songs are boomerang sermons: what we sing away, comes back through our ears.[34]

So we should ponder, before expressing any, "I believe." Indeed, some might believe songs you sing, simply because they believe in you. So, we have a spiritual responsibility to ourselves and to others over what we sing. It's a difficult area, where otherwise the mind could relax. Facing bad songs, coping mechanisms include singing alternative words, and charismatics may have the happy option of disengaging brain and letting the spirit rip at low volume! Indeed, some have argued that singing in unknown language should be second nature.[35] Really bold spirits might up and congregationally challenge bad songs. When good songs hit just the right spot, they allow us "for a few golden moments, to see spirit and flesh, delight and labour, skill and worship, the natural and the supernatural, all fused into that unity they would have had before the Fall" (Lewis 1981:129—slightly decontextualised).

British Pentecostal scholar, William Kay, argued that good songs seem to increase the mystic sense of oneness with God, yet that both *Apostolic* and *Church of God* networks, may be damaging their ability to attract youth because of too ingrained a comfort with prioritising older hymns over newer songs (*Pentecostals in Britain*, 2000:45, 232).[36] Christian networks, and local churches within them, need to be vigilant, blocking or correcting the bad and encouraging the good and relevant. Folk singer Barry McGuire happily admitted he'd been brainwashed, jovially adding that he had had dirty brains, but let's not be brainwashed by grubby songs.

One way to avoid the damage of bad Christian songs is not to sing any Christian songs. Many secular ditties are actually safer than

---

[34] After writing this, I have come across the idea that songs are (perhaps) more important than sermons: "be singing what you sang on Sunday.... songs are our soul food" (Getty and Getty 40-1).

[35] See Howard Ervin's *These Are Not Drunken*, 1968:232.15, on ōidais pneumaticais as spirit-inspired singing (Eph.5:18-9; Col.3:16; 1 Cor.14:14).

[36] I don't call Christian networks, *Churches*. The Methodist *Church*, the Roman Catholic *Church*, the *Church* of This or That, is all counter-biblical. There is one church (*kuriakē*) of many networks/communions of differing perspectives, and differing proportions of Christians meeting in local churches (*ekklēsiai*).

The Impact of Songs

Christian ones, since obviously not claiming full insider authority for the most meaningful of themes. Their pretensions are lower. *Row, Row, Row Your Boat*, never intended to be more significant than, say, *Jesus Will Return in Our Generation*, a belief some songs imply.[37] Singing what we believe usually reinforces our belief, and reinforced belief usually sings in an expanding spiral. This is all the more reason to be concerned about singing unbiblically. Networks that have moved into heresy have done so, not because believers in their churches have all deeply reflected on the issues, but because dominant leaders have led the way into error, and been followed on trust. Their errors have generally been put into song. Singing is a corporate way to inculcate error, and truth, and often a mixture of both.[38] With many Christian song writers, untrained in sound doctrine but personable and musically talented, there is danger for the people. Songs impact us.

Afraid of challenge, Miss Emma Woodhouse told herself never to paint portraits where there were "husbands and wives in the case" (Jane

---

[37] Some accuse Paul of having had that belief for his generation. The closest text, deemed to support this idea, is perhaps 1 Ths.4:15, simply because Paul used the self-inclusive 'we' for those mortal at Jesus' return. Is that even judging Paul by our style of talk? Paul would have known Jesus' prior ignorance, and probably deemed his own execution likely. Moreover, if we come the literalist with this 'we,' then let's include all his initial audience in it, as if Paul expected none to whom he wrote, to die before Jesus returned: *reductio ad absurdum*. All he intended was to contrast the lot of a type of Christian, *viz* all those still mortal (as he and his audience happened to be at the time) at the parousia, with that of deceased Christians. Should we say that Noel Richards' *He Has Risen* (1993) *literally* implied that Noel expected to have died before the resurrection: *We ourselves could not be raised / From the grave we shall arise*. Do *we* sing that, expecting to have died? Language is more fluid, and more scope should be given to Paul.

[38] Arius, for instance, was a C4 heretic who claimed that God's noncarnate son was created within time. Arius was winsome, wrapping heresies into the then CCM, and singing them in his bid to boost their public approval rating. Taking the musical high ground, he rocked the world. Paul of Samosata, a C3 heretic, had likewise been a popular Christian songwriter. His songs were about God choosing a good man, named Jesus, to empower by his mind (*logos*) and to adopt as his son. They got it wrong, but sounded cool, and cool is good.

Austen's *Emma*, ch.6)—too many tender toes. It is dangerous to challenge songs: one can hurt and be hurt. Hurt we must, but harm we mustn't without serious warrant. Some adopt songs for sentimental reasons. Some responses to challenge, but it is not for me to tell tales, can indeed be quite ludicrously lamentable. Westernism[39] often exalts musical stars to ambassadors for society: they are idols beyond their musical expertise. Western Christians all too easily make the same mistake about musically talented and personable Christian performers. For instance, if a new song's signed *Darlene Zschech*, who, especially if not a songwriter, dares question it?[40] Yes, she may be an inspiration, but to bow down to her as the darling of heaven, is no lesser idolatry than to bow to Astartē. Do her songs merit automatic air time in church?

If the pope speaks *ex cathedra*, few Catholics would demure. We have many papal songs. Yet even those we love might need challenge. "I like worship songs. If I didn't like them, I wouldn't get so annoyed about them.... I believe that the modern worship song is an immensely powerful vehicle for worship, and a major factor in encouraging, sustaining, and strengthening the spiritual lives of millions of Christians around the world" (Page 5). Songs can be powerful. They can be prophetic. Yet even when prophets speak, or sing, we should evaluate. Why shouldn't local church leaders oversee their own play lists, as a duty of pastoral care?[41] Yet this can be risky, as they can be accused of beating up on Yahweh's anointeds (1 Chr.16:22/Ps.105:15), especially by those respecting named singers above named pastors: many more have known Darlene's name than her senior pastor's, and heard her sermons but not his.

---

[39] When Parrinder 237 speaks of Westernism, then defines it as "perhaps by implication, Christian" it misses the mark.

[40] Yet we don't have to be carpenters to spot a shoddy table (Page 3).

[41] Churches could even invite congregational feedback when each new song is introduced, and tailor lyrics to their congregations. A radical overhaul of our system would be panels set up, preferably interdenominational as with Bible translation, that lyricists would send material to for assessment by professional theologians and poets.

The Impact of Songs

Another Pentecostal, David Allen, perhaps a little peeved each time his preaching played second fiddle to song leaders, wryly noted how little NT witness there is to songs, compared to spoken proclamation (Allen 186).[42] To this extent, the power of songs can be used to abuse the greater good. This is not simply at particular times, such as a visiting speaker sitting it out. More generally, it can foster the idea among Christians, that songs are the new canon, replacing even Scripture. Is evangelicalism needing a new Luther?

In Augustine's days, there was a debate about how close songs should be to speaking, rather than joyous singing. Saint Augustine confessed how the beauty of singing Christian songs had blessed him, especially soon after his reversion to Christianity (*Confessions* 10.33). So, what did he think about the enchantment of the music overshadowing the lyrics? Well, granting the words were true, he deemed it best to let either music or lyrics get the upper hand for others: horses for courses, so to speak, or at least ponies for youth, and horses for adults. But for him to put music above message would be to sin.

Similarly, songs were a mixed blessing to C S Lewis, who desired "fewer, better, and shorter hymns; especially fewer" (Lewis 1981:126). Lewis argued that one blessing which stylistic preferences offer us, is the opportunity to defer to each other in love. This aspect of Christian service is where, say, one who prefers classical music defers their passion in favour of the rough and ready singer, and *vice versa*.

But this is an indirect song effect, which comes through cultivating a servant heart, rather than critiquing the lyrics. Might not such blessing be devalued, I ask, by singing theologically undermining songs simply to please the other person: should we serve poison in love? Neither Augustine nor Lewis taught that a good tune meant a good song, and their insights remain helpful. "Thrum—thrum—thrum—went the strings of the Witch's instrument…. It didn't come into

---

[42] Though worded as if the spirit's descent was *not* far superior to preaching, his meaning was perhaps that song leaders were too prone to mistake their own spirits for the real Holy Spirit, and too prone to assume that a strong sense of his presence needed musical rather than spoken response. His descent at Pentecost received a preaching response, though there is not an assumption that response must be preaching.

[Jill's] head that she was being enchanted, for now the magic was at full strength; and of course, the more enchanted you get, the more certain you feel that you are not enchanted at all" (Lewis 1985:151). As in C S Lewis' *The Magician's Nephew*, contrasting the Witch's evil enchantment with Aslan's good enchantment, may the only songs to hold us spellbound be good songs.

Consider Soaps. They can carry immorality, for some soaps like jokes are dirty: joke-soap can turn the clean, dirty. Though in seeking to justify themselves, TV Soaps might claim that they *reflect* their society, many Christians are concerned that they also *reinforce* what they reflect, or, perhaps worse, seek to reinforce the evil they reflect. Presumably by reflecting sin but not righteousness, bad soaps seek to actively exalt sin and to debase its prime dampener, Christianity. How many soaps really feature wise Christians? That has long been the back stage strategy of the anti-marriage lobby, in that marriage is a concept that morally precludes interpersonal sex outside its own matrix. As C S Lewis warned some generations ago, "the Christian doctrines on this subject are extremely unpopular" (Lewis 2002:3.6.104). To debunk the doctrine of sin is to debunk the doctrine of being a sinner, which short-term can feel liberating, and long-term is nihilistic, the implosion of humanity. To debunk marriage as sacred, is to debunk its inner message of judgement of our lifestyles, and to treat it as simply human law without moral content. Once meaningless, you can play around with the term to your heart's content, legislating all kinds of nonsense, pretending that the idea, God, is dead. Dethroning marriage makes deadly sense.

Similarity between Christian characters in soaps and reality are purely coincidental, when based on corporate christophobia (fear of Christ) and hagiophobia (fear of holiness). This you will know unless you are under the spirit of the age's spell. Nihilistically, if we wish away God, we wish away goodness. And how long Western civilisation can haemorrhage away morality, and yet retain some preserving image of God, is moot. But in the context of this book, are we intellectually any less guilty than bad soaps, if we fail to see that what we sing also reflects and reinforces? We must ask not simply what is, but what ought to be. Are we content with the numbing thrum, thrum, thrum, seeing perhaps the splinter in society's eye, yet not the log in our own? Do we "strengthen what [we] still have before it dies" (Phillips: Rv.3:2)? Church, as well as society, has truth decay.

In making sense of creation and creator, good teaching makes sense. In living the godly life, it also makes sense. While this book mustn't major on what most songs don't do, it must mention that there is a dearth in songs about how we ought to live, since the dearth creates death: Lk.6:46. I have said that songs are sermons. Did not Pliny say that the Christians he interrogated sang holiness reinforcement into themselves? Today, song content should reflect and reinforce holiness as well as good old fashioned common sense. They should exclude the anti-intellectual and the immoral, and exude the best of intellect and ethical lifestyle. They can be, and should be, servants of the best, and at their best. Thus they will well impact us and those who read us.

We should combine good lyric with good action, engaging body and soul in them. "How can you sing...*Amazing Grace*, how can you sing prayerfully of heaven and earth and all God's wonders without using your hands? My hands demonstrate what I feel like inside. My hands, my feet. I throw in my whole body to say all that is within me. The mind and the voice by themselves are not sufficient" (Mouw and Noll 1905-7 of 3791).

Evangelism in Luton

As to effects on non-Christians, quite a few church songs, like unknown language, will assure them that we are mad. Page told about a Christian wedding that took place in Luton. A Christian spoke. Non-Christians started to think that Christianity might make sense. But when the singing began, eyes glazed over. "As we sang songs about two-edged swords and anointing oil and lots and lots of sheep, we...showed them that when it comes to song lyrics, Christians speak an entirely different language" (Page 1): befuddled evangelism was counterproductive. Epiphany lights flashed, and Page realised that he didn't really understand the songs either. Page thick, songs slick? No, it's simply that we are far too likely to not bother with the detail of mere words, when songs have a good tune and are led by good people The Pied Piper effect. Insider talk is pretty meaningless to outsiders, and can baffle insiders too (Page 102). Like Trinity in *Matrix 3*, Page finally saw above the clouds, saw the light. For my part, I think it's worth waking sleepers from their sleep. Nonsense is poor evangelism.

Attack of the Mûmakil

I am a son of Duinhir, I'm called into the fray / The mûmakil are kicking, they must be fought today / O brother, sister, join me, and do not be afraid / John Bunyan's done, though giants run, we must not be dismayed. But, you may ask, why fight a few daft problems? Spiritual people have a long record of singing spiritual songs, so surely they can be trusted? Anyway, the songs are for us, not for serenading non-Christians, aren't they? So does it really matter if we sing silly love songs, so long as we sing and rejoice? Isn't that joy the true impact we're after?

Personally, I'd love to yield to the clamour of both Political Correctivism, and Church Correctivism, and celebrate the abnorm by denying that there is a norm. Go with the flow, love and peace, man. However, the questions above tend to ignore the lasting impact of songs, on both non-Christians and on Christians, and I would seek truth. Yes, Christian songs can endanger Christians. Eastern Orthodoxy still carries weekly warnings against some people it deems to have been arch-heretics. Swedish singer, Evie Karlsson (nee Tornquist), sang about a spark enabling folk to warm up to a glowing fire. Scandinavians will definitely appreciate that image. Yet Australians can ban sparks for fear of bushfires. Like sparks, songs can warm today, but burn tomorrow. I warm to the Scandinavian glow, yet fear the Aussie fire. Folly and bad doctrine can burn or smoulder, its way through Christianity. To use an illustration from Tolkien, the mûmakil have made it to the Great Gate of Minas Tirith, and we're getting used to seeing them in our fields. A form of multiculturalism gone mad? Mûmakil threaten both us and those we encourage to know Christ, so fight and sadly slay them.

When in prison, Paul and Silas combined praise with evangelism (Ac.16:25). Christian singing multitasks (1 Cor.14:15; Eph.5:19; Col.3:16; Jas.5:13; Rv.15:13). Good songs are very important to our individual lives, and are potentially of great value to others (encouragement, maturation, solidarity, evangelism, etc). Roman Catholics focus more on the community level, even spanning the millennia, while Protestants focus more on the individual level.[43] Yet singing can also devalue all these areas. As with spoken public prayer, attention to the *form* of songs should not distract from the overriding importance of good *meaning* in songs: bad theologians can write inspiring songs, yet such songs can sustain and spread bad theology. "All [singing] presupposes an underlying theology; conversely, our theology will have a decisive influence on our [singing]....it is also true to say that our [singing]...will also influence our theology" (Carson 1992:95).[44]

"But wherever the mûmakil came, there the horses would not go, but blenched and swerved away; and the great monsters were unfought, and stood like towers in defence, and the Haradrim rallied about them" (Tolkien 3.5.6:828). Metaphorically, their kind are still with us today. I would rather not fight the mûmakil, but they must be fought. The sons of Duinhir went right to the fight, but they were slain for their pain. Like spoiling a gay party with straight talk, iconoclasm can easily lose friends. To rephrase an old Kentucky song, *You are always to be found, a singing in your glory, without my frowning face round, 'till then you're hunkey dorey*. It's like what Lewis said about Christianity: talk about the hunky dory, about all being well and the world under a benign grandfather god, and folk will smile. But talk of God having his plans for us, into which we ought to fit but seldom do, and those same folk will frown, the day spoilt. Similarly, for shooting down a Christian song, you can be accused of murder, lyricide. However, for the sake of the people, the more important the songs are, the more important it is to get them right. Kendrick said we should aim to produce quality Rolls Royce songs, and I'd agree with him, even if his own cars need to be tweaked. Hopefully those newly in the business will make Royces, not lemons.

A song might suck, but some folk say, Hold your tongue. Yahweh challenged Job to put up or shut up, and Job shut up (*Job* 40:5). But when Jerusalem tried to silence Jeremiah, he spoke up. I think that we are under some obligation, here. So the hand some would have hold its tongue, I raise first in confession, leaving my tongue to wag:

---

[43] Mouw & Noll 1788-91 of 3791

[44] Where you see '[singing]' Carson wrote 'praying': I've kept his principle but not his theme.

Power and Christian Songs

I confess that I am indeed no musician. But my tongue shan't challenge music: the worst of songs can have the best of music.

One blogger told herself off for critiquing songs which some use as worship springboards, deciding she should only speak out against theologically disturbing lyrics, those inconsistent with God. That is more or less where I am at and I'll happily side with such bloggers, though I shall suggest some other principles for all Christian lyricists, in the hope that these principles will help lyricists produce better songs for the future, should the lord tarry. About the last thing I wish to do is to discourage folk from singing to please God, but there is clear blue water between that, and alerting them to songs that undermine the biblical revelation of God, and/or fall below a good standard whether of lyric or of logic.

In fact, my quote above from Tolkien is misleading, since whereas the mûmakil approached Minas Tirith as undeniably hostile beasts, the towers of strength I oppose are often deemed our longterm friends. Either way, they can have a mammoth impact. There are good songs. There are bad songs. There can be good in bad songs. There can be bad in good songs. If you ask me if I am an enemy of songs, I would say that I am a friend of prayer, that understanding prayer helps understand songs, and that we need to understand both before we talk of sides. I am an enemy of the bad. Before tackling songs (Part 3), let me tackle prayer (Part 2), to set up the context.

Part 2 Prayer and Christian Songs
Chapter 3 The Trinity and You
From QuadCap to OneCap

Before I knew the Matrix Trinity (hopefully we missed her fall in *Matrix 2*),[45] I knew the Eternal Trinity. Yet in the west, Christian sight has grown dim, and by and large recent generations know not the trinity. Many songs born in these generations show faulty understanding. The translation convention of substituting, in the OT, God's name by *the LORD*, sometimes even without explanation, is part of the problem. The *International Children's Bible's lord*, ignores both God's name and Tyndale's quadcaps method, *LORD*, showing a childish conception common among adults. God's name deserves a shout! Usually song lyrics follow the ICB style, even if they're cut and paste from an adult English version. If ever we are to visualise the trinity in sung and spoken prayer, we need to spend some time learning the doctrine.

The Unknown Lord

Various factors have tended to suppress God's name. Besides the Jewish hedge put up around God's name 'for safety's sake', the Greek OT which adopted the hedge (though it often employed an anarthrous technique to imply that kurios sometimes doubled as the name), was used by Jesus himself. Many great Christians have used the KJV or earlier authorised versions, but does this make them our benchmark? I do not think these are good reasons not to go back to a Hebrew distinction, especially to combat modalism. Tactically you should deploy the weapons and defences that fit the given battle. It's draining the concept *trinity* into an unbiblical concept of Jesus, which is a battlefield now. After all, if our thinking about God is sloppy, how can we sort out our incohesive and incoherent world? God must not be nebulous to us.

The term *lord* can function, in one part of a song, to refer to the father's son, and in another to refer to the son's father, jumbling up

---

[45] See www.movieguide.org/reviews/movie/the-matrix-reloaded.html, and *Matrix Revelations* (ed. Steve Crouch):
http://www.movieguide.org/reviews/movie/the-matrix-reloaded.html.

the persons and the singers. As said, to some extent this slip is due to English versions that replace God's name with *the LORD*, which sounds (and in lyrics often looks) the same as for Jesus being *lord*, and can encourage folk to think *Jesus*, rather than to think *Yahweh*, whenever they read the OT. Like the ancient pharaoh, many Christians would ask who Yahweh is, and explain that they don't know him (Ex.5:2). I think *Yahweh* aligns better with *God* than with *lord*. Even Chris Idle cited Zp.3:16 as about the *lord* (not LORD) singing, then related it to *Jesus* instead of to Yahweh as trinity.

Nick Page showed similar oversight. It's easily done. Following some brilliant points that worship isn't songs and time slots (it's bowing our whole lives to deity)—the revelation must be ingrained in heart and head—Page underlined his definition of worship as "showing God how much we value him", restating this as "showing Jesus what we think of him" (Page 24), agreeing with the Redmans that the focus of worship "should be Jesus.... It's really all about him" (44).

Stuff and nonsense, sir! God *is not Jesus*—God *is a trinity*.[46] David Allen, referring to Edward Irving's orthodoxy, commented that Irving's controversial Christology "did not, however, lead him into 'Jesusism'—that rather sentimental attachment to Christ sometimes found in charismatic circles that leads to a tendency to neglect other members of the Trinity" (Allen 102). I think Allen was right about contrasting the Charismatic Irving to today's Charismatics. Some, in sentimental attachment to Jesus, overlook father and spirit. And detetragrammatising God's name to *the LORD*, then often further misshapen into *the lord*, can also easily move us from the trinity.

The Who Lord

Lord is sometimes a word for we know not whom. Wham, bam, slam, let's start singing the first few lines, wherever they lead. It's blind man's buff. How often are songs simply introduced from the front, as

---

[46] True, Jhn.1:1,18; Rm.9:5; Tts.2:13; and 2 Pt.1:1 say that Jesus is Theos. On these texts, I grade the NET (A); NLT (A-); NRSV (B+); ERV/NIV (B); CEB/NOG (B-); NCV/NJB (C+); NKJV (C-). My point is that the emphatic biblical emphasis is that the term either speaks of the father, or of the corporate trinity. "Jesus is God" is misleadingly simplistic, and the error of the Witnesses is nearer the truth than many would like to believe.

if the congregation only needs to pick up the tune? As if prior thinking is irrelevant? There is surely scope for letting congregations overview the full lyrics, before being invited to sing.[47] I like to see the map before beginning the journey: orientation. OK, first up, imagine a new song is to the *lord*. Simple. But I'd begin uncertainly, like Saul's "who are you lord?"

Alas, visualising, I have painfully often sung heartily to the father, only to discover midway that the song's *meant* to be about his son, or perhaps *vice versa*.[48] Imagine, guys, that meeting your secret passion on a dark night, you begin pouring out your heart, telling her how beautiful she is, and that you've always admired her from afar. *She* then interrupts to inform you that it's actually her mother you've met, not her daughter! Fortunately it's so dark that all the mother sees in the darkness is the glow of your red face. Oops, you should have checked first. Don't blab in the dark.

As a singer if I hit choppy lyrics to someone else, I stumble, dazed, shell-shocked, having sung my song to the wrong person: my brother is not my father. Nowadays, I'd rather let the OHP bit by bit scroll through an unfamiliar song, and check out who it's to, before I engage in actually singing it. Of course, by which time it has finished, and folk are sitting down. Ah, *c'est la vie*. Each song could be headed by its target audience (visualisation)—I have abbreviations such as TD3, referring to songs sung to the spirit.

The Confused Lord

A song by Carman, *Lord of All*, begins *Lord, you are wonderful*.[49] So, as the band sings I listen, unsure as to direction: *Who are you, lord?* Someone will guess that *lord* means Jesus. Someone else will guess that it means his father. *Lord of all* might refer to Yahweh (the lord of all the earth: Ps.97:5 *et al*), or to Jesus (*kurios pantōn*: Ac.10:36; Rm10:12—where it means the pan-ethic lord of redeemed Jews/Gentiles). *Cuz/That Jesus Christ is*,

---

[47] One couple offered some sound advice: "If you are using a new song, teach it. Email the congregation in advance if you can...", though feedback options to sing it modified, or even not sing it, were not considered (Getty & Getty 119).

[48] The unfazed include unitarians and fuzzy trinitarians.

[49] Incidentally a polydirectional song—bits to Jesus, and bits about Jesus.

suggests in normal English that we are singing *about* Jesus, not *to* Jesus, so seems to prove we're singing to the father about Jesus, only it then refers to Jesus as being *lord of all*, so he's the one being sung to about himself in the third person. If our mind is not engaged, it will not confuse.

A song by Lincoln Brewster (2002), *All I Really Want*, also begins with *Lord*. Its chorus begins God I praise thee,[50] which seems clear, until we see that *Jesus Saviour friend of sinners* is probably the only person being sung to—as if he is God, alone God. Neither father nor spirit are wanted, *only* Jesus. *Here I Am* (*Majesty*),[51] seems sung to the father about the lamb's blood, only to thank the father for laying down his own life! The father is crucified, and while Tertullian weeps we whoop it up. Visualisation of the uncreated persons is basic for good lyricists and singers. Fuzzy songs; fuzzy singers.

The Limited Lord

I heard someone say today that salvation's neither based on good works nor on the torah, but on *Jesus only*. They oversimplified. On that point, it's far better to say it's not through Jesus only, but through Jesus the only pivot: the trinity saves. Though it's dangerous talk, like walking on the cliff edge, my real beef is when folk take Jesus-only talk into the ontological. The former is unitarianism in function—only God the son does the basic of salvation. This may be called Onlyist. The hard form is to deny the personal coexistence of the father and the spirit. This is unitarianism, with a small u. The denomination calling itself Unitarianism, has a different approach, but shares the basic idea that God is one person.

Some non-denominationally hard unitarians, hold Jesus alone to be deity. They limit intrinsic eternality to Jesus, ignoring the father, the spirit, and the noncarnate son, and tend to talk as if one person, Jesus,

---

[50] Grammatically, *thee*, spoken to God nowadays, implies he is one person, but it would fit if only to the father.

[51] By Stu Garrard & Martin Smith (2003). It turns girls into guys, saints into sinners, and the father into his son. Added value: the reason (rather than an outcome) for being forgiven, is that we can forgive, and having transmorphed from the father, *we*, not the father, are Jesus' desire—lucky him and what excellent taste!

had paternal and helper *modes*, a trinity of *masks*. Arguably, "...most Western Christians are practical modalists" (Letham 212). Those who know and welcome modalism at least tend to be consistent in their belief. And they, with knowing smiles, reckon that self-confessing trinitarians, by singing Jesus-only songs, are instinctively closet modalists, needing to come out. Regrettably some Christian songs are pitched somewhere between what the Bible says, and the systematisation done at Nicea and Chalcedon.

IMO trinitarians who sing such songs simply sing substandard: the standard itself is fine. Failure to visualise the trinity leads to songs falling below par in prayer and in theology. The lord was limited in what he could do (Jhn.5:19), and remains so. We must look beyond the limited lord, as he taught us.

So, how can you train your visuals? Have you ever, using a countdown watch, spent 10 minutes talking to the father, then, like on a telephone, said 'goodbye' and spent 10 minutes talking to his son your brother, then ended with a 'goodbye' and spent the next 10 minutes talking to the spirit? 30 minutes not asking, just talking? It's likely to be painfully slow at first, like a shy first contact, but such prayer time builds up some gut feeling that the father is neither the son nor the spirit, that the son is neither the spirit nor the father, and that the spirit is neither the father nor the son. Sadly, getting to know the real father as distinct from the real son and the real spirit, can make confrontations with spiritually foggy songs increasingly irksome, but it can put us in better touch with the Athanasian Creed.

The true LORD

Michael Saward, an Anglican, defined hymns as "a series of connected verses, usually addressed in worship to one or all of the Persons of the Holy Trinity, logically developing a Christian theme, usually in metrical and rhyming form, to a tune capable of being sung by a congregation".[52] Hymns can address all the persons of the trinity biblically. To jump to a term I'll look at a little later—the term theo-directional (TD)—if you wish to analyse Christian songs, at this stage you could use **TDo** for open songs to deity, where *God* seems to you to mean the trinity,

---

[52] In Idle's *Hymns in Today's Language?*

Prayer and Christian Songs

TD1 for songs to the father, **TD2** to the son, and **TD3** to the spirit. If analysis results in revealing, say, a **TD23** song (son and spirit), yet the song implies they're one person, then mark it down as antitrinitarian. Chris Idle's comment that it "seems to rule out hymns by Unitarians, of which we sing not a few" (Reform), suggests that many songs are covert unitarianism. But we sing 'em anyway. Hey, if the emoticons are good, why fuss about words? All you gotta do is thank the father for dying on the cross and the spirit for sending Jesus, and smile that smile! Jesus Onlyism, Oneness teaching, is unitarian/nontrinitarian,[53] in the sense that it holds that deity is one person who plays three different parts (father, brother, and helper) and whose name we can simplify as Jesus. Jesus is all I need and all that thrills my soul is Jesus. True, or false? False. Let's not forget the trinity

One brilliant song is Mark Altrogge's (1987) *I Stand in Awe*.[54] As worship to Yahweh, the Eternal Society, the Land of Trinity, it exudes a sense of the mountain descending upon us, the weight of glory. We are imperilled, and cry for mercy. As Malacandra might say, in our best thoughts there are such things mingled which, if angels thought them, their light would perish (Lewis 181). My spiritual diet would put any healthy angel to shame. Isaiah was a profit; I am a loss. Woe is me. Altrogge's song really chokes me up.

I wept when I discovered that Altrogge, a few years later, gutted it into a mere Jesus song.[55] Imagine wholehearted singing stanza 1 to Yahweh, feeling dwarfed by awe, only to have stanza 2 jump out and crucify your vision, blind your mental direction. It's as if Leonardo da Vinci had decided a few years later to paint a Hitler mo onto the Mona Lisa, and became Leonardo da Vandal! Visualisation might have saved Altrogge from such insipidity. Tyndale's LORD is Yahweh; the Lord is Jesus. Yahweh is vaster than Jesus, as society exceeds an individual. Ultimately deity is not a person. Let's move to one person.

---

[53] C17 Unitarianism was more into Dynamic Modalism, the idea that the human Jesus was adopted by God.

[54] I'd simply tweak *Holy God*, to *Holy One*. Altrogge's name now disheartens me.

[55] The bastard second stanza includes: *You are beautiful beyond description, Lamb of God, who died for me.*

Chapter 4   The Holy Spirit and You

If you are a Christian, you are in a relationship with the Holy Spirit, but is it a by the way, or an intimate, relationship? Are you aware of him each day? Do you talk with him each day? If not, why not? Could it be that you are too Jesus-focused? Is that possible? Is that bad? Well, not according to some songs, that's for sure. I freely admit that the spirit is somewhat hidden in Scripture. For instance, while the first and second person have family identities, namely *father* and *son*, and to us *father* and *brother*, the spirit lacks such a family designation. There are reasons for this, such as now having a family relationship with deity in terms of father and brother in heaven, and also having a here and now missional relationship with the spirit—he is the paraclete, the helper in mission.

John's Gospel works on the picture that the father and son are 'in heaven' and us and the spirit 'on earth', us thus having a 'vertical' and a 'horizontal' link with deity, a life to live and a job to do. And there is perhaps also an apocalyptic reason: two 'packets' have been opened; a hidden 'packet' remains. Like *Revelation*, this can remind us that there is so much more to deity beyond the sunset. *Still round the corner there may wait, a new door, or a secret gate, and though I oft have passed them by, a day will come at last when I, shall take the hidden paths the run, east of the moon, west of the sun.* Ah, we walk in divine poetry. Yet hidden though he be, he should be an ever-present part of our relational lives: real life is meeting. Jesus never casts out the spirit!

<u>Reflections on Prayer</u>

But what do the songwriters say? Only Jesus can satisfy your soul, only Jesus brings redemption, only Jesus satisfies, Jesus only is our message, Jesus only will we see, Jesus all in all we sing, Jesus only is our saviour, Jesus only is our healer, only Jesus can our every sorrow know; he alone can truly help us. This is a simple string from a number of unitarian songs: the only trinitarianism glimmer in the fog is one which has us ask Jesus to fill us with the spirit. Are the father and the spirit redundant and insignificant to us, complications we can well do without? Does this reflect the picture in *John* of Jesus having ascended to the father, and the spirit engaging in the work of

Prayer and Christian Songs

NT salvation, being Jesus' agent on earth? In fleshing out trinitarianism, we need to relate to the spirit. This fellowship, this natterland, protects us from Jesus Onlyism/Oneness, and accords with Scripture. And after all, why sidestep the spirit? Even Jesus worked by God's finger, the Holy Spirit (Lk.11:20/Mt.12:28).

Unitarianism pervades our prayer-songs, too. I sometimes fear that we misunderstand prayer almost as much as we misunderstand trinitarianism. "Most folk pray how I pray, so my way's OK," can equally be said in Witness, and Mormon, circles. Parochial ways can be globally wrong. Whatever the ads, ten million cats can be wrong. Martin Luther's revelation, that assurance of forgiveness came through trusting that God would welcome all who directly come to him, was a minority report. Many still think such assurance is arrogant and hope, rather than know, they're God's. Global majorities can be wrong. Christian songs are often prayers. Belief shapes, and is shaped by, prayer. Let's look more generally at prayer, sorting out some basics.

Prayer is talking in God's direction. I call this being theodirectional, Godward, and will later look at this in some depth. Let's put it like this:

| Theodirectional | Unidirectional to deity | You are praiseworthy, God |

Prayer, if with biblical belief, will form a virtuous spiral, but if with unbiblical, will form a vicious spiral. What relates to prayer relates to deity, and what relates to deity matters. Laziness of mind impedes logic: to love deity with our mind, is a moral duty leading to joy. Without the mind it is mere happiness, excitement without exploration. But attention to the form of prayer, should not distract from the overriding importance of good content in prayer—even bad theologians can pray faith prayers, and see evil mountains removed. But who would argue that the less biblical we are, the better we can pray, or that blessed are the heretics, for they shall not obtain truth? Surely it is the best of both worlds to have great theology and great faith prayer. Antibiblical prayers can sustain, and spread, bad theology. And "all praying presupposes an underlying theology; conversely, our theology will have a decisive influence on our praying....

It is also true to say that our praying (or lack of praying) will also influence our theology" (Carson 1992:95). Many are the songs we pray.

Quasi-Requests

Prayer comes in many shapes and sizes, sometimes with a dollop of artificiality. For example, let's looking at asking God. I focus on the congregation and say, "let us now ask God." Fine. I then focus on God and begin, "please..." What if I bring together these two focuses: "Let us now ask you, God, please..."? I have *asked* him *if* I may *ask* him. This quirk has a knock-on effect on sung prayer. Rather than "father, please go with me and help me," it's "father, <u>I ask you to</u> please go with me and <u>I want to ask you to</u> help me." The bits underlined aren't asking, but *informing*, the father, that the speaker is making a parallel request: I'm *telling* you that I'm *asking* you (or at least wish to ask), for such and such. Must we prime God like we prime a congregation, that request is coming? Do we seriously visualise God as listening?

Consider which sentence is more natural: "Jackie, I ask you to please go with me, and I ask you to help me," or "Jackie, please go with me and help me."[56] Must Jackie process two kinds of information—I am *telling* her that I am *asking* her? Convoluted! Theologically worse, would be, "father, I would like to ask you to..." to which he might reply, exasperated if he were capable of exasperation, "well, OK, you've told me you'd *like* to ask. Now, are you, or are you not, going *to* ask me?" Such grammatical quirks, with their level of unreality and artificiality, tend to make deity seem obscure.[57] It is important that our songs do not sound as if he were artificial to us. Let's pretend that God is really before you, as he was before Moses at the burning bush: how would you ask him? The crunch word is *really*. When we ask him for things, do we really believe he *is* before us, or do we believe it's more like texting him, with the hope that he'll read the text sometime? Because our physical senses don't detect him, do we

---

[56] Some would recognise the archaism here: *I pray thee* = please.

[57] Natural speech can to some extent reflect this approach. "Jackie, I'd like to ask you a favour. Please feed the cat while I'm away." We prepare Jackie for a request, then make the request. But does God need preparation?

believe he is less really before us, than a fellow human being? Lack of visualisation, of picturing belief, badly infects Christian songs.

Whom Should You Ask?

Children, even if born to Christian parents, were not by first birth born into God's family, and should not be taught to pray in Jesus' name. If as individuals they have been, or become, born into God's family, it's another matter: dual citizenship comes with personal faith-welcome. But prior to that, they should at most pray to God as God, not God as father. It's been thus throughout human history, for any adults not born into God's family. He was *Yahweh* to his people; *Elohim* to others.

For Christians, the primary biblical pattern <u>is asking the father in the son's name</u>, that is, asking in the authority and persona of the son. To ask the father in the father's authority and persona, doesn't quite cut it, though some pray "father, we ask in your name". Petitionary prayer is based on understanding the work and person of Jesus.[58] God the son became a human being, and walked with man as 'Jesus.' In the shadow of the cross, he taught disciples to move to direct access with the father, and to base it on his (Jesus') own authority—*in his name* serving as a way of saying *in his mission*. This special relationship of working family, which we are to enjoy with the father, is clouded if

---

[58] Some object that petitionary prayer is a philosophical contradiction. If God is all knowing he need not be informed, and if he is all goodness he need not be asked. If your neighbour loves cats and knows you're going on holiday and leaving your cat in your garden, why ask them to feed the cat? In the case of the human neighbour, one might say it's courtesy. In the case of God, one might say that although he will work out his cosmic plan, he allows us to interact with parochial issues in order to mature our focus on the spiritual. He wishes us to invoke him into our lives and thus to mature. Petitionary prayer can also be to attune our hearts to godliness, to think as God thinks, so it's getting *us* involved, not simply aimed at God being involved. Prayers that end "for your sake" miss that requests are for *our* sake. Please heal me for *my* sake, and heal them for *Jesus'* sake!? Jesus gave himself for us for *our* sake (Jhn.17:19).

we make petitions to Jesus (Jhn.16:26-8). Roman Catholicism makes similar mistakes when asking Mary to help out.[59]

In fact to be *in Jesus' name*, petitionary prayer, whether sung or spoken, doesn't need to say the words "in Jesus' name," or "in the name of your son." It simply needs to be from those in Jesus asking for what's in Jesus' will. Indeed, for prayer that's synched to Jesus' mission, whatever we ask for that's needed for that mission, will probably be in God's will (father and son are one in will: Jhn.10:30), and will therefore be granted. I say 'probably' because even here mission is part of a bigger picture. He can allow obstacles to us doing mission, in order to work on us or on others. Paul had wished to visit the Thessalonians (1 Ths.2:18), but God had allowed Satan to stop Paul for a while, perhaps both to build up Paul and to build up the Thessalonians. God's strategic will. Even his will, in the sense of his desire, has intrinsic limits: he *wills* all human beings to be saved, yet allows the rebellion of rejection. Love will woo, but will not violate, our heart choice. My book *Israel's Gone Global*, covers this in much more depth. Still, we hope our requests are in Christ's mission. If they are, we don't need to tell his father that they are. If they are not, should we try to deceive God? A *please* and *thank you* should suffice.

---

[59] Catholics sometimes argue that asking *saints* (they mean spiritual postmortal VIPs) to intercede, is no more daring than asking a Christian friend to do so, and indeed that saints are more likely to influence God. Fair doos. I'd say that if you ask a Christian friend to pray for you (each is biblically a saint and a priest), then you should still ask God direct. Similarly, if you ask a deceased saint, you should also ask God direct. The main point is that if you are a Christian, you too are a saint and a priest, and should not cop out of asking direct. Besides, you should know you're in God's family, and that you don't need anyone else to get him to hear you. But within a context of our active priesthood, meditations on very spiritual persons, and their mediations, can help our prayers (Jas.5:17-8). Perhaps God intends that Christians on Earth's stage, since they can gain from mutual support and maturation, in a way which perhaps the heavenly audience cannot, should share each other's needs in this way.

Prayer and Christian Songs

Person asked	Bless me	Bless us	Father's name	Jesus' name
Father	✓	✓	✗	✓
Son	✗	✗	✗	✗
Spirit	-	✗	✗	✗

A somewhat popular yet disturbing feature, is asking the spirit to bless folk. Biblically the spirit is the person of deity alongside us who inspires, not receives, our requests (Rm.8:15,26-7). Some heretical old hymns are now respectability coated with the gentle dust of tradition (eg Baptist James Edwin Orr's *Search Me, O God (1936)*: *O Holy Ghost..send a revival*; and Apostolic/Elim's E C W Boulton's *Floods Of Revival, Lord let them fall..Spirit Divine, O quicken us now*). Chris Bowater's *Holy Spirit, We Welcome You* (1986), prays *let the breeze of your presence blow / that your children here might truly know / how to move in the Spirit's flow*. Besides asking the spirit not for *his* but for *the spirit's* flow, this song asks us to buy into God the spirit being God our father! Oh come now. It's right to welcome him, but not as being our father, nor to welcome Jesus as being our sister. We are heirs of the father, and co-heirs with his son; Jesus is not ashamed to call us his brothers and sisters, but not his children![60] Trinitarianism is decaying in the West. Prayer-songs can reflect and reinforce this decay.

Father, Lord, or Spirit?

Ultimately the father is lord (Jude 1:4), and he is spirit (Jhn.4:24). In ch.4 I'll cover prayer to *the* spirit, the third person of deity. Suffice it now to say that although he is the perfect paraclete (helper) on earth, we're not told to ask of him, and if anything should see him as helping us ask the father. As regards praying to the lord, in our state of decaying trinitarianism, is calling God *lord* best dropped, while we seek to rebuild trinitarianism, confining *lord* to Jesus? Easily prayers which start with the father, pop in the fact of his ultimate lordship, then unconsciously move to dwell on Jesus (the NT focus of strategic lordship), while we still vaguely picture one *person* (the lord!) being spoken to.

---

[60] Rm.8:17; Heb.2:11. Mk.10:24 does not refute my point: Paul and John also called *disciples* their children, but as regards God's family all are brothers & sisters.

This is Oneness, something the Athanasian Creed's bit about "confusing the persons" warned against (see *infra*). For example: "*Lord God, you* said 'if I your *lord* and teacher have washed your feet....'" Our brother, not our father, washed human feet. Such prayers encourage the heresy in numerous songs that we are children of Jesus, or of the spirit. Yes, Jesus called his disciples his children. But hey, they weren't even born anew into God's family! And in the same sense some disciples were *children of John*, or of Paul. It was a cultural picture for disciple to teacher, not a trinitarian use expressing eternal parentage. Relationally, the biblically highlighted position is trinitarian: we are children of the father, brothers and sisters of Jesus, and work with the Holy Spirit our helper.

Athanasian soteriology might be a bit iffy, but its theology is insightful. Here, slightly reworded, is part of the Athanasian Creed:

> ...the global faith is this: That we worship...God in trinity, and trinity in unity, neither confusing the persons, nor dividing the substance.[61] For there is one person of the Father, another of the Son, and another of the Holy Spirit. But the deity of the Father, of the Son, and of the Holy Spirit, is all one, the glory equal, the majesty co-eternal. Such as the Father is, such is the Son, and such is the Holy Spirit. The Father uncreated, the Son uncreated, and the Holy Spirit uncreated. The Father beyond our full comprehension, the Son beyond our full comprehension, and the Holy Spirit beyond our full comprehension. The Father eternal, the Son eternal, and the Holy Spirit eternal. And yet they are not three eternals, but one eternal. As also there are not three beyond our full comprehension, nor three uncreated, but one uncreated, and one beyond our full comprehension. So likewise the Father is almighty, the Son almighty, and the Holy Spirit almighty. And yet they are not three almighties, but one almighty. So the Father is God, the Son is God, and the Holy Spirit is God. And yet they are not three gods, but one god. So likewise the Father is lord, the Son lord, and the Holy Spirit lord. ...yet not three lords, but one lord.

This is an exposition of triunity, of oneness relative to *society*, and threeness relative to *persons*, and an implicit recognition that we are

---

[61] For example, not saying only one is lord, only one is saviour, only one is God, etc.

dealing with patterns for understanding that which we can only partially comprehend (1 Cor.13:9-10). Not each a lord, but each being lord; not each a god, but each being God. Even "in the name of the father, in the name of the son, in the name of the spirit," can suggest three names, rather than the one threefold singular name of Mt.28:19. Trinitarianism allows best insights in this age.

Nor is the OT a justification for calling Jesus *lord*, for the English rendering of *Yahweh* as *LORD* is not inspired by deity, though Intertestamental Jewish Religion superstitiously used lordship terms to avoid God's name. Even for the sake of argument granting OT justification, the NT position remains clear: it is Jesus who for this age has been given the function of lordship (Php.2:9-11; 1 Cor.8:5-6), and the spirit is delegated central command, lord, at ground level. While arguably overkill, if we never call the father *lord*, and never ask the *lord* for anything, it can open up/keep open trinitarianism.[62] This seems to have been Paul's rule of thumb.[63] The Athanasian Creed makes valid points on ontology, relates to each person each area of definition, and implies (without investigating differences of our interaction to each by the different basic titles of father, son, and spirit) the ABC of a triangle. All lyricists should have a dust free copy on their desks.

Adding Back the Spirit

Hillsong is only one forum where old Sabellius recruits singers. Lots of songs have Onlyist tendencies. While it can seem a little bit hard to knock a devotional song for having a little bit of unitarianism, the cumulative effect of many such songs can undermine what I hold to be core biblical teaching. Take a different example, where wilfully or

---

[62] The "lord have mercy", *kurie eleēson* (Latinised as *kurie eleison*), would be better as *patēr eleēson* (father have mercy), although we might still think it strange asking for mercy from one who has had mercy on us by making eternal life, which Christians have chosen, available. Did a penitential sense of distance inspire this phrase, now embedded in the church courtesy of the East?

[63] Eg, in *Romans* there are 38 justified Greek NT references to *lord* (*kurios*). 9 are citations of the OT, put the Septuagint way as *lord* (4:8; 9:28-9; 10:16; 11:3,34; 12:19; 14:11; 15:11). 16 are new references clearly to Jesus (1:4,7; 4:24; 5:1,11,21; 6:23; 7:25; 8:39; 10:9; 13:14; 14:9; 15:6,30; 16:18,20). The remaining 13 are probably about Jesus (10:12-3; 12:11; 14:4,6,8,14; 16:2,8,11-3,22).

not, the trinity has taken back seat. We all know that Jesus is the *only* saviour. Thus, the KJV rightly says, "To the only wise god our Saviour, be glory and majesty, dominion and power, both now and ever. Amen" (*Jude* 25). But the NIV reads "to the only god our Saviour be glory, majesty, power and authority, through Jesus Christ our Lord, before all ages, now and forevermore! Amen." We thus side with Gail Riplinger[64] and dismiss the NIV for moving the text away from its witness to Christ's deity, since as Gail said about this text, "our Savior is Jesus; therefore Jesus is God" (Riplinger 371).

That at least is clear. Or is it? In fact, besides good textual evidence for the NIV, I think Gail overlooked here the simple fact that the KJV, which her book advocates, speaks of "God our Saviour, and Lord Jesus Christ" (1 Tm.1:1), as different persons. In other words, Jesus is not our *only* saviour in a wider trinitarian setting, so why insist that *Jude* 25 calls him saviour, unless it's clear that that's what Jude called him in that context? In different ways and for different reasons, we can easily drop into unitarianism. Is the Holy Spirit not saviour, too? All three are saviour. All three share that *name*. The Athanasian Creed is wise.

Whatever our hobbyhorses, it's helpful to see that "the theology of the NT revelation is Father, Son and Holy Spirit, one god.... In every activity of each of these three 'persons' of deity it is always...God who acts; the NT principle was subsequently formulated in Catholic theology by means of the formula: opera trinitatis ad extra sunt indivisa [that is, the works of the trinity are entirely undivided.] That is to say, the personæ [that is, persons] must not be rigidly separated from one another and identified with particular divine functions (for example creating, redeeming, sanctifying), for all the personæ act in every divine work" (Richardson 123). Let's add back the Holy Spirit as saviour.

We should question *Jesus-only* statements, and ask in what ways *if any* the father and spirit might be involved—for example the father secures, the son procured, the spirit cures. We must bear the trinity in mind, and heart. How do we do this with the spirit? With him whom C S Lewis said we might find "rather vaguer or more shadowy in [our minds] than the other two" (Lewis 2002:4.4.175)? By minds and hearts fed by God's word and proper songs, that's how. To this end

---

[64] I give her greater mention in my, *The Word's Gone Global*.

I'll spend some time in looking at a seldom covered area of theology (pneumatology), namely how the spirit should be incorporated into our devotional life. In fact, any movement away from Jesus Onlyism, whether towards the father or towards the spirit, is gain. Perhaps too, incorporating the spirit into one's daily thinking will make it more natural to incorporate the father, whereas broadening from fellowship with father and son is less obvious. What is our relationship with this shadowy figure?

Trinitarian Fellowship

Relationship can mean fixed, static relationships: for example, Earth to Sun; satellite planet to host star; the hated daughter remains a daughter until death parts.[65] It can also mean *vibes*. For example in the relationship of employer to employee (impersonal idea), there could be a bad or good relationship (in the sense of vibes). The two people could swap job roles (static relationship change) and retain their bad or good relationship, their dynamic relationship. This sense of vibes can usefully be called 'fellowship.' Christianity is about beginning fixed family relationship in the first sense (Mt.28:19) and building loving dynamic relationship in the second sense (1 Jhn.1:3; Php.2:1).

Many evangelical Christians begin fellowship only with Jesus. As he is the 'door' this is easy to understand—we meet the entrance door before we meet the room. Some, seeking what he is the way *to*, meet the father (Jhn.16:27), and perhaps progressing to binitarian fellowship, progress further into trinitarian fellowship (Jhn.14:16). A few might even meet the one guiding them towards the door before arriving at the door. The spirit is at work around and about us. For Christians, he is in fact a work colleague, whether or not we know it. That's a fixed relationship. But a dynamic relationship, fellowship, is Christian too, and I'll go into this. When we sit down after a day's spiritual work and put our feet up, he's with us in the next chair, so to speak. But first, to say again, the father is first.

---

[65] There are no families or spousal reunions in heaven—the redeemed are family.

Father First[66]

Jesus is the way, not the destination, nor the navigator. The trinity distinctions include an authority structure. The spirit was working alongside Jesus (Mt.12:28), indeed had worked since creation, and would soon in a new covenant way, represent Jesus working alongside the disciples (Jhn.14:15-31): *Acts* continues Jesus' mission of teaching and other acts (Ac.1:1). Christians and the spirit would be witnesses together (Jhn.15:26-7), and the very fact that he was manifestly with them was manifest evidence that they—unlike for example the Jewish Sanhedrin—were those who were obeying God (Ac.5:32).[67] The issue of whether the spirit was sent primarily by the father, or equally by the father and the son, helped create needless division between East and West.[68] This was within the big issue of whether the Western side of

---

[66] In so far as we don't pick this up, Jesus has failed! Reasons we ignore him:
1   bad traditional teaching that's never been ironed out;
2   the father seeming unapproachable (Heb.12:28-9), while Jesus, being incarnate, seeming approachable (Heb.2:17). Romanism perhaps implies that Mary is even more approachable.
3   1 Jhn.1:3

[67] Does not Ac.5:32 mean the obedience of accepting Christ, from which flows obedience in Christ?

[68] More can be said. Source or sender? If the Nicene Creed simply meant mission, East & West would be fairly happy. But if speaking of ontology, the Filioque Clause sounded like father & son were equal sources of the spirit. The West failed in consultation & humility, and unilaterally insisted that the East accept into the Nicene Creed the clause 'and from the Son' (a.k.a. *filioque* clause). The East rightly objected to unilateral and ambiguous changes to the creed, and rejected as heresies the ideas of papal authoritative primacy, and of any father/son equivalence which undermined the uniqueness of the father as the sole or primary Fount. Perhaps a better balance of Augustine (West) would have fitted well with the Cappadocian position (East) that the spirit proceeded "'out of the Father through the Son'" (Young 64). The West thought that even in its *eternity* sense—which it didn't mean—it fitted with biblical teaching on the trinity. Pope Leo 3 attempted to restore the original creedal form while believing the filioque theology, but failed. In 1054 came the so-called Great Schism between East & West, each side cutting the other off, excommunications withdrawn in 1965 by Catholic and Orthodox leaders, though the Schism remains. Jhn.15:26 speaks in a temporal sense of mission:

the church—represented by Rome—had more authority than the Eastern side—represented by Constantinople.

As regards the spirit, God's son was involved in the sending, and his cross was crucial, but he had come in his father's *name*: (Jhn.5:43; 10:25): the father was first. Incidentally, baptism was 'into,' or 'relative to,' the one name, showing a joint lordship of the trinity (Mt.28:19): the spirit is joint-lord. Rightly, the father is mentioned first. When the son has sorted out global control once and for all, he will hand it over to, yes, the father (1 Cor.15:28).

Distinctive Plurality

Fellowship with the spirit is a norm (2 Cor.13:13/4; Php.2:1), even if these verses mean fellowship produced among Christians by the spirit. Besides joint-lordship, Mt.28:19 symbolises disciples' immersion into *companionship* with the trinity. Remember, the Athanasian Creed went to some trouble to say that the global church should worship the trinity, the eternal society, and that alongside the father and son, the spirit shared deity, glory, being, eternality, transcendence, lordship. But remember also that each trinity member is distinct, so that our relationship to each varies. As said, the ABC of a triangle, not, I may add, an AAA of eternal cloning. Today in church someone thanked God for sending, the lord for having come, and the spirit for living with us. Now that's trinitarianism: three persons, one society. On the other hand, some thank God for coming and dying, and that by his wounds we are healed. Wrong, God is unscarred and unmarred. Tertullian of Carthage was frustrated by this confusion of persons, often expressed in crucifying the father in our talk—what's called patripassianism. Unitarianism posits one person expressed in three ways, or else affirms the personhood of spirit and/or son but denies their deity. Songs can work with or against trinitarianism. There are many types of singing to/about deity, some of very high standard. In what ways can we sing to, or about, the spirit, as being an eternal individual within the eternal society? Let's explore.

---

was the son co-equal or secondary sender? Who has primarily sent us? Are father and son of equal *weight*? Indeed, was the sending not a standing back and letting the spirit move into his field of global operation?

Chapter 5   Praying to the Spirit

I have long written on this question. As far back as 30th June 1989, I had a reply from Rev. Keith W Munday (AoG), Rushden, Northants. He spoke of my "most interesting observations on meditation and music. They were most appreciated. I liked the thought of 'perceived reply' in mediation and I think this is quite valid when we are truly in the Spirit.... The thought of Trinitarian worship. I have been exercised on this line, wondering if we have given sufficient thought to the Holy Spirit.... The essence of your thoughts is so rich I am still enjoying them. I hope you will not mind if I quote some in subsequent writings! With every good wish, Yours in Christ, Keith W Munday." May you too enjoy.

<u>Request</u>

"Spirit of faith, come down", prayed Charles Wesley. Let's skip the usual question of whether we're asking for what's already happened. Let's simply ask, should we ask the spirit, our personal paraclete and guide, for how we'd like him to help us today? I probably didn't even think about this question until I heard Yonggi Cho (Korea) in 1976. He took the line that besides being personal, the spirit, as *allon paraklēton* (Jhn.14:16), was our onboard helper (*paraklēton*) and exactly like (*allon*) the one he succeeded as helper. Overlooking that he was using *Classical* rather than *Common* Greek, Cho assumed that it followed that since before the cross the disciples asked Jesus (paraclete 1) for things, that after the cross disciples are to ask the spirit (paraclete 2) for things. Cho seemed to me to make sense, and I followed his thinking, expanding the ways in which I spoke to/with the spirit.

I still do talk with the spirit, and we should definitely have him in mind. Nevertheless, I've come to see that asking him for things faces a huge problem, in that Jesus said that requests were to be put direct to the father (Jhn.16:23-4; see Mt.6:9-10/Lk.11:2-4). Sure, a few other NT writings mention requests to Jesus, though they are linked to terminal matters rather than run-of-the-mill requests (eg Stephen's dying vision, and John's eschatological vision).[69] Jesus passed to the spirit the

---

[69]   For Paul the trinity is 'lord,' though Jesus' lordship is stressed. 2 Cor.12:8 appears in context to indicate Jesus, though Paul's case was extreme, perhaps potentially terminal. In extremity he either justifiably or unjustifiably asked the

role of helper/paraclete. But was that why Jesus wouldn't take on board further requests? To go Cho's route fails to account for Jesus' explanation that there dawned a new contact with the father (which proved Jesus' success as The Way). It was that which would preclude requests to a paraclete.

So, on the one hand, Jesus didn't say, "Ask your new guide." And on the other hand, he implied, "Don't ask your guide." A positive disinclination; a negative inclination. Nor do I think that Jesus, missioning as a human being, ever asked the spirit for things, though they missionised together. Generally, requests should go to neither lord nor spirit, but to God. This puts into perspective our principal relationship (Jhn.20:17) and seems to me to make better sense of requesting "in Jesus' name."[70] Requesting the father also helps avoid the errors of either picturing it as a toss-up as to which of three equals should be asked (that is, father, son, or spirit),[71] or of picturing Jesus as greater than both the father and spirit, or even picturing 'Jesus' as another name for the father,[72] and thus presumably for the spirit too.

Do you read these footnotes? Number 69 raised the idea that Paul, in line with John, asked the lord indirectly, not directly. Were they in line with Jesus? Looking forward to his crucifixion, Jesus was explaining about a changeover, about new times (Jhn.14:28). Before he died, his disciples still looked to him for help as thaumaturge (wonderworker) and rabbi (teacher/mentor) but, in the shadow of the soon coming cross, he knew that they should soon have the direct access he had always known: a relational upgrade of truly epic proportions. I do not know whether Jhn.16:23a means that they soon wouldn't

---

lord direct (was he rebuffed?), or asked God directly, therefore the lord indirectly in line with Jhn.14:14/16:23-4 (see below).

[70] When seeking our father's help it reminds us of our filial relationship (and thus servanthood), and is God's signature behind our commands. To ask Jesus "in Jesus' name" is thoughtless, nor does a royal petition such as asking the king "in the king's name" cover the strangeness of such speech, nor is it Scripture's meaning.

[71] A view called Tritheism—that is, 3 independent gods.

[72] A view called Modalism in the sense of God being one person who acts like three.

need to ask himself *for* things (NLT), or *about* things (ERV). I do know that 16:23b means that immediately they had welcomed his resurrection, thus were spiritually born into his family, requests were to go direct to his heavenly father. Direct contact was all part of the spirit's new covenant role (Jhn.7:39). It is by the spirit that we touch base with Abba. To ask Jesus, is, technically, to deny the cross. The rule of thumb is that the father is God, Jesus is lord, and we ask God, not the lord!

But what of 14:14? Some would say it only applied before the cross. After all, since the verse immediately before and after had a pre-crucifixion setting, weren't they simply being asked for any last requests before he died? Admittedly I do not see what kind of requests Jesus might have expected. Some would say that the text isn't a problem anyway—go with the KJV/NKJV for simplicity! Have scribes complicated, or simplified, the text? But even with the complicating word 'me' that's found in the Nestle-Aland/UBS text (also known as the NU or CT), but not found in the Greek text used by the KJV, if Jesus will respond *indirectly* by the spirit (though the text says directly), need we say more than that Jesus is *indirectly* asked (though the text says directly)? That is, we are to ask the father directly, and it's the spirit who directly responds, but indirectly it's as if only Jesus is asked, and answers. You may ask, why would Jesus have spoken in direct terms if he were an indirect party?

I suspect the answer is that he who would soon become the essential hub between the one asked (the father) and the one answering (the spirit), flagged himself up as the coordinating motif. After all, it's the Holy Spirit who directly does things, not Jesus. Even in his earlier miracles, it wasn't Jesus working by his deity, but Jesus working by the spirit (Mt.12:28), just as we can. It's a case of reading the wider immediate context, in order to get the meaning. Even in Western society, a building contractor can say that they will build you a house. This doesn't mean that they will directly build every part of it. It means that a dozen or so people of different skills (bricks, electrics, plumbing, etc) will be hired by the contractor to do the work. What literalist would sue contractors for not doing it all by themselves *as promised*? That would be the literalism that caught out poor Shylock.

We should neither hold Jesus to be the one asked, nor the one who responds: he is the middleman in the context of his mission and of us working as his agents. You can go year on year without ever having a biblical reason to ask Jesus or the spirit to do anything. Jesus taught us to pray, *our father*, not *our paraclete*, not *our brother*. Take Paul: access to the father, through Jesus, by/in the spirit (Eph.2:18). The one able to superabundantly do (3:20) is not Jesus as so often assumed, but the father (14), unto whom is glory *in Christ Jesus* (21). Throughout his letters, Paul confirmed Jesus' teachings on prayer.

So, unless my feelings exceed Jesus' authority, I cannot justify directly asking the spirit. Besides the texts which preclude asking Jesus, and prefer asking the father, there's Rm.8, which seems to me to exclude asking the spirit. The spirit is the one who points us to the father (15). The spirit is the one who confirms us to be God's children, heirs alongside Jesus (16-7). And the killer text is v27: the omnipresent spirit is the one pictured as on the ground guiding our prayer, rather than being at the other end receiving our prayer. Pictures make a point.

Gratitude

"Thank you spirit", sang Rebecca St. James. Being pleased for what he has been done, we should thank our helper,[73] even though he acts according to his nature—that is, does what he is without making a conscious choice "to love or not to love."[74] Giving thanks doesn't make him happy or in any way reward him. The expression of gratitude increases our sense of connection. This helps us become more like Jesus, so pleases the father who delights in our wellbeing. Interestingly, when facing his death Jesus gave thanks. The very term *eucharist* means thankfulness. His was pleased to help us. Recognise deity's givingness and his needlessness. Our father's lovingness at the cost of giving his one-of-a-kind son. Our brother's lovingness in wholeheartedly welcoming his father's plan that he should become

---

[73] The spirit as saviour is "as essential to our salvation as the father, as essential as Jesus" (Carson 1986:150).

[74] Consonance, rather than compulsion or choice, best explains why he acts as he does: he does what he is; he acts naturally.

Praying to the Spirit

one with us, die for us, and rise as the first of the new humanity.[75] Our helper's lovingness in willingly taking on board the new covenant role of being paraclete to us—even we of humanity which rebelled and crucified the lord—and for lovingly guiding us even though we often give him grief. In poor human analogy, could you love someone who you knew had butchered your best friend? If there is eternal pain within the trinity, that pain is shared by the spirit. Yet he loves us.

When the perfect comes, *thanks* will probably be swallowed up in *praise*. In other words, we'll no longer focus on the acts done, so much as revelling in the praiseworthiness of the doer. His acts show his graciousness, which is of course praiseworthy. But for now we thank one to whom we are in debt beyond an iota of repayment. Each day the spirit walks with us is gain, and worthy of thanks. Are we such nice people that we should imagine that he is privileged to walk with us? Are we so wise that we don't need his guidance, his helping hand? Do we not need the transformation into Christ's likeness which the spirit brings to our lives? Are we not at least common beneficiaries of that greatest of individual miracles he has done for us, conversion, new birth into the messianic kingdom?

But for now, *Thank you* militates against human arrogance. In fact, even the little things God does for us are delivered by the spirit, though we often think they're directly by Jesus. The biblical big picture is one where God's son, having become Jesus, handed over to the spirit and has 'left', never to return until the end of this age: *maranatha*.[76] Yet Jesus is somehow 'here', and in prayer we often invoke him to 'come' in a non-eschatological sense. So, is he, or is he not, 'here'? Does he, or does he not, 'come'? You are reading or hearing my book; you are reading or hearing me. For where my book is, there am I also. Similarly, where the spirit is, there is Jesus. In situations into which the spirit is invoked, Jesus is invoked into. When you see or hear the spirit, you see or hear Jesus. It boils down

---

[75] Jesus' death was proactive, not reactive. It was planned by the father (Ac.2:23) in line with the son (Eph.2:15b), and so presumably with the spirit—a societal plan. And Jesus understood the plan (Mt.16:21), and fully agreed (Jhn.10:30).

[76] Some think this word states an already fact: *viz* that our lord has come. IMO it states a future fact, our future vision, and Yes, our lord shall come (Rv.22:20).

to a case of identification, representation. The Bible explains, but we are slow to understand. We often fail to thank the spirit because we simply do not see it's him at work with us.

Praise

"Sweet Holy Spirit, Sweet heavenly dove", prayed Doris Akers. What really is *praise*? It is an expression of admiration:[77] a man might praise a young woman's beauty or a work of art, without wishing to possess her or it.[78] Such admiration is healthy and (unless expression is imprudent or undermining) to let it flow is quite right—according to nature, as the ancient Greeks would have said. One might almost say that praise harmonizes logic and spirit, as both 'head' and 'heart' come together in praise.[79] Praise is a spiral of blessing! Indeed, despising praise can cause internal injury.

In praising the Supremely Praiseworthy, we are transformed by contemplating and accepting the source of all virtue. Some overlook this, and so might misunderstand why deity seeks our praise. He is not the Supreme Egotist,[80] and it is for our good that he encourages us to 'feast' on himself, so to speak: if he could create a more praiseworthy object for us to behold, then he would, and would

---

[77] I illustrate the distinction and link between praise and thanks thus: an artist freely gives me one of their fine pictures. I thank them for their generosity and praise their artistry. Thanks, is for doing, never for being. It's kinda daft to thank God for being God—it's not something he has done for us!

"If you will thank me…let it be for yourself alone. That the wish of giving happiness to you, might have added force to the other inducements which led me on, I shall not attempt to deny. But your family owes me nothing. Much as I respect them, I believe, I thought only of you", said Mr Darcy to Elizabeth, having raised Elizabeth's fallen sister (Austen 299).

[78] It's like *Obituary* (*The Rifleman*, S2.E4), where McCain explained to his son that looking at a pretty woman is "like looking at a sunset or a pretty picture painting. You can admire and appreciate them without wanting to own them."

[79] Logic is probably to spirit, as Eve to Adam, both *from* and *spouse*—or, sadly, living apart. In *Star Trek: The Motion Picture* (1979), Spock finally realises that logic alone is lonely. Loneliness logically implies a lack of something potentially available and needed by our nature—we are incomplete without other.

[80] Though dated, C S Lewis' *Reflections on the Psalms* is extremely helpful here.

command us to render to It our highest praise. After all, is it not clear that Levitical offerings made to him, were not food for him? Praise to/of the spirit is obviously right, for even impersonal virtues are said to be worthy of praise (Php.4:8). Would it be right to praise a woman, a picture, yet not the Holy Spirit? We are right—please excuse the anachronism—to *Praise Father, Son, and Holy Ghost.*

Worship

"Holy Spirit, we welcome you", prayed Chris Bowater.[81] What of *worship*? Since the spirit is a member of deity (and is rightly understood to be lord, 2 Cor.3:17; Heb.13:6),[82] we may rightly worship him, that is, ascribe to him the majesty of eternity which belongs to deity as deity: ultimate and supreme glory to the Most Holy (Is.6:3; Jhn.12:41; Ac.28:25-6). In *John* he is intentionally missing from references to the father and son (for example Jhn.14:20-4). This is perhaps to emphasise the truth that we are pictured as in heaven, simultaneously *with* our brother and our father (Eph.2:6-7), and at the same time living in our world with our guide (Jhn.14:26; 16:7): in one sense (spiritual) we have arrived, but in another sense (mortal) we still travel. Worship of the spirit is not ruled out.[83]

Adoration

"Spirit, we love you...and adore you", prayed Donna Adkins.[84] The trinity is *love,* so it follows that adoration of the spirit is a natural part of our walk with him (Gal.5:18,25). Moreover, the spirit is closely linked to love (Gal.5:22; Rm.5:5). It stands to reason that the spirit doesn't walk with us simply in obedience to the father and son: he loves us too.

---

[81] Down sides: Chris' prayer song included the ideas that we ask the spirit for things (misdirectionism), that the spirit is our father, and that the spirit should be told about some other spirit's flow.

[82] The corresponding verb of Heb.13:6 is used of Jesus (2:18), but it also applies to our helper (Gk. *allon paraklēton*) on earth (see Jhn.14-6). Carson held that *allon* is a pointer to worship, love, and (probably) thanks (Carson 1986:52).

[83] The KJV's expression *of himself* (Jhn.16:13) is simply an older way of saying 'off his own bat', or 'self-determination'. Many versions improve, and the NET/NKJV are especially good.

[84] On the down side, she treated the three persons too equally.

While the father is the one who invited us to come, and the son is he who blazed the trail for us, it's the spirit who directs us along the way. On this journey we wilfully stray many times into spiritual Bad Lands, but he stays with us (though free to leave) and suffers with us,[85] as did God's son who also came freely to save us into the journey to life, and the father in giving up his son. Like the son (and the father), he loves us. He doesn't love us because of our *value*—we had no value, but do have preciousness—but perhaps loves us *into* value. Value is a tricky term: I value beyond computation the irreplaceable priceless love of parents, yet compute whether a replaceable computer is enough value to me to pay the price. The spirit neither values us as items, nor for relationship, though he makes us useful (valuable) towards blessing others. He loves us because *he* is gracious and *we* need his love. So, it is natural to love him, the loving spirit.

Dedication

Holy Spirit, I serve you? Yonggi Cho used to have a seat reserved for the Holy Spirit. That's never been my thing, but nor have I pastored a megachurch. I see how it can be good pretence, a game of make believe in the order of C S Lewis' *Let's Pretend* (Lewis 2002:4.7), so long as we don't believe that the spirit literally sits in the chair, feet on the floor. If the chair stands as metonymy for the spirit being with us in platform work, that's fine. Cho's main point was his accountability to the spirit. That's fine. He taught that ideally we move from the spirit being merely a resident, to him being the president. That's great.

It is not so much a case as giving him everything, as being prepared to give him all that we have and are, and seeing that such is really his, anyway. Yieldedness. Abraham was asked to sacrifice his special son, the promised heir. He was about to do so literally, when Yahweh stepped in, showing him that it was the yieldedness he sought, along with the faith, and that he himself did not need literal human

---

[85] Him suffering is often denied by those who like me deny *patripassianism* (which in modalist hands means that the father was crucified), and by those who philosophically have moved from the extreme of passionate and fickle deities, to the extreme of one dispassionate and staid deity—the emotionally unmoved mover of all.

sacrifice (unlike some so-called deities of the day) and himself was the provider, not the receiver. And true dedication is not boastful. Sing along with Reuben Morgan, if you must, but do you *really* give the lord your heart and soul?[86] Reality check, please. It's actually refreshing to confess that we don't totally yield, perhaps never have, and perhaps never will within mortality. Scripture speaks of us becoming more like Christ, the totally yielded one, but it doesn't, I think, say we achieve the goal as mortals. Let dedication be tempered with modesty, and plain good sense. Granted our limitations, should we yield to the spirit? I'd certainly say yes. He is the tactical lord on earth. To yield to him is to yield to the lord, which is to yield to God.

Apology[87]

"God, remove the cobwebs from my life", prayed the church deacon, week in, week out, year in, year out. Eventually, as he sat down after asking for this yet again, another regular attendee jumped up and begged, "no father, please kill the spider". *The Heart of Worship* (Michael Smith (2001)) flags up a common misconception of *worship*: we've sung our songs, we've done our worship, we go home to our lives. Smith has us apologise for this God-ignoring attitude. Well, it's a lesson some of us will need, but to sing it yet again implies that, like the church deacon, we haven't learnt the lesson! If I sing it once, then sing it again, it shows I hadn't really learnt the lesson. I shouldn't be *coming back* again: kill the spider. Oh, apologies to arachnophiles, by the way. And my apologies to he who made spiders, not least since our inner Shelob creates cobwebs more than a cave full of Shelobs.

Many of us are indeed troubled by a weekly build of webs, a weekly turning away. But is Smith's lesson really one which, learnt one week, must be learnt again the next *ad infinitum*? Let there be different apologies, for different sins. Then, if we really don't need to learn again what *it's all about*, let's sit out the song rather than negatively

---

[86] http://www.worshiptogether.com/songs/i-give-you-my-heart

[87] Apology logically should relate to all the persons of deity: we find that baptism, which is symbolic of our initial entrance into God, is *into*, or *relating to*, the corporate name of all three (Mt.28:19). Yet if apology is the main part of our talk with God, then are we living as he intends?

confess. If it only applies to one in the church, let them sing solo! Weekly singing Smith's song implies a weekly cycle away from, as well as return to, *the heart of worship*. At the very least we should be working our way through Shelob's Lair and towards the eucatastrophe, not mere cycling through life. Incidentally Smith's is also a unitarian song—*it's all about you Jesus*, ruling out the father, the spirit, and the nonincarnate son (the Logos), so has missed the heart of worship by a long chalk. The really good bit reminds us that apology can be the way forward. Anyway, this is all a bit general about apology. Ought we to apologise to the spirit for our sinfulness?

Hold onto your answer. First, are you a sinner or a saint? Scripture has at least two definitions of *sinner*. And as one psychology professor put it, "we are—all of us—disordered. We do not like to think of ourselves as disordered, and this too is a reflection of the fall" (Yarhouse 40-1). The first definition is of human beings outside of God's family who are, and do, wrong by their very nature. If this is you, you need to welcome God's welcome into his family: you are a sinner given an evangelical call to heart and mind turn (repent) and accept God the father to become your heavenly father.

The second definition is of persons inside God's family who are, and do, wrong in spite of their new family nature. If this is you, you have welcomed God's welcome into his family: you are a saint given a pastoral call to repent from daily sin (decontaminate) in order to live a life that best pleases your heavenly father and you. To you, on the one hand confession's not an issue to get strung up over, a truth Joseph Prince might flog to death, but on the other hand it is a serious issue. As Peter Gillquist put it, an obsession with confession is not called for, so much as us walking in God's light: God in the background will be decontaminating us. Put another way, living with Christ will make us more Christlike. We will understand our moral imperfection and our family belongingness. For saints, apology is as family members, clearing the air. For saints, sin as the barrier to God, has been overcome. The mega apology of life-change conversion (metanoia) is followed by daily micro apologies of a different sort, and for a different reason.

Praying to the Spirit

Thus, the paternoster speaks of being daily restored to good fellowship—forgiven as we forgive.[88] Will my heavenly ticket be revoked whenever I wrong God, and only reinstated if I forgive those who wrong me? No, we're not talking hell (*hadēs*) here. It's simply that being reluctant to forgive will degrade our daily family life with our father. So it's important to keep the two types of sin listed above (the rebellion against family, and the rebellion within family), distinct in our minds, and to see that all Christians have passed from ultimate condemnation (*katakrima*: Rm.8:1), but not ultimately from condemnation—we too should condemn our sins. It is to saints that I put the question, ought we to apologise to the spirit?

The *Our Father* (paternoster) addresses the chief party aggrieved, namely our father to whom we should apologise for our daily sins. This is kids, during family time, admitting to themselves and their father their disobedience.[89] In effect, it is also asking their father to help and heal them at the moral level. It seems reasonable to me, even if it isn't biblically underlined, to also apologise to the spirit, whom our sins also sadden. He walks with us from earth to heaven, so to speak. On the one hand I doubt that Is.63:10 clearly specifies the person we call the Holy Spirit, since it would not have been so read by Isaiah's initial audience, to whom monotheism was taken to be monopersonal, not tripersonal. On the other hand, Eph.4:30 was written to those to whom the individuality of the Holy Spirit had been revealed, so they would have seen that the person called the Holy Spirit could be grieved. They were in a higher class than Isaiah. They could see that Isaiah's generality meant that grieving Yahweh was grieving the eternal society of father, son, and spirit. Apologies to each person we needlessly grieve, is not remiss. When we misguide our guide, is it not courteous to apologise to him?

---

[88] For his Jewish readers Matthew put this in the Jewish cultural way of something owed, a *debitum*/debt (Mt.6:12). God was their people's father; he is our personal father.

[89] When Jesus spoke about us not forgiving, I reckon it's about an attitude of unforgiveness, rather than forgiving, that he meant. If it takes an apology (request) for God to forgive, it likewise is required for us to forgive. Resentment, bitterness, can hinder our fellowship with God.

Chat and Complaint

Chat is not explicit in Scripture, though arguably it's implicit in the Yeshuic Covenant, insofar as we in Christ are individually children in God's family. In God's home mayn't we be homely? The Bible teaches that in one sense we are home (in True Canaan), yet in another sense are still travelling there (True Exodus): we combine the good we've got with the better still to come. The Eucharist symbols of bread and wine symbolise the quick-baked bread and the vicarious blood that prefixed the exodus. The elements also symbolise the bread of travel (manna in the exodus) and the wine of arrival (the joy of the Promised Land). We, in his kingdom on earth, are travelling to his kingdom in heaven. And travelling with the spirit, may we not chat as we walk the road? Well, it seems reasonable to me. Perhaps the big hurdle is moving mentally from mere formality with God, to family informality. This should be with family awareness that our father is busy on a salvation job, which we should share in under his direction and with his help, even as did his uniquely unique (*monogenēs*) son.

Complaint is well attested in Scripture. On the one hand, it can be good. Habakkuk sat in his watchtower awaiting signs of invasion, and complained to Yahweh, because Yahweh caused Babylon to invade evil Judah, yet Babylon was more evil. His honest complaints received honest answers. Jeremiah, pressured into becoming a prophet (Jr.1:7-10), was given a task which turned him into the butt of every joke of the enemy within. The danger he prophesied didn't materialise straight away. Tormented in mind, he still couldn't bring himself to reject his prophethood and still believed he would be vindicated (Jr.20:7-13). Our lord, dying, recalled words of dereliction (Ps.22:1): hallowed complaint. On the other hand, complaint could flow from rebellious attitude, and Jesus warned a seemingly appreciative crowd that they might fail to make the true Canaan, even as a generation that made it out of Egypt failed to make it into the physical Promised Land. Alas, thinking themselves Israel, they didn't see that they were living in symbols of Global Israel. Seeking national renewal only, they deserted him, losing spiritual as well as national renewal. The term *gonguzō* (I complain) in Jhn.6:41,3, is also in Nb.14:29.

Praying to the Spirit

Summary

Songs can be a powerful way to sidestep the trinity. Isn't it terrible that the Witnesses dump the deity of the father's son? We thank Jesus that we're better than them, since we merely dump the deity of his father—*you alone are God, Jesus*. Where the song leader leads, we will follow, follow, we will follow on—all hail the god of good music. Anything for a simple life: why should God complicate life?

Yet facts are stubborn things; and whatever may be our wishes, our inclinations, or the dictates of our passions, they cannot alter the state of facts and evidence. It remains a brute fact that God is tripersonal, triunity, so songs really should affirm, not disaffirm, this. Each deity person can fellowship with us on a daily basis.

We may picture Jesus as the one who connects us to the father and the spirit. To look at various ways we can fellowship with them, having noted that co-operation is one way, I have looked at verbal, contemplative ways, particularly related to the Holy Spirit. Not totally ruling out any minor prayer requests to him, I have nevertheless highlighted that the biblical injunction is almost totally to ask the father, neither the lord, nor the spirit. Excluding request, we may talk to/with the spirit along the lines of thanks, praise, worship, love, commitment, apology, chat, and complaint.

Part 3 Problems and Christian Songs
Prologue
Like a good sales rep, songs often carry us along, and reps can be right. Yet as Sue Brown remarked, "music appeals primarily to the emotions and...carries words past the critical faculty into the affection where they may do either good or harm" (Carson 1996:509). Charming songs are persuasive. Therein lies their danger. The Haradrim felt secure riding on the backs of the mûmakil, or rallying around them, yet they fell before the might of Gondor. Leaders tell us to sing along. They say it's what we need to know. They shove so many things quickly on our plate, then say to eat it if we wanna grow. But after the feast, after the fire, let's take a little time to cogitate, to think, to let the brain cool down. Don't put me down just 'cause I'm not a youth. I am a student on the path of life, seeking out the truth, which I wish to share. Sure, other voices might be right, and it's easy to buy in to the beat, to go with the flow. If we do so, we sometimes have those second thoughts, doubts, but who likes to be a minority report? Nevertheless, I have bit by bit followed my doubts, and have, I feel with God's help, come to a few thoughts about the spirit.

- He sings along with many songs I would rather not sing;
- He doesn't vindicate the wholeness of the songs he sings with us, for he sings a kind of lyrical and perfect harmony to our faulty songs: he looks to their heart and the singers' hearts, rather than to the outward details (1 Sam.16:7);
- He is happy for those who wish to sit the song out, to do so (Rm.14:23);
- Those who sit the songs out should, on the whole, not stop those who wish to sing them, as they can be enjoying the spirit of the songs (that is, their vision) even if the words are mixed up.

I have also come to see five basic factors in good songs.

Good...	What's said...	Factor
vision	conveys a right community vision	Community vision
music	has artistic backing	Musical art
use	as vision, inspires the singers	Community action

Good...	What's said...	Factor
structure	is said rightly	Grammatical quality
words	is right	Lyrical correctness

I'm more than happy to say that songs can carry blessing, indeed carry singers into blessing, and bring back a bit of heaven to earth. I've had it, been there, passed some on. Some songs might be dire, yet have that one phrase that can be like a window opening to great revelation and meditation, or have key words that fit the sermon. But to use Kendrick's analogy, the Rolls Royce should have good steering, good onboard entertainment, good suspension, good engine, good everything a car should have. Indeed, superlative, not good, or it's not a Royce. As persuasive a sound as they make, as relevant the sound is to the audience, the congregation, I shall nevertheless expand on my own journey into song critique, as things once persuasive, have become less so to me.

I sincerely believe that some of these points are viruses that infect the value of songs, both to nonbelievers and believers, and shall employ a demerit system according to my idea of their seriousness. I will begin by giving all songs 100%, then deducting points for problems, yielding a **Problem Avoidance Grade**. I shall cover what I deem to be various problems. Yet I also sincerely believe that as C S Lewis said, besides some things being biblically up for debate as to whether they are right or wrong, we might reasonably disagree about whether they are important or not.[90] His position here was not the error of subjectivism, since it presupposed the existence of an actual right and of actual importance. It merely acknowledged that our opinions will sometimes be mistaken. In short, on some or all of my points below, you might well dispute, and might be right, so long as your reasoning holds good within biblical parameters. My next few chapters are somewhat rough distinctions. For instance, an archaism not only violates current grammar, but can misrepresent God as archaic.

---

[90] D A Carson put *adiaphora* as *disputable things,* adding that it doesn't follow that if there is one disputer that the aspect disputed falls into a hands-off *adiaphora,* a moral or belief *laissez-faire.*
http://themelios.thegospelcoalition.org/article/on-disputable-matters.

As personal humour, you can sing *I have confidence in me*, for confidence, not from confidence. It can be nice to sing what we know is false, even as it can be nice to read fantasy. But do we believe the fantasy, and do we claim to have a confidence we don't know we lack? Some songs boast about us. Some say they're lies. How should we define a lie? Some say it means any untruth, but suggest that sometimes lying is moral, at least to save life wrongly endangered: few Christians would try and justify sinfully motivated lying.

So, might some lies be morally justified? Under that definition, maybe they can. In Victor Hugo's, *Les Misérables* (1862), Hugo commented that Sister Simplice, horrified at having told a lie to save Valjean, deserved to be "credited [in heaven] for her falsehood" (1.8.5): she risked her loss for his gain. Corrie ten Boom argued that telling Gestapo that Jews weren't hiding where she knew Jews were hiding, was a morally justified lie: she risked her loss for their gain. Shiphrah and Puah were hardly honest with Pharaoh. Are altruistic lies good for the soul?

I prefer to roughly define a lie as knowingly telling untruth in order to wrongly deceive for the prime and likely gratuitous benefit of the deceiver, unbeknown to the deceived—evil motivation behind deception. Not all untruth is a lie, and (unintentional or intentional) may be morally fine. I *thought* that what I said was true. It wasn't. Did I *lie*? No. Sure, I misinformed you, but I was misinformed and spoke as truly as I knew. On the stage, the professional comedian was only joking, and neither wished to be taken seriously nor to be called a liar—no permanent deception was seriously entertained and the audience was enriched. My intended untruth about where Valjean was hiding wasn't a lie, because it wasn't deception for my selfish gain (or lack of loss) at another's expense. When puddings are trotted out, my wife calls me a pig. I am not a pig, but neither is she lying. For my part, I fight shy of calling Christian songs, lies, even if I think they're intellectually untrue in parts. It's too negative a word.

So, "'when I became a Christian I stopped telling lies, and started singing them'" (Page 25)? Does *The Daily Herald* proclaim, "Christian convert sings a pack of lies"? No, that'd only be good headlines for a cheesy newspaper. Whatever truth is in this, in my books *lies* is too strong a word. It ain't true, but it ain't a lie. We join not in a pack of lies, but

Prologue

in a congregation of believers. It is likely that lots of lyrical mess is, to many, unhelpful but harmless, even as youngsters can miss saucy innuendoes harmful to adults.

Still, lyrical quality, though not the main element, is important, and is what I'll focus on. With regards to accuracy, special emphasis should be placed on ensuring that lyrics are theologically sound. When Christian songs are for congregational singing, songs of solidarity, it is important that their quality excels, in style, substance, and significance. Yet many songs are generated by those who lack one or more of these virtues. It can even boil down to the singer, not the song. As Charles Gildon put it in 1706 (*The Post-Boy Robbed of his Mail*), those who sing the psalms of David should have David's spirit—and one might add his embryonic theology. Gildon objected to booze-filled men singing spirit-filled songs, their vices contradicting the virtue of the psalms. But not all Christian songs are fully virtuous.

"Let's try to write better ones," said Graham Kendrick, adding that "much of my life is taken up with sweating over songs and lyrics to try to make them as near to a Rolls Royce song as I possibly can, because I believe it does bring a greater release of worship".[91] Wait a bit. Didn't the Welsh Revival degrade into a new idolatry, into hedonistic worship, so to speak, by boasting the pleasures of the Rolls? Didn't it leave the Rock of salvation, for the Rolls of recreation? Didn't it trip-advise the journey rather than the destination, the means rather than the End? Is asking Kendrick to drive, risking spiritual pride?

Yes, there is that risk. But living is risky. Should we die to escape the risks? Or should we live with the risks? Human loves are unsafe, too. Should we follow Augustine and petrify our human loves? Or should we remain human and risk our hearts being broken? An island never cries, but nor does it ever laugh. Chris Idle said he'd prefer that folk "went to heaven singing drivel, than go to hell singing great hymns" (*Reform*). He also said that great hymns, songs, and sermons, will help more get to heaven than drivel hymns, songs, and sermons, will. I don't advise risk avoidance, but I do advise risk reduction, the thrills

---

[91] www.crossrhythms.co.uk/articles/music/Graham_Kendrick_The_veteran_worship_man_from_plastic_ukulele_to_praise_marches/36338/p3.

without the spills. This can cause songwriters even more sweat, but their pain will be our gain.

Don't ban the band. For the life of him, 'General' William Booth just couldn't see why the devil should have all the good music, nor can I. Doesn't the popular music scene use a morally neutral language in which Christians should excel? Our message is the best. Why boast in how badly we can wrap it in music? Kendrick's idea of great music and great song, as long as songs are based on good theology, can go into making a Rolls which God will be happy to drive. But I see few Rolls on the road. A lot of popular models spluttering along, a lot of entertainment, but little edification, little critical thinking, and a lot of nonsense. Nonsense, of course, covers more than shoddy theology, though theology is crucial for believers. *Nonsense* is also a key word of Page's book title.

Shoddy style is bad for evangelism. Showing a joyful face to nonbelievers is good. Showing nonsense—or what appears to them as nonsense—is not. Even glossolalia can seem nutty (1 Cor.14:23). The greatest Day of Pentecost had arrived. Christians, having waited in Jerusalem for God's new age promise, were finally spirit filled, switched on for the covenant mission. Yet the joy and the drama that began the mission, seemed to some the excess of drunkenness (Ac.2:12-3).[92] To insiders, it was divine wonder. Left unexplained, it could have killed the church. Onlookers were divided between those who suspected it meant something, and those pretty sure it meant nothing. The evangelised asked for an explanation (1 Pt.3:15).

The inability to explain the inexplicable was Nick's Luton Epiphany, not the Jerusalem Epiphany. Biblical imagery can be strung together in meaningless ways, mixing metaphors, and chopping and changing between words to deity, words about deity, even words from deity,

---

[92] In this episode of the spirit, the unknown-to-the-speaker languages were languages known to the visitors from around the Empire, and the theme of praising God (not preaching) was directly understood. Thus, the charge of being drunk and disorderly was soon answered by Peter the preacher. Paul's point was that generally the spirit didn't match the languages he generated to the audience, so it's best to tone things down among non-sympathetic audiences.

Prologue

besides often confusing the persons of the trinity. One can cut out words from Scripture, throw them into the air, and make a song from how the words land. It is not logical but it is human. Call it art. I call it heresy. I call it confusion. The saying goes back to Tertullian that some heretics had crucified the father, by which he meant that they didn't consciously visualise the father and son as two separate persons, and so spoke as if God the father had been crucified. Christian songs can confuse Christians and non-Christians.

We should ask, since singing transmits a message, whether our songs are fully clear and fully true. Lyrics can be inspired and can inspire, but this is no guarantee of perfection. Some stand in need of repair; some are irreparable! Let's look at what goes into good songs and into bad songs. Theologically, we may wince at Graham Kendrick's *Shine, Jesus, Shine*, which addresses Jesus, the spirit, and the river (which river?)—anyone and anything it seems except the father, unless he is the river![93] Still, it backboned a London 'praise march' in 1985, which sparked off a national 100,000 plus event, and is still on some playlists over 25 years later—no mean achievement. Earlier, in 1980, Dougie Brown was praying to *the river* to wash over him, even to make him new—was that to make him a Christian? Some Christians still deem these songs to be blessings. I guess it boils down to the fact that the spirit dances with imperfect dances, and sings with imperfect songs— if they have his vision. For my two left feet, it's sometimes better to sit out the dance. Put another way, the spirit can enrich even through poor prophets, and thankfully walks with imperfect people, but aiming for perfection should make getting there more likely.

---

[93] Theologically clumsy, *Shine Jesus Shine* prophetically encapsulated a heady eschatological and evangelistic vision to stimulate God's church.

Chapter 6   Grammatical Problems

"Speak...to one another with psalms, hymns, and songs from the spirit. Sing and make music from your heart to the lord, always giving thanks to God the father for everything, in the name of our lord Jesus Christ. Submit to one another out of reverence for Christ.... Christ loved the church and gave himself up for her to make her holy, cleansing her by the washing with water through the word, and to present her to himself as a radiant church, without stain or wrinkle or any other blemish, but holy and blameless" (NIV: Eph.5:19-21,25-7).

Ø: Mixed Themes

In some ways, previous generations have been better than ours, and some of the old hymns were packed with themes. They can be metanarratives, in a few stanzas covering from *Genesis* to *Revelation*, and beyond. Actually, too jam packed, at least for many of us. They feature inconsistencies, not against each other, but against a multitude of competing messages. I don't think we should boast that they're too complex for today's church to handle, but they probably are. There are some good reasons to simplify. In line with good homiletics, it makes good sense that each song should have a strong theme and stick to it. Modern songs can still be mixed bags of apples and oranges. For analysis, since such glitching doesn't always stand out like a sore thumb, it isn't always straightforward, and I no longer factor this into my grade charts. However, I flag it up as significant.

Perhaps today's songwriters look less at the big picture metanarrative and thematic overload. But some still mismatch themes and write in confusion. If you juggle themes, you might drop a clanger. Consider a fictitious song—*Judas went and hanged himself / Go thou do likewise, thyself / Well done, O Good and Faithful Servant*. All biblical lines, but cut and paste simply doesn't yield any biblical sense. Lyricists should first ask what the lines mean or meant, in their contexts, and only if discovering a theme, string them together. Judas wasn't commended for hanging himself, and had he been a good and faithful servant would not have hanged himself. That God used his rebellious disposition to a good end, simply parallels to having used the evil of Joseph's brothers to move Joseph to a salvation base for them (Gen.50:20). Nevertheless, if I tweaked those lines, and added a

Grammatical Problems

great tune with contemporary A1 music, marketed it in an attractive package, I guess it might catch on. I dunno, maybe I could make it sound like Judas obediently hanged himself just to please God!

Seriously, any apparent unity of theme (for example, peace) should be a genuine unity. Some songs are like the Spot the Odd One Out quizzes. All too many song writers assume that pick and mixing biblical texts will work out fine. One quasi-biblical hotchpotch is *He Is Our Peace*, woven from Eph.2:1 (about Jesus), and 1 Pt.5 (about God). Kandela overlooked that two types of peace are at issue, and that internal peace (1 Pt.) is not based upon racial peace (Eph.), though messiah is the common denominator. Apples and oranges are in one orchard. Instead of holding together two texts that speak of individual inner peace, or two that speak of global covenant peace, she failed to meaningfully relate A to B. As a rule of thumb, ask what the song means, and how each expression links in.

Quite frankly, biblical hotchpotch can demand a level of Bible familiarity that many singers and lyricists probably lack. When Robin Mark wrote *Days of Elijah* (1996),[94] was he in a contest to get in the most Bible allusions? A unidirectional song would either be all to deity, or all to man. His was a polydirectional song,[95] and polydirectional songs may be put like this:

| Polydirectional | Part to deity, part to man | You are praiseworthy, isn't he? |

This song makes numerous eschatological assumptions, which if the feel-good factor wasn't there, would raise obvious questions. Some might even say that biblically, Elijah's Days means the whole church age, and that salvation, though quoted in Isaiah's future tense (Rm.11:26), has already come from Zion.[96] Some eschatological songs imply that the last two millennia were so much wasted time until WE

---

[94] 19 biblical references in 16 lines, *per* Page 88-9.

[95] *Poly*, from the Greek word, *polus*, carries the ideas of many/much. If a song is only bidirectional (two directions), *polydirectional* might seem to be overkill. However, songs can have several directions, and rather than speak of bidirectional, tridirectional, and the like, I have settled for *polydirectional*.

[96] My *Israel's Gone Global* book, covers this more. Keith & Kristyn Getty's *Oh, How Good it Is* (2012), rightly says that "the redeemer has come".

Problems and Christian Songs

came, and that WE know that the lord is no longer Yahweh but Jesus, who after the C21's mass speed-evangelism, will promptly return. How on earth did God get along without US? Are we infected with pride? I don't think it's even improved by Donnie McClurkin's addition that his favourite god is Jehovah.[97] Since it's not unusual for lyricists to let proper standards slip, singers should usually do their own checking before opening mouth—beware and be aware.

<u>A: Incompletism</u>

For this, I deduct 5 points. For beginning a line with a pointless start creates an incomplete statement. That was meant to sound wrong. Imagine simply saying to a stranger, "Because you're a stranger." You'd be thought a strange stranger, because *because* is like an unconnected bridge in the middle of the ocean, not really making sense either end—or at best like a jetty. This is how some songs are structured. For example, *I Exalt Thee*, lifted from Ps.97:9 (KJV),[98] when

---

[97] www.lyricsmania.com/days_of_elijah_lyrics_donnie_mcclurkin.html. Though God is not a god, getting his name in is good. Page 96, which is mostly correct, misleadingly states that *Jehovah* isn't in Scripture—the ASV/NWT have high *Jehovah* quotient. What he probably meant was that the hybrid *form* of God's name, *Jehovah*, is inauthentic. But any form of God's name is better than no name. Few songs challenge centuries of side-tracking God's name. One can still sing *Guide Me O Thou Great Jehovah* (William Williams: 1771 English edition), and Merla Watson's (1974) *Jehovah Jirah*. Pete Lawry wrote *Yahweh! Jehovah Is The Lord Our God* (1983): exclamation indeed! *Second Chapter* has a Yahweh song.

So too has Reuben Morgan (Lam.5:19), although I am unhappy with his song, and he has a long history of the "you alone are God, Jesus!" theology, characteristic perhaps of *Hillsong*. Why should we be baptised in the same heretical baptism wherein (I fear) *Morgan/Hillsong* are baptised? While Morgan has sung to the father (*Still*) and spoken of the father's son (*The Fear*), see his *Mighty To Save*; *You Alone Are God*; *Inside Out*; and *Let Us Adore*, for clear expositions of Onlyism/Oneness. *My Redeemer Lives*, et al, probably also stem from Onlyism. Several of his songs (for example *All the Heavens*, and *Eagles Wings*) are ambivalent. I allow that trinitarianism is difficult to get our heads around, since it's counterintuitive, and that allowance must be made for Morgan's head, for his heart may mean well.

[98] Pete Sanchez Jr. (1977) *For Thou O Lord art high above all the earth / Thou art exalted far above all gods / I exalt thee*. This ignored the KJV marker

Grammatical Problems

the psalmist's thought began in the previous verse—"Zion rejoices...for (that is, because) you, Yahweh...." Part A, connective, part B. Besides its language being archaic, the song begins with a connective, a bridge from nowhere, and going nowhere.

Sanchez should either have kept the connective *and* connections, or dropped the connective *along with its* connections. The *issue* is Zion's joy *for/because* Yahweh is the Most High. "For you're wise. I'll trust you", isn't real life talk unless something came before it. "You're wise! I'll trust you" makes sense as related stand-alone statements. "Because you are great, therefore I'll trust you" at least makes some sense, or, say, "you've sorted it out for you are wise. I'll trust you." A simple *Yahweh you are most high / above all the earth / you are exalted far above [our/human] gods / I exalt you my lord*, would have been fine. Similarly, many plaques have featured Jhn.3:16. Some begin, "For God..." Some correctly begin, "God..." The latter show some awareness of the incongruity of beginning with a connective: *for* carries on from v15. It was a "because of what's just been said." If you say the word *for* is not redundant, I reply that therefore neither is v15: keep both or drop both.

Another form of incompletism is the expression, *worthy*. If someone says "I give you," you might like to know what, and why. If someone says "you are worthy," you might ask, "of what?" A clip around the ears, a promotion, a rejection, a compliment, death? Are you to be left wondering what you're worthy of? In *Revelation*, we read that because of his deeds and help, the Lord God was worthy to receive the submission of human glory and honour and power (4:11): we defer to him. Likewise, because of what the eschatological lamb had done, the Lamb was worthy to receive power, wealth, wisdom, strength, honour, glory, and praise (Rv.5:4,9,12): all gifts submitted to their source. What are you worthy of, and why are you worthy of it? *You are worthy*, like *I give you*, is an incomplete thought. But then, for

---

(periphrasis), and God's name (that is, it was detetragrammatonised). David Hodges' medley incorporates this, but adds, *Your name is Jesus...your name is father*: so Hodge replaced Yahweh with Jesus as *the father* (not the son), leaving us his *children* to rejoice at how easily we can change eternal ontology.

Problems and Christian Songs

Christian songs it doesn't matter—does it? Religious verbiage goes a long way.

Darlene Zschech's polydirectional *Worthy is the Lamb* (2000), has a lot of thanks, and lists items of praiseworthiness, yet features a repeatedly undefined *worthy is the Lamb*.[99] We can sing "you are worthy" till our eyes glaze over, yet never go anywhere. Praise isn't repetition. Praise is a journey going somewhere. *Revelation* completes all its *worthy* sentences: *worthy to* walk in white (3:4); *worthy...to* receive...*because* (4:11); *worthy to* open the scroll (5:2); no one...*worthy to...* (4); you are *worthy to...because* (9); *worthy...to* (12).

B: Archaism

For this, I deduct 10 points.

B1: KJVism

Good old familiarity. In David Lean's *This Happy Breed* (1944), you end with the sense that the family houses no longer feel the same, inevitably changed over time. Likewise, words tend to change meaning. For example, *conversation* in the KJV days meant how folk live, but nowadays means how folk talk (see Php.1:27). No doubt how we talk reflects how we live, and how we live reflects how we talk. Still, keeping translation up-to-date will better witness to God. Many hymns are based on KJV language, and need translation in order to avoid confusion. There are nouns and verbs that aren't biblical, are simply from the KJV tradition, and now, being dead, no longer speaketh. Christian Humanism understood that folk should not hold the present as definitive, yet should go back to source for perspective and clarity: understand the past to understand the now. The bigger picture is not just of source words, but the original scriptures, and

---

[99] *Darling of Heaven* to one side, *crown you now with many crowns*, is an incomplete statement—needed because *we crown you with many crowns* wouldn't fit the music? Also, *worthy is the Lamb*, if to the Lamb, should be *worthy are you, Lamb*. Even so, she still didn't even answer the question, "what are we saying he is worthy of?" So, another incompletism. Incidentally, while I don't insist that Hillsong convert to trinitarian, some lines might have been better so. Is the grace from the father mediated by the son, and isn't it the spirit who applies (washes by) the blood, in Levitical terms?

Grammatical Problems

this has been far better reconstructed than in the days of King James, allowing better versions in today's languages.

As to individual words, Mary's soul did *megalunō* the lord (Lk.1:46). This isn't the same as magnifying it, though it was in KJV days. "'Magnify' today means to make something very small appear very large. So when we magnify God it sounds to a modern ear like God is a microbe under the microscope" (Page 97). Some song leaders first explain that we can't make God any bigger, then have us sing "come magnify the lord with me." Philosophers might say that God is the source of size, himself trans-sizeable, hence omnipresent, transcendent. Why have *magnify* in Scripture, as the NKJV/NRSV do,[100] if it needs converting into today's terms? Must we keep the familiar?

"Just as certain parts of the traditionalist wing of the church want to keep the King James Bible and the 1662 Prayer Book because 'the language is so poetic,' a lot of modern traditionalists want to keep the same old vocabulary in use in their worship songs. These people wouldn't speak that way and wouldn't want their preachers to use the same antiquated language, but they don't want to have songs in a modern language" (Page 104). For some it will remind them of their youth.

Once upon a time, many believed that the NT writers made up their own words because they didn't know proper Greek. Then archaeology discovered large amounts of NT type Greek, which showed that Greek had acclimatised from the highbrow Parthenon, to the common market place. In other words, generally the NT writers had simply used the common Greek, rather than the cultured, classical Greek, in which to speak to the common people in the streets. Is this not a pattern for lyricists? In my early days of discipleship, which was within Pentecostal Evangelicalism, the choice of Bible version was either the KJV (archaic), the Living Bible (street talk), or the RSV (God alone was archaic!). All can be good; all offer lessons.

On balance, I reckon that songs should be up to date. Neither Olde Worlde English nor Latin is sacred, though *relevancy* under deity is, as the Catholicism appreciated when it moved away from Latin. When not in Rome, why do as the Romans do? Biblical language was

---

[100] Others: *praise* (ERV/NCV/NLT/NOG); *glorify* (CEB/NIV); *proclaim the greatness* (NJB); *exalts* (NET).

Problems and Christian Songs

the common, relevant language of the people, so to be biblical is to be current: KJV Onlyism, even in style, is unbiblical. Old hymns that are worth keeping can often be transmitted, either by reworking their themes into new songs, or upgrading their style of language. On the latter, much work has been done, as in the *New Catholic Hymnal* (1971), and *Hymns for Today's Church* (1982/7). For simple changes in meaning, the task is to analyse what parts should be changed, then generally within the limitations of rhyme, metre, and authorial ideas,[101] to decide how they should be changed.

Some expressions have exceeded their best-use-by date. Languages live in flux. For instance, did *the LORD of Hosts* mean the Master Chef? Did it mean Radegast, perhaps to whom John Scotus was served up in 1066? Or did it mean that Yahweh was the commander-king of more than enough armies to protect his people?[102] Take another example. In revising the RSV, the NRSV translators decided that "I will accept no bull from your house" could be improved on, and that's no bull.[103] Other archaic words common in lyrics, include *exalt, anoint, seek, extol, bless, fortress, tower, burden, robe, garment, canopy, gates, captives* (Page 98).

We can add more, such as the mystique term *minister*, especially as a noun. Today's English requires *servant/helper*, and for the verb, *serve/help out*. Does the spirit minister to us, or does he help us out? How many teach that only some Christians are *ministers*, or *priests*? That some specialise in full time church service does not warrant them alone being called *ministers*. There are many more changed words, such as *chariots, swords,* and *Onwards Christian Warriors*

---

[101] This can be complicated by variants. Songs used to get more changes as they travelled the globe, so tracing back to the original wording involves research, and authors might have written variants. Also, where authorial theology seems wrong, should one correct it or propagate the theology deemed wrong?

[102] This expression (eg in Is.1:24) is of the suzerain king, Yahweh to his people, having potential command over many armies: invincibility. Roughly, versions divide into 4 groups: the formal equivalent (*LORD/God of Armies*: CEB/NLT); the functional equivalent (*LORD/GOD all powerful*: ERV/NIV); the archaic formal (*LORD/God of hosts*: NKJV/NRSV); and the technical which shows the Yahweh-covenant connection (*Yahweh Sabaoth*: NJB/NOG).

[103] See Bruce Metzger's *The Bible in Translation*, 2006:159, on Ps.50:9.

Grammatical Problems

never made fame.[104] And with the Christmas donkey, the idea of Jesus born in a *manger* is often trotted out.[105]

Some Christians love antique things, antique talk as in Richard Adam's *Watership Down* where the rabbits welcomed the warren smelling of the rabbitry of generations past—the familiar and secure. But antiquity can lull us to sleep, and say to non-Christians, or new-Christians, that Christianity is really for Dark Age traddies. It's something the Wesleys tried to avoid. "The language of the hymns of Methodism is distinctly the most modern diction to be found in C18 verse. It is comparatively seldom that we encounter any of the verbal mannerisms of the period", mannerisms which perhaps aged Watts more quickly (Bett 34).

But modern C18 is not modern C21. As originally written, they're yesteryear's songs, not today's songs. Language relevancy had a long history in Roman Catholicism, though it proved difficult to demote the 'Tridentine' Latin Language Mass in favour of Mass in the local languages of the masses involved. Some Roman Catholics still oppose the change as a unique selling point lost to the masses.

Biblical language was the common, relevant language, and translation of Scripture and songs needs to take account of language changing with time. The Bible has a long history of translation, ideally by quality translators, into local languages for local folk. Even the Quran has translations, and Muslims recognise that no translation can be perfect. Elizabethan English in church is fine if it's Elizabeth 2. Linguistic spices, snatches from other languages, some ancient, still exist as meaningful additions to current English. However, a snatch is not syntax. It is an addition, not the basic structure.

A well-crafted song in olde worlde language, for an olde worlde feel, can have a positive impact. For example, Cliff Richard's *Millennium*

---

[104] But Sabine Baring-Gould's (1865) *Onward, Christian Soldiers*, did.

[105] Are McKeehan & Heimermann Jesus freaks, if they believe their 'best friend' was born in a manger? Are they in good company? A catchy song, but they didn't understand that *manger* meant *feeding trough*. Jesus was possibly born at Joseph's parents' house, on the ground floor where guests' animals could be sheltered, then placed in a *manger* to sleep. It's *manger* (CEB/NET/NIV/NJB/NKJV/NLT/NOG/NRSV), [*feeding*] *box* (ERV), or *feeding trough* (NCV).

Problems and Christian Songs

Prayer was a throwback to the KJV (sadly with subcanonical material mixed in), though he properly translated *trespass* from C1 Jewish speak, into general idiom—at least if 'sin' *is* general idiom in a world that disdains absolute judgement. Whether full modernity of language would have improved its evangelistic quotient, is moot. Its Christian witness was unpopular to christophobes, yet it was a strong witness to the general public. Likewise, Handel's *Messiah* still stirs us.[106]

A number of old terms have all but left the public domain. Consider a Christmas carol by Charles Wesley, *Hark How All the Welkin Rings*.[107] Whereas it's fine for longterm Christians who have cracked the code, in public singing should we not bias towards non~ and newer~Christians? Do we still welcome the welkin? And what does *Hail, the Sun of Righteousness...risen with healing in his wings*, mean to the average person in the pews, or to those we'd wish in the seats? *Hail* is *welcome/hello*. The rest is a reference to Mal.4:2 (Mal.3:20 in some versions). The NKJV reads, "The Sun of Righteousness shall arise with healing in His wings": the capitalised *His* shows it was taken to mean messiah. The NIV reads "the sun of righteousness will rise with healing in its rays." The NCV, "goodness will shine on you like the sun, with healing in its rays."

If not its only meaning, its core meaning was that the radiant sun symbolised messiah who would come with spiritual life and enlightenment, like the invigorating sun-rays of a new dawn. This would be the pivotal Yahweh Day. Because of its very profundity, it should be conveyed in clear language. As a general rule, if a thing's worth keeping, it's worth updating. In churches where nonbelievers hear this at carol services, if sang unchanged, is there added explanation, or do they leave believing it's about "a chicken with a medical degree" (Page 86)?[108] If we wish to connect with lyricists of

---

[106] www.youtube.com/watch?v=SXh7JR9oKVE

[107] Nowadays better known as *Hark, The Herald Angels Sing*.

[108] At least it's better than my pet hate, *Away in a Manger*. I suspect that the Mothers' Union, or such, invented the myth of a cryless baby, to whom mothers may croon without disturbance. A sickly song, for a docetic child? R T Kendall compared "no crying", with *Once In Royal David's City*'s, "tears and smiles like us he knew"—"it was the first sign of human likeness" (Kendall 67).

bygone Christmases, we should wish to revamp their wording so that today's singers may sing as mentally in tune with, say, Wesley, as his original singers were.[109]

B2: Ye or You?

Though the 1611 KJV was written when Early Modern English was the style, and *you* had replaced *thou*, it was pitched in the previous, Middle English, style, "more or less bound [to] the language of 1525" (McGrath 274). Like a ghetto child, it was born old. In this style, there was a singular *thou* (nominative)/*thee* (accusative, or dative), and a plural *ye* (nominative)/*you* (accusative, or dative). But if formal, rather than informal, it was always *you*. If a genitive form, the informal singular was *thy*/*thine*, otherwise it was *your*/*yours*. In 1611, common English, influenced by the French *vous* (*parlez-vous français?*), had turned to using the old singular forms for addressing family and inferiors, but the KJV, locked into Tyndale, as the Bishops' Bible had been, used the singular for God, human beings, and demons—celestials, terrestrials, and infernals.

Today, singular or plural, the normative, accusative, and dative forms, are *you*, and *your*/*yours* genitive. Even the standardising revision of 1769 kept some of the previous Middle English, including variants of *you*/*your*/*yours*. What is second nature in one's mother's tongue/language, can be far from second when it's far from your mother. Yet some still argue that Middle English beats Modern English, because it could differentiate between singular and plural forms of 'you.' Not that the KJV always did so. After all, why does it have *your god* (Dt.1:30), followed by *thy god* (31)? The Hebrew text doesn't change. Or *thy god* (Dt.6:15), followed by *your god* (16)?[110] I guess it goes at least back to William Tyndale, ringing the changes for the sake of style: vary style, keep interest. Whether or not it is a sad fact, the fact is that most today do not know the difference. Even

---

[109] We might also consider changing from the prospective view to the retrospective view. From carol reincarnationalism, to incarnationalism; from re-enactment, to remembrance. His birth is not expected, and I have done a remake of *Hark the Herald*, in chapter 12.

[110] Dt.6:16 is "thy god" in Mt.4:7/Lk.4:12. Compare also Ex.20:2/Dt.5:6 (*thy*), with Lv.25:38/26:13 (*your*).

among KJV readers, many probably don't realise the difference, not having been taught Middle or Early Modern English. I for one see no good reason for songs, where a singular is clear in context, needing a Middle English singular *thou/thy/thine*. And no good reason to toggle between the two types.

OK, here's an example of a toggle: *Jesus,* thou art *precious...your worth I see... in everything* you're *precious*. For consistency we could have, *Jesus,* thou art *precious...* thy *worth I see... in everything* thou art *precious*. Or, *Jesus,* you *are precious...your worth I see... in everything,* you're *precious*.[111] But why start with art? Put another way, if this song had been written in the current consistent style of the last option, would there be any sense in rewriting it in one of the other ways? If the reply is "no sense", then writing it as it was, was non-sense. And why on earth should Christianity vie with postmodernism for the nonsense trophy? Let's not be daft.

Now, besides sounding odd to newer ears, the thy/thou style is often misunderstood. Consider: "I appoint unto you a kingdom... that ye may eat and drink at my table.... Simon, Simon, behold, Satan hath desired to have *you*, that he may sift *you* as wheat: But I have prayed for *thee*, that *thy* faith fail not: and when *thou* art converted, strengthen *thy* brethren" (KJV: emphasis added). All well and good, but whom did Satan seek? "'Simon, Simon, listen! Satan has demanded to sift all of you like wheat, but I have prayed for you that your own faith may not fail; and you, when once you have turned back, strengthen your brothers" (NRSV). That is almost perfect.[112] The *you* to be sifted is *humas*, a plural you; the thee as prayed for and to strengthen, is *sou*, a singular you. So, Jesus prayed only for Peter (*sou*) to sort out the others (*humas*). I think I missed that in my KJV days, but to say that the 'number' distinctions are always important is going too far.

We can have the important issues brought out by other means. To say that anachronisms are more theological is inept: we worship a being who is plurality, though his emphasis is oneness. Granted, if ever our language reverts to having plural vs singular pronouns, we should then biblically prefer the singular. Indeed, to pointedly prefer

---

[111] *Jesus Thou Art Precious* (date and author unknown—possibly Pentecostal).
[112] For Lk.22:29-32, the NRSV is best.

Grammatical Problems

a singular to a neutral pronoun, might seem the way to go for unitarians, such as Witnesses, that pointedly deny that deity is societal. In the years when thine was fine, the singulars (deity is one being) never denied his plurality (one being of three persons), but were an emphasis choice. Those years are long gone. Nowadays, the non-numbered pronoun nicely covers the fact that deity is plurality in singularity, the eternal society.[113]

To say that the older singulars are more reverential, is unbiblical: *thees* and *thines*, and more importantly their Hebrew and Greek equivalents, were used equally for man and for deity. To say that anachronisms sound better, is unbiblical: anachronisms are confusing and off-putting—the scriptures were written in then contemporary language. Finally, there have been pronominal distinctions between deferential and familial forms of address. Tolkien noted how in The Shire "the deferential forms had gone out of colloquial use" (Tolkien 3.F2.1107), one reason Denethor found Pippin, who thus addressed him as an equal, amusing. Songs before 1931 didn't use the common language 'you,' for deity.

Among the first lyricist to move into the common use of 'you,' was 'Jan Struther,' who wrote both *Mrs. Miniver,* and *Lord of All Hopefulness* (1931). This hymn, addressing God as the *lord*, slipped in an informal pronoun: *give us, we pray, your bliss in our hearts*, instead of *thy bliss*. Gradually folk realised that there should not be two languages, an antiquated and a contemporary, and that the Bible had been written in the language of common people. But qualms lingered. Even the *New English Bible* (1970), hesitant, reverted to archaism to have *deferential* pronouns for deity. While old pronouns rarely feature in new songs, many old songs need updating for the sakes of

---

[113] Society is plural: Jhn.1:1 has the idea that the Word was with God [the father], and was God [in substance], both worked out in detail in John's Gospel. Many examples can be given of the plural singular: for example, molecules only exist as pluralities; four one dimensional lines of matching length, at right angles, make one two-dimensional square, and six squares of matching size, at right angles, make one three-dimensional cube; it takes more than one person to make one family.

non/new-Christians. Some hymnbooks, for example *Hymns for Today's Church*, target this aim.

B3: Sageism

In that it's no longer the way we now talk, sageism is an archaism, howbeit a recent one. It is a serious misunderstanding, an unintentional divide and exclusion of some for whom Christ died. Though curiously, some boys, girls, and women, were deliriously excited in 2003, when they became men![114] Some people just don't see that once upon a time songs rightly used expressions such as *men*, and *every man*, inclusively. Nowadays, they're only *parochially* inclusive. It's not that I welcome the folly of transgender ideologues, who now seek to degenderise semantics, thus human thinking, and whose care for those who actually suffer from gender dysphoria is questionable. It's just that English has within the norm changed its pattern, and older songs should be brought into line.

In inclusive settings, *men* often sounds both sexist (excluding adult female human beings), and ageist (excluding pre-adult human beings—commonly called children). I have coined this term *sageism*, to combine sexism and ageism. For Lk.5:10, the old NIV had 'men' (sageist), the NIV Inclusive, had 'men and women' (ageist), the NIV has 'people' (inclusive). Catch-up has been staggered. Some songs proclaim salvation for men and women, but preclude it from children—or so it can sound to children.

Equality is not a great and glorious god, so much as a fickle god of virtue and folly. Great evil has been done in its name. Albert James Lewis suffered some blindspots. Once he asked if so and so was invited to the regiment get together. On being told no, he said that he felt it was unfair, regardless of the fact that so and so had never belonged to the regiment. Politics has shown that same blind spot, legislating as in, what is intrinsically out. It was like A J Lewis when it came to legislate that homosexuals of the same sex should be invited to marry. Alas, outside its limited domain, Equality becomes a tyrant. It is wrong either to ignore it, or to be enslaved to it.

Within its orb, let us discriminate, asking the right questions. For instance, what about contexts where *men* and *kings* might be what is

---

[114] See Garrard & Smith's (2003), *Here I Am* (*Majesty*).

Grammatical Problems

both said and meant? If so, to change to *people* and *monarchs* is misleading. Equality, keep out! It is also sexism to needlessly remove a contextual gender component, potentially scandalous to the exclusive gender. Likewise, C20 maternity units were for *women* to give birth, not *people* to give birth. These are examples of sexism in *exclusive* contexts. Normal differences should not be squashed. Removing exclusive talk about boys, girls, men, women, would be sexism, even ageism, as much as speaking in exclusive terms when the inclusive is meant. Sageism works both ways. Avoiding both errors, we should ask whether gender/age terms, in our songs, are properly exclusive or inclusive.

Chapter 7   Theological Problems

"Sing...psalms and hymns and spiritual songs among yourselves, and making music to the lord in your hearts. And give thanks for everything to God the father in the name of our lord Jesus Christ. And further, submit to one another out of reverence for Christ.... Christ loved the church. He gave up his life for her to make her holy and clean, washed by the cleansing of God's word. He did this to present her to himself as a glorious church without a spot or wrinkle or any other blemish" (NLT: Eph.5:19-21,25-7).

C: Blessing God

For this, I deduct 5 points. Among words that can mislead, figures the word *bless*. I don't say it's a big issue, only that it is an issue. And since it blurs the distinction between God and man, it may be deemed a theological issue. Versions that still speak of *blessing* God, sacrifice Heb.7:7, an axiom which generalises that blessing is never from the lower to the higher. The basic Hebrew, *BRK*, functioned, through differing forms, sometimes as *to bless*, and sometimes as *to kneel* (to revere, praise). It is generally agreed that the sense between forms, the between kneeling before, and being knelt to, that of God blessing humanity, and humanity *blessing* God, differs.

English Bible versions should reflect this. To assess their policies, I have looked for phases, such as *bless the LORD*, and *blessed be/is God*. Cutting to the chase, it's ones like the CEB/NJB/NKJV/NRSV on the problem side, and ones like the ERV/NET/NCV/NIV/NLT/NOG on the solution side—a few minor problems with the better versions are fairly liveable even if not loveable, and should only prove a problem if folk prooftext to 'prove' that we can bless God.

"Those finite verbs...that speak of God as 'blessed,' may very well be qal forms, artificially levelled by the Masoretes because the distinction between the verb patterns had been forgotten (for example, 2 Chr.20:26; Ps.26:12; 103:1), and would mean 'kneel to, revere, exalt.' If such be the case, the distinction between 'bless[ed]' as God to human (piel) and 'revere[d], esteem[ed]' as human to God (qal; cf. NIV 'praise[d]' in such cases), would be apparent. Where the verb appears in a human-to-human context, the qal passive participle would indicate a meaning of 'praised, exalted,' thus 'blessed' (for example, Gen.14:19), while the piel

Theological Problems

would signify 'bless' in the formal sense" (William Williams: VanGemeren 2001:H1384 (barake1)). That is, it's likely that the Hebrew text came to lose its distinctive forms between praising God and blessing people. Theodirectionally (ie unto deity), we should sing praise, not bless. Going back to the Redmans' *Blessed Be Your Name*, *Praised be the name of the Lord* improves one step, *Praised be the name of the LORD*, another, *Praised be the name of Yahweh*, yet another, *Praised be Yahweh*, perhaps being the best. But can we ever bless (or praise?) this song too highly?

D: Buddy, Boyfriend, and Baby

For this, I deduct 5 points.

D1: Buddy Jesus

Jesus is my lord, my big brother, and the biggest singer in my family (Heb.2:12), but he's no friend of mine. Shock horror to some, yet commonplace to others. Let's define some ideas. In ultimate eternity, even as girl/guy love will be as redundant chaff, so, I suspect, will mere friendship. In the here and now, these are both wonderful expressions of love, yet when the perfect comes, the imperfect is retired. Aioniologically speaking, this is the problem I have with reunions "on the other side", a mere continuance of human loves.

We should not squeeze our definitions into the Bible. What are its meanings of friendship? First, what do you make of Lincoln Brewster's *What a Friend I've Found* (2002)?[115] It is attractive. Those bereaved from, or who have never known, the richness of either a mother's love, a friendship love, or a spouse's love, can warm to the idea that deity can role model, surrogate, these human loves. I'd love to be ardently committed to the idea of Jesus as my best friend. Does this make him so? What of folk passionate to the idea that the Blessed Virgin is their mother, or that Jesus' body was broken? Does their

---

[115] *What a friend I've found / Closer than a brother / I have felt your touch / More intimate than lovers / Jesus, friend forever / What a hope I've found / More faithful than a mother / It would break my heart / To ever lose each other*. It has fairly good rhyme, although lovers (perhaps "a lover") doesn't quite rhyme with brother/forever/mother/other.

passion make things so? We should never believe simply to fulfil our wishes and the theologies built around them.

But if Jesus is our buddy, as I used to believe, then I believe it can only be known by extrabiblical revelation, for I believe that it isn't biblical revelation. And I'm a little reluctant to ground my doctrine outside of Scripture, especially if in line with my wishes. I now see that the definition of friendship[116] in John 15, is about promotion from servants to confidants, allies, *if* they maintained their obedience. A follow Christ through the cross, then he'll show us his plans, so to speak. Jesus would talk new covenant to those who would walk humbly in mission with him.

This friendship meant that his inner group would soon enter the Christian plan for life (Jhn.17:3), which they would open up to the world and put into written form, the New Testament.[117] Possibly it applies directly to each sibling who submits to his lordship, the path of discipleship we may all travel. But if you really insist on citing Jhn.15 for calling Jesus, *friend*, do you equally insist on having promoted *him* from your slave to someone you share *your* plans with—so long as he obeys *you*? Because that's how it pans out *if* you're talking as *he* talked about his disciples.

Talking about the word *hetairos* (friend), K H Rengstorf said that "the absence of the word elsewhere in the NT shows that it is not thought to be appropriate to Christians, for in relation to Christ doulos is the proper term for believers, and in relation to one another adelphoi" (Bromiley 265). Let's face it, Jesus talked of unilateral, not bilateral, alliance—not about us being buddies, but of something asymmetrical. Scripture likewise says that Abraham was a friend of God, but it doesn't say that

---

[116] Here the term is *philia*, which purely for convenience we can confine to the idea, *friendship*. By NT times the contrasts of Classical Greek had blurred. Philia & agapē could be used interchangeably: Jesus three times asked whether Peter loved him (v17, *philia* x3), yet John's record used *agapē* twice, and *philia* once (Jhn.21:15-7); love (*agapē*) can be against God (Jhn.3:19); and God loves (*philia*) his son (Jhn.5:20).

[117] Yes, there was also Paul. Yet he made sure to check with the first batch of apostles, and had a very special foundational call as an apostle. The basic plan had been given before Pentecost.

Theological Problems

God was a friend of Abraham. The loud silence speaks volumes. A unilateral, one-way thing, a privilege granted by the higher, not by the lower. The OT lacked a buddy theology.

Nor is Pr.18:24 an exception, since it does not imply Yahweh. In the NT, *Friend of Sinners* (Mt.11:19/Lk.7:34) means one who helped them, not their best buddy at the boozer. Joseph Scriven's (1855) *What A Friend We Have in Jesus*, has *friend* as *benevolent rescuer*, a friendly ally. Scriven understood the point about friendly help (all our sins and griefs to bear) for Christians. And the level of friendship perhaps depends on how open to God we are. With deeper discipleship comes deeper understanding of his nature and his covenant plans. The closeness of the spirit who represents Jesus, is another matter, but isn't buddyism.

Contra Buddy Theology, I suggest *The Four Loves* (C S Lewis), and *Difficult Doctrine of the Love of God* (D A Carson). *Friend* has a range of meaning (for example Facebook, buddy, friendly fire, befriend): Scripture should be read contextually and exegetically (perceptively), not eisegetically (reader response). Reader response has always been big. In the fifth century, a heresy-hunting Eastern archbishop (a.k.a. patriarch) of Constantinople, born in Kahramanmaraş, Turkey, and educated in Syrian Antioch (a.k.a. Antakya, Turkey), flagged up his concern that Mary was being worshipped as deity (would Islam not welcome him?), and suggested that church-speak should be more careful.[118]

---

[118] Ordinarily what a mother conceives is fully part of herself and her husband, but the incarnation was not ordinary–Joseph had no genetic input. With the incarnation her genes went into only part of the package (some think it helps to visualise man as body/soul/spirit), accommodating the pre-existent personhood which is beyond, and now has an integrated mode within, creation. There was never a time when God's son was not, but Jesus began in time (Jhn.1:14), becoming the christ: a unique blend of creation and transcreation. Mary was thus the mother/bearer of Christ, the human, anointed, child. Whether his humanity blended in her temporal personality into his eternal personality, I leave aside. Yet note, theologically the first sinless Adam (the man) had no mother but was perfectly human. The last/second sinless Adam's mission required entering the human gene pool, but perhaps he didn't need a personality input from his genetic mother to be fully human.

Problems and Christian Songs

The majority feared that taking his advice would lead to her son no longer being worshipped as deity (would Witnessism not welcome him?). The ruckus that was raised showed that the *Mother of God* idea had its devotees, and the bishop's suggestion that Mary was simply *Christ's* mother, horrified them. Today that individual, Nestorius, is still cursed (blacklisted) in Orthodoxism, though I doubt that he minds. Reading as we wish to respond, tends to misreading.

In similar vein, are those who have claimed Jesus (the father, and spirit, are frequently ditched) as *friend/husband/father*, more likely to charge than change? I happily encourage the deep intimacy between God and his children, which his son's death enabled and the spirit's indwelling promotes, but Christ doesn't wish us to go all mushy on him, nor to overlook his command position.

Can the warm fuzziness of buddyism, devalue divine intimacy? Chris Idle noted how so-called *Liberal Christianity* (a.k.a. quasichristianity) likes to encourage feminine terms such as *mother*, and enjoys the "delightfully ambiguous 'Partner' and 'Lover.' Charles Wesley of course wrote Jesu Lover...but even then brother John was not so keen, omitting it from his 1771 book." (Reform). The West has a large antimarriage lobby,[119] some of which infects the church, suffocating to death terms such as *spouse* and *marriage partner*, with *partner*, and the almighty *Ms* which undermines *Mrs/Miss* distinctions—distinctions highlighting marriage, so derided by *Ms* ideologues.

How does one socially engineer away the idea that marriage as sacred, alone set up by God for interpersonal sex (IPS)? Easy, suggest that that's uncaring, unscientific, bigoted, and using various other negative slurs on the slide into the moral void. Then throw in reams of feely talk to promote the idea that IPS is amoral, an as-you-like-it, with-whom-you-like-it, for as-long-as-you-like-it. *You, like, it*, being the operative words. People being loyal to people is out. Hedonism

---

[119] Marriage has stood a litmus test of relational loyalty, and carries God's voice that unwedded interpersonal sex is wrong. Like all of us, those who like unwedded interpersonal sex, dislike being condemned. Their basic method to justify themselves is, having formed an ideological network, to denounce & degrade the concept, marriage, and the even bigger claim of the divine authority which demands their obedience.

Theological Problems

and autocracy are in. Devaluing this way, western governments are, for now, tentatively tethered to truth by the tenuous concept of mutual consent.[120] I fear that buddy theology songs are joining this fuzzy flow, closing down to God and his lordship.

Idle (Reform) noted some other unhealthy trends. For example, a drift from the spirit as a person who both helps and commands, to that of a more Star Warsy influence in the air. "The spirit becomes a convenient motif embracing multi-faith, new-age, and do-it-yourself, philosophies; he, or (increasingly) she, is ignored no longer". "'Fatherless' hymnals" are being engineered in. Commendably, anti-drunkenness songs rightly condemn the cause of drunkenness, but various anti-HIV songs condone, not condemn, immoral sexual transmission of HIV: "when they speak of hysteria, hatred and fear, we think we know who is being caricatured.... [But] it is like having a section of hymns devoted to lung cancer or road-accident victims, without any reference to possible causes."

Idle also noted a "new stream of 'divorce' hymns" in which the "'spirit' apparently releases us from old obligations and ties in the name of freedom and fulfilment," free love—meaning our worship of human emotions rather than obedience to Love himself. Objective truth is out. Westernism becomes the greedy sea which shall one day yield its dead. All this can flow from a buddy approach to deity, a descent from lordship into the wishy-washy.

D2: Boyfriend Jesus

Then there are romanticising songs into girlfriend-boyfriend types. One blogger picked up a Vineyard song: "no mention of God, Jesus, or the cross—just 'I' and 'You.' How is this a worship song to God? It could

---

[120] Unwritten policy: first force Ms/Mrs, or Miss/Ms, options, and as Ms acclimatises, drop marriage distinctives Miss/Mrs: semantic deconstruction. The endgame Ms simply says that marriage doesn't matter, even if mutual consent does. Yet the new position is tenuous and temporary, since if *God* is an invalid or irrelevant concept, there is no absolute ground for *mutual consent*. To add international flavour, Ethiopia has Ato for Mr, Woizerit (Wzt) for Miss, and Woizero (Wzo) for Mrs: semantics recognises marriage—disrecognition is the vanguard of attack.

Problems and Christian Songs

be me singing it to a girl!" (lestyouforget).[121] Is Jesus our boyfriend? No. There must be clear blue water between God and girl/guy. Was *Let My Words Be Few*, co-attributed to Matt Redman's wife Beth, because he needed her permission to turn a song he'd written to her, into one written to Jesus? I'm not the first to ask, and yes, it is cheeky, yet it's asked to make a point. Matt acknowledged that it wasn't ideal for church singing.[122] Too much syrupy sweet candy and not enough meat and potatoes, is bad for our health. What of Scott Haslem's (1999) *Keep Falling In Love?*[123]

What of C19 Horatius Bonar's *I heard the voice of Jesus say... Lay down, thou weary one, lay down thy head upon my breast.* It was probably based on a dubious translation, sadly kept in the NKJV of Jhn.13:25, that in today's ears makes John seem effeminate. (All the Russian guy-to-guy kissing in Tolstoy's War and Peace, can sound like that!) The cultural reality was that Jews lay on their sides at the low Passover table, and to whisper a question to a neighbour immediately behind you, you'd roll from your side to your back, then twist your head, to more or less face them. And in John's context, it was not about weariness, but about John's whispered enquiry about the betrayer's identity. It is extremely unlikely that *Jesus Boyfriend*, was Bonar's theme.

God is beyond biology, time, and space. Biology exists only within his creation, and for humanity has male/female expression, roughly synchronised to the nonsexual genders of masculine/feminine. Some

---

[121] http://lestyouforget.wordpress.com/2008/04/11/bad-worship-songs

[122] https://www.youtube.com/watch?v=qFljv_wit4k

[123] *I am found in your embrace, covered by your love / Beyond my deepest dreams I know your love so strong, Spirit come [why?] / You lift me up to heaven's door, you restore my soul / I can't live without your touch, I need you so much, need you more / You're my rock and my redeemer / The rock on which I stand / I keep falling in love with you, Lord / Every beat of my heart, breath that I take / Through the seasons that change, your love remains / My hiding place, my home.* Or Oneness Pentecostal Lanny Wolfe's (c.1975), *I keep falling in love with him over and over and over and over again / He gets sweeter and sweeter as the days go by / Oh what a love between my lord and I.* To some extent someone's meat is someone's poison, since some are touchier than others. Loving God is to be enjoyed, but not perhaps the idea of frequently falling in (and therefore out) of love for him.

Theological Problems

languages have about 30 genders, linguistic markers (Carson 1998:78). God is the fount of what we perceive to be masculinity and femininity, even though the incarnation for mission and identity, was incorporation into male humanity. Jesus had, and has, a male human body. The trouble is picturing Jesus as male (a biological aspect) and then romanticising. Thus, though there are many kinds of love, talk of loving him *can* sometimes sound like loving a male human being, along gender lines.

Talk of *loving God* is safer, for it is more likely to be read across along the same nonsexual lines, as *loving humanity*. Some unmarried missionary women are told that Jesus will be their husband; nuns are oft called brides of Christ. Why not just as easily say that he, or perhaps *she*, will be the *wife* of single missionary men and of monks, and that to subsequently marry a mortal, a nun or missionary woman must first *divorce* Jesus? A point of *Genesis* is that God reckoned himself a poor substitute for an Eve, and that she was a poor substitute for him: neither should play *substitute*, but together should form a triangle of love: husband, wife, God.

But whether married or not, of course, analogically a Christian man or women is somewhat like a bride enabled to bear spiritual fruit (Rm.7:4), but—even as I am not the mystic body of Christ but the church is—biblically the bridal image is retained for corporate entities (2 Cor.11:2). That is, he is husband to the global church, not to its individuals. Individuals are not the church in their individuality, only in their full togetherness, and form churches in localised corporate togetherness.[124] A point of *Revelation* too, is that ultimately the expression *bride* is linked to the church over the millennia (Rv.19:7): the eschatological wedding supper. Jesus-Boyfriend songs might not be too dangerous, but I think they are silly and, to some, sickly. It is better, as someone else said, to see the relationship between Christ and the church as compared not to a boyfriend and girlfriend but to a husband and wife, and to see that the wife is not

---

[124] Only these two meanings of church are biblical. Calling a Christian network *Church*, demands, IMO, repentance, whether *Church* of Rome, *Church* of the Nazarene, Elim *Church*, or Anglican *Church*.

any individual but the one church. Christians are part of that community that is betrothed to him, his wife awaiting their wedding. Nor do we find refuge in the *Song of Songs/Canticles*. It has had a number of treatments. Some have even claimed to see Martin Luther's nose in 7:4! Some Judaics treat it allegorically as if between Yahweh and Ethnic Israel, and some Christians as between Jesus and the Church. Which side started that game? I think Tewoldemedhin Habtu was right to say that its primary message is in the surface reading. Namely, sexual desire as "God-given and beautiful when practiced in the context of a heterosexual, [lifetime] committed, and loving, relationship", with the possibility of a hidden spiritual-level of broad applicability (Adeyemo 797). Similarly, the C4 monk Jovinian controversially argued that it typified a straightforward love story of celibacy previewing the joys of chaste marriage awaiting the lovers: this makes excellent sense.[125]

I treat the Baby Jesus theme under Decontextualisation, and give it a slight to middling demerit. Besides being goo gahism, ideas of him wearing Pampers and yet prayed to, holds true faith and evangelism up to ridicule.

E: Polytheism

For this, I deduct 10 points. True, most can cope with a gap between what folk say, and what they mean. So, so as long as there is no theological gap, is the verbal gap really material, or is it mere nitpicking? Well, nitpicking can usefully prevent lice infestations, since nits become lice—not nice.

The term *god*, in some contexts, should be capitalised. As an absolute, for instance: *God is*. But in a relative setting, a smaller g conveys the idea: ultimately there is one god, God, and the gods of the nations are idols, though poetically *gods*. Many songs have an [*our god is...*] structure. My god is wonderful, your god is precious, our god is healer, etc. Many songs have a predicative (wonderful/precious/holy) god, etc. How's your god today? In Western talk, this can sound like a

---

[125] Jovinian denied the ideas of Mary having remained a virgin after bearing Jesus, and argued that marriage was no less holy than the virginity of nuns (Chadwick 76). I like that guy.

Theological Problems

throwback to polytheism, the idea of many more or less equal gods and goddesses. As a Roman Catholic well said, "we do not even believe in a god, for this would imply a possible or conceivable multiplication of gods: but only in God" (Tyrrell 76). I'd allow Tyrrell a little slack: there is a god, but he cannot be a comparative god (adjectives compare), but I share Tyrrell's concern of a semantic cliff-edge.

And as Karl Barth said, "any god postulated or dreamt up by man, even the loftiest and most impressive, is alien to the Christian faith and can only be repudiated by it as a non-god" (Barth 43). I still think that the title of ex-Atheist Antony Flew's final book, should have been, *There is God*, or *God Is*, not *There is a God*. Instead of speaking of their rival *concepts* of God, some Muslims speak of *the Christian god*, and some Christians of *the Muslim god*, yet both sides agree that there is no god but God. Life is crazy. Muslims and Christians both converge (there is only one god) and diverge (is he is monopersonal or monosocietal?).

C S Lewis noted that "'mine' in its fully possessive sense cannot be [truthfully] uttered by a human being about anything."[126] He then, poetically, pictured demons being spitefully gleeful over the ways in which us humans can wallow in pride and confusion, over this term which has "finely graded differences that run from 'my boots' through 'my dog,' 'my servant,' 'my spouse,' 'my father,' 'my master' and 'my country,' to 'my god'" (Lewis 1975:21.109).

Too easily we can reduce all the senses to that of 'my boots,' the 'my' of ownership of the inanimate, and even exchange the responsibility of regard, to the irresponsibility of disregard. When Richard Harries wrote, *C S Lewis: The Man and His God* (1987), did the title not say something about Harries' theology? Jack's god wasn't Richard's, and I hope neither had one. Does *my* lucky god get me for an hour or two on Sundays. Of course, all other hours are *mine*. McCoy exclaimed, "my god, Jim," not to deify his captain, but as concerned surprise. Who McCoy's god was, *Star Trek* never said, but is it not safer to avoid *my god* talk?

---

[126] Does power make true ownership? I capture a wild horse. Does that make the horse truly mine? *The Horse and His Boy* (C S Lewis) gives the lie: "The earth and everything on it belong to Yahweh" (CEV: Ps.24:1).

Problems and Christian Songs

Yet it's in the Bible, isn't it, so it must be right. Is it? Well, not as the highest levels of revelation.[127] The Bible contains tertiary education, as well as earlier secondary education. While many biblical passages could reasonably be translated in terms of *God, who is mine*,[128] many remain in their polytheistic setting as contrasts between *my god* and *your god*. Scripture was not written as a philosophical treatise, though philosophy should be based on it. Of the Bible versions I've examined, I particularly commend the CEV for seeking to redress this issue.[129] Quite possibly Ethnic Israel had grammatical and/or theological safety mechanisms that maintained, once attained, philosophical monotheism. Generally, when *we* talk, it should not be in polytheistic context (contrasting *gods*), since that's not our worldview, nor is it where Scripture was leading to. Do we still talk to each other of *moo moos* or the like (1 Cor.13:11)? Let's talk and sing as if adults.

Unless careful, talk about God's attributes can confuse possession with source, reflection with radiance, and the immanence with transcendence. Though technically water is a liquid state of a molecular compound, a batch of H^2O, let's just talk *water* here. A substance cannot have an amount of what it is; water cannot have water. I agree that an amount may have a percentage of the substance and a percentage of impurities, a mixed compound. The sea has a percentage of water, of salt, and of plastic bottles. But as a substance, water is defined *as* water, H^2O, not *by* water. We do not rightly speak of wet water as an adjective, a type of water, though to us water has a characteristic of being wet.

---

[127] I readily acknowledge that the NT contains archaic speech patterns, for instance about idols. Nevertheless, it does not ride on the simple idea that Rome had its gods and that Christians had their covenant god. Indeed, Gal.4:8 taught Gentile converts to reject such silly ideas. And 1 Cor.8:5-6 underlines that while Gentiles talked irrelevantly about gods and divine lords, yet Christians were into true meaning—one lordship, Christ, who revealed one kingdom, his father's. *The god of this age*, is only poetically pictured as a god (2 Cor.4:4).

[128] Rm.15:6: (eg Geneva/Bishops/KJV) or (eg CEB/NIV/NRSV)? Similarly, Rm.15:5: (NIV), or simply, (NLT)?

[129] In my chart in *The Word's Gone Global*, the highest version is the CEV, given the A+, followed by the NLT grading C-.

Theological Problems

Likewise, whereas poetical language might say that deity, the tripersonal, is beautiful, philosophical language would say that deity *has* no beauty since deity *is* beauty.[130] Source, not possession. Think of it this way, that Measure cannot be measured, that Standard cannot be compared to Itself. God is Goodness, Holiness, etc, not simply a good or holy *kind of god*.[131] Yes, he is always good towards us, and holy to us, but that's talking verbs. It can be difficult for one whose adoptive mother language is philosophy, to speak poetry, when it seems to clash. Indeed, Church history has some big examples of the (philosophical?) East and the (prosaic?) West, mistrusting the other because a key word by one side, though used orthodoxly, was wrongly thought by the other to be heterodox, since the other side used that word another way.

A lesser issue today—just to give a current example—is one where to some the expression, *born again*, is sacrosanct, and to others it's a mere Nicodemian jest perhaps implying a repeated type of birth, instead of a new kind of birth.[132] What if the latter believed that the former believed in reincarnation? I repeat that talking the same language, with the same meaning, is important. Why sing of our type of god is, when in fact we believe that God's the only god on show?

I suspect we lack the cultural grammatical and/or theological safety mechanisms, which the biblical writers would have had as second nature. In our day and age, why attempt their talk patterns of multiple gods, with the evolved nuances of Yahweh as distinct above all other gods, and even the other gods as being secondary, not even

---

[130] That is, the higher excludes the lower. This is not the same as 'Beauty is Deity,' a deification of an attribute.

[131] Perhaps interestingly the definitions of God as Love and Light come in *First John*, a letter written in response to a philosophical (proto-Gnostic?) attack on God's nature: see 1:5; 4:8/16.

[132] See my book, *The Word's Gone Global*, which examines the idea that 'born again' was a jocular misreading of Jesus; that only those born *from above* (Jesus' meaning) are Christians; that even had it been dominical, 'born again' would not define a *type* of Christian. It remains moot as to whether, in our age of apostasy, the term 'Christian' requires explication.

sentient, constructs? And if that's not to be in our talk, why differentiate by *my*/*our* god?

Indeed, nowadays the West has so moved from gods-talk that when it does, it talks a different language. For instance, in the West, what does "gods of the nations" mean? We are likely to reply that our TVs are today's gods, but that's hardly what the psalmists meant, even if we do sacrifice our children to Molek.[133] It can be putting entertainment and escapism before living relationships, and drip-feeding the spirit of the age, but it is not believing that TVs, or other electronic gizmos, actually house incorporeal nonhuman spirits that have evil intentions. Gods-talk is not what it was.

Therefore, when handling the older type of talk, I think that we should at least bias towards a more philosophical way of presenting the biblical data, avoiding lyrics that could seem to contrast one god with another, each dressed in polytheistic clothes. I actually have some sympathy for Bultmann's demythologisation. I say again, some monotheists, such as Christian and Muslim, wrongly contrast themselves as having different gods. Some say that the Christian god isn't their god, Allah. Christians might reply that their own god is loving, some, biblically and semantically confused, that he is Jesus. But it is not *the gods* that differ. God is the only god in show: *the gods* is purely a semantic figment. What differs, are the *concepts* about God. I refuse to sing that my god is such and such a type. I have, I vainly hope, no god. I have God, and he has me, and I am glad.

F: Voxdeism

F1: Soft Voxdeism

For this, I deduct 25 points. At this level, it is a type of misvisualisation—we visualise ourselves as deity.[134] One example is

---

[133] I happily endorse www.movieguide.org for good guidance about movies. All films ideologise; some demand worship, and the entertainment industry can function as Westernism's Molek.

[134] Divinisation (not *divination!*) is itself a useful term in the context of our transformation into God's true likeness, though Mormonism misjudges God's 'start' and our 'end'. The created can never become uncreated, and the

Theological Problems

Kendrick's *I Will Build My Church*, for which we visualise ourselves as Jesus, then switch back to being mere mortals, howbeit empowered to command spirits to obey our words. I guess the latter is a bit like Ezekiel, only he acted under explicit orders, so that he truly echoed Yahweh's creative words (Ezk.37). Kendrick's song doesn't add to Scripture,[135] but it does expose singers to the danger of doing so.

Prophecies are sometimes unwisely phrased in the same dicey format, *I the LORD you god, say....* This can make judging the prophecy, feel like judging God, although when prophesying some feel so close to God that it seems a natural way to speak—seeing from his perspective. As with god-talk, some justification can be claimed from the Sinaitic prophets who made us familiar with that format. But I deem it unwise to tread where the canonical prophets trod.

F2: Hard Voxdeism

For this, I deduct 50 points. Such songs actually add words to Scripture, making ourselves out to be God scripting new canon. One example is Bell and Maule's *Will You Come And Follow Me?* This merrily creates new canon in every line. I am fussy about what we sing as Scripture, and wary about false ideas going forth as deity's *ipsissima verba*. I sadly acknowledge that one of my favourite authors, Sir Arthur Conan Doyle, believed in a *New Revelation*—occult (psychical) revelation is merely demonic.[136] Sadly some Christian lyricists stray the same unhappy way.

---

uncreated is intrinsically noncreated. But let's neither pretend to be deity nor able to speak new revelations.

[135] Though Kendrick 'gives' *hell*—a term some think poor translation—dominical affirmation. Voxdeism can canonise our misunderstandings.

[136] Raphael Gasson's *The Challenging Counterfeit*, is a helpful exposé of Spiritualism, since written by a former longterm well-meaning medium who, having rather reluctantly become a Christian, could see both sides of the fence. I have critically rewritten as this, as *Revisiting The Challenging Counterfeit*.

G: Unitarianism

By and large errors in this area—I speak as a trinitarian—are simply based on lyricists living in poor theology, even as misvisualisation is likewise based on living in poor praying.

G1: Soft Unitarianism

For this, I deduct 65 points. Soft unitarianism differs from the issue that is later looked at under the idea of prayer misvisualisation, in that the latter can operate within a trinitarian framework, and is essentially a problem of prayer. Unitarianism (Islam is one form) visualises God as one being, one person, one monopersonal, nonsocietal, being, so is *theological* misvisualisation.[137] Biblical revelation has various ways of handling the concept, *trinity*. The terms *Yahweh*, and *God*, tend to focus on God the father, as ultimate source—*monarchia*. Theologians speak of the eternal generation, and eternal spiration, of God the son, and God the spirit, respectively.[138]

I have argued in *The Word's Gone Global* that Jesus-is-deity texts exist, yet their fewness implies that that focus is not where the Bible is at (1 Cor.8:6). So, to be biblical, we may say that Jesus is deific, but will seldom voice that fact, but if voicing, will always do so in the context (as does the Bible) of his father being supremely God. The Athanasian Creed noted the combined interaction of all three persons of deity.

Soft unitarianism tends to limit interaction to one person, the *Jesus-alone-does-this* song. In principle, I leave the father-alone songs alone, since the Bible tends to highlight the term *deity* to him, even though the New Testament, as a whole, advances understanding into

---

[137] In my books the theological standard is the biblical, although in some sense we may speak of, perhaps commend, *Islamic theology*. The Letters to the Seven Churches, shows how truth & error can be held in the same hand.

[138] Perhaps the term spiration was based on the idea that God's son actually breathed out the spirit into his disciples, misreading Jhn.20:22. To move from the economic trinity (ie the trinity working in time & space) to the essential trinity (the trinity as Being, beyond time & space) is also questionable. However, the biblical terms for *spirit* overlap the idea of air, wind, breath, allowing some justification for spiration as a rough & ready term.

trinity dynamics. In short, trinitarianism holds to the ultimacy of the father, not of the son. Soft unitarianism I automatically limit to a soft-fail (35 points is U+).

G2: Hard Unitarianism

For this, I deduct 75 points (25 points is U). This rises about Jesus-only in function, to implicit Jesus [alone] being God. It therefore lacks a safety surround of father or spirit, though it lacks explicit emphasis words, such as 'only/alone'.

G3: Hyper Unitarianism

For this, I deduct 90 points (10 points is U-). Hyper unitarianism differs from the issue that is later looked at under the idea of prayer misvisualisation, in that the latter can operate within a trinitarian framework and is essentially a problem of prayer. Hyper differs from soft, in that it specifically teaches that Jesus alone is God, or that the father died on the cross, or that the spirit is coming back for us, or some such nonsense. In short, it assumes that the father and the spirit are needless terms, or are an actor's masks that Jesus uses.

Songs denying the deity of the son and the spirit, but not of the father, are also hyper-unitarianism, raising issues of ontology, not merely of activity. Hyper-unitarianism I automatically fail badly. Christians can be unitarians, whether visualising Jesus as being his father and acting successor, or God's son as being less than deity, but I reckon that unitarianism seriously undermines good theology.[139]

---

[139] Eastern Orthodoxy perhaps makes most of creedal anathematising of such heretics. It has done so (in wording which reflects Paul's), perhaps not wishing heretics to be ultimately damned, but wishing cancerous heresies to be removed from the church on earth by major excommunication and warning (Gal.1:8-9; 5:12; 1 Cor.16:22).

Chapter 8   Proseuchological Problems

"Speak...to one another in psalms, hymns, and spiritual songs, singing and making music in your hearts to the lord, always giving thanks to God the father for each other in the name of our lord Jesus Christ, and submitting to one another out of reverence for Christ.... Christ loved the church and gave himself for her to sanctify her by cleansing her with the washing of the water by the word, so that he may present the church to himself as glorious—not having a stain or wrinkle, or any such blemish, but holy and blameless" (NET: Eph.5:19-21,25-7).

H: Misdirection

For this, I deduct 15 points. Since Part 2 has covered this point indepth, I'll only give a slight summary here. Misdirectionism can lead to, but falls short of, misvisualisation, the mental fusing about the members of deity.[140] Misdirected prayer nevertheless misunderstands both our static relationship with deity and deity's dynamic relationship to us. Therefore, songs encouraging this malpractice encourage a serious loss of biblicality.

Jesus taught requests not to himself, but to his father, who after the cross would become messianically *abba* to, and only to, each Yeshuic believer. In the new covenant, Yeshua himself should no longer be directly asked by his disciples, because the father himself would love them in the personalised individualism of that new covenant—direct contact. Jhn.16:23 makes this clear, and even without preferring the simplified TR version, 14:14 fits well into the framework of asking the father directly (= asking Jesus indirectly), and the spirit directly responding (= Jesus indirectly responding)—trinity involvement.

Paul's way of joining the terms *God/father*, and *lord/Jesus* (1 Cor.8:5-6), and mentally keeping these two persons distinct yet united in one tripersonal being, is perhaps the wisest way forward. I suggest we avoid the Dominus Factor, introduced by Wycliffe into English, drop calling God *lord*, follow the rule of thumb that the father is God, Jesus is lord, and ask only God (not the lord), in Jesus' *name*, us being a part of Jesus' family and mission. And though talking with the spirit is part

---

[140]   Latin: *neque confundentes personas, neque substantiam separantes*; English: neither confusing the persons, nor dividing the substance. Athanasian Creed.

Proseuchological Problems

and parcel of Christian life, biblically the spirit is the one alongside us who inspires, not receives, our requests (Rm.8:15,26-7). So, ask only the father, and don't call him *lord*. I mark down the Dominus Factor.

I: Misvisualisation (prayer)

Even hands-free phoning adds danger to your drive. To some extent this is because of visualisation. We blank off from the road as we focus on the inner voice of the phone, and in our minds follow where it leads. Some even look at their phone as if it's doing the talking, so don't hear the road. Asked about our bank account, we might visualise Wall Street—and next moment, Crash. For so much in life, visualisation is second nature. My concern here is for prayer, and our face-to-face relationship with deity. Heb.12:2 encouraged some who looked to return to the safety of Judaism, to seriously visualise Jesus. In short, the Bible encourages good visualisation for good theology. However, some songs encourage blindness, and in prayer songs, looking unto Jesus might, surprise, surprise, cause us to stumble.

Songs can lead us into various types of misvisualisation. At a low-level, if we *hallelujah* God, we're asking him to praise himself. That's by being blind to language. At mid-level, misvisualisation tricks us out of praying prayer. By toggling between prayer and non-prayer, sometimes at bewildering pace, we simply don't recognise prayer. That's being blind to prayer. A classic example of this is when after a song that's entirely to deity, the congregation is told, "now, let's open in prayer". "Der, isn't that what we've just been doing?" you may ask. Or, when an offending offering bag shakes under our noses during a prayer song—obviously we're not to pray prayer-songs because they ain't prayer! Prayer is being sung into the air, but not unto God.

Sometimes, by throwing in a song about God, or a psalm about him, folk even interrupt the flow of a prayer time. Is this because they don't visualise that prayer is actually directly to somebody, so they don't mind interrupting our talk to/with deity?[141] What makes it even worse

---

[141] Interruptions can be justified—I recall Sam Fry's "I forbid that there prai-er" (Blackmore 470) on hearing of King Charles 2's death. But some are just too eager to stick their oar in, prioritising that over prayer.

Problems and Christian Songs

(hyper) is, if besides overlooking the prayer nature of song, we also overlook the nature of the persons of deity, confusingly switching between members of deity. We address the father, call him, lord, then thank him for being crucified, what scholars call patripassianism (conceptually crucifying the father). While such misvisualisation between the members of deity also happens in non-prayer songs, I have chosen to ignore marking it down except when it figures in prayer-songs, where it makes worse the already bad.

I1: Soft Misvisualisation

For this, I deduct 15 points.

YuYu

If I sing, "You (pronoun), you (pronoun) love me", I am misvisualising, blindly telling I say not whom, that they love me. I think that this almost lack of visual, just about comes under the umbrella of misvisualisation. Yuyu basically blocks corporate visualisation, since it doesn't give us the person or being being sung to. It operates as an ambivalent *you*, or even *lord*. Paul sought clarification: *lord, who are you* (Ac.9:5/22:8/26:15)?[142] Any song—any prayer—addressed to *the lord*, should make it clear who that lord is. Such ambiguity is a kind of "we hate nouns" (WHN) song.

A prayer-song should make it clear to whom we are praying, so that we can visualise aright. Is it to God in general? Is it to the father, his son, or to the spirit? Or is it a clear combination of them? "You you you" doesn't help us visualise as one: I pray "You help me", to the father; you sing it to our brother; she sings it to the spirit. This leaving it to guesswork can also lead to a singer guessing one person, only to discover as the song progresses, that the prayer's directed to another person. So, I'm praying a song and picturing the father, then the next line on the overhead says "thank you for dying for me"! Oops, father, sorry, should've been singing this number to Jesus, goodbye and I'll switch to him now.

---

[142] Luke's triple record of this phrase might be based on Paul's gravitation to the term. Paul would usually refer lordship to Jesus rather than to the father (1 Cor.8:5-6), a good pattern for our days of creeping modalism.

That's embarrassing. Ultimately, a song which says "you sent your son" clarifies the addressee, so is not a yuyu song, but hopefully clarification should come early into the song, lest we have to re-visualise, redirect the flow, having been singing to the wrong person. It's good to run through a song before beginning to [prayer] sing it.

Noyu

An opposite hiccup is the "we hate pronouns" (WHP) songs. This too hinders visualisation. If I sing, "Lord Jesus (noun), Jesus (noun) loves me", I am misvisualising, blindly telling one Jesus about another Jesus. But, if avoiding the WHN of Scylla and the WHP of Charybdis, I sing "Lord *Jesus* (noun), *you* (pronoun) love me", I'm visualising, picturing Jesus in front of me. This course also takes in the possessive case. Say I meet two friends, one's John, one's Jack, who has a book I'd like to see. So, which shouldn't I say—"*John*, please pass me *Jack's* book", "*Jack*, please pass me *Jack's* book", or "*Jack*, please pass me *your* book"?

Of course, if I'm not looking at them and not really visualising them, I might absentmindedly say "*Jack*, please pass me *Jack's* book", but that wouldn't be real life. Yet some prayer-songs reflect this absentmindedness, this unreality. It's part of a bigger problem with prayer. In Leo Tolstoy's *War and Peace*, Princess Mary's prayer is answered by God who absentmindedly talks about himself in the third person: "If it be God's will to prove thee in the duties of marriage, be ready to fulfil his will" (3.3). As in the amazing story of the three big holes, well, well, well!

Why ask "*God*, we would see *God's* glory," when instead you can really picture yourself before God and ask, "*God*, we would see *your* glory"? What is so wrong with pronouns? Yet in the nineteen eighties, Chris Bowater wrote a song to the *Spirit of Praise*, asking him to let him know *Holy Ghost liberty*. Chris' wording was absentminded misvisualisation, and, even in that decade, rather old hat. No *ghost* need haunt the picture. Two decades earlier I'd been asked if Christians believed in ghosts. I said no, and was told I was wrong, because Christians believed in the Holy Ghost! Got me there, at least if we're singing from the good old KJV. Pneumatology aside, wouldn't *let me know your glorious liberty*, sound more like the spirit was *actually* in the singer's sight? In short, formally Bowater's song turns from singing *to* the spirit, to singing *about* the spirit, thus lacks prayer focus.[143] Devotion is better if our heads and imaginations sing from the same song sheet. Then nonbelievers might be more likely to suspect that we really do believe that we're singing to deity. What an amazing idea!

OK, we've looked a bit at theodirectional songs as unidirectional, and have contrasted them to polydirectional songs. Let's look a bit at what some call manward songs, and I call anthrodirectional. It may be put like this:

| Anthrodirectional[144] | Unidirectional to man (yourself, and/or others) | God is praiseworthy, isn't he? |

Hallelujah?

Hallelujah is an anthrodirectional word in itself, to be sung only to each other. You see, it's a Hebrew word, inviting people to praise Yahweh. The *hallel* bit says *praise*. The *u* bit urges *creatures* in the Thomist sense (Ps.148), generally humans, to do the praising. The *jah* bit, which some prefer as *yah*, is a shortened way of saying the creator's name, *Yahweh*,[145] which we used to spell as *Jahveh*. Put together, we can see that *hallelujah* urges fellow human beings to praise Yahweh. In fact, since his name has a heavy tie in to covenant, you may say that it's covenant praise. In short, it is a word TO praise, not a word OF praise.

If leadership says *hallelujah*, the biblical lay response is "yes, let's do so!" and then to get on and praise Yahweh, rather than endlessly repeating the injunction, *hallelujah*. Otherwise, it's like saying to a group of youngsters, "let's cross the road, let's cross the road, let's cross the road, let's cross the road, let's cross the road," without the

---

[143] I wrote to Chris about this song. Chris replied that *Chris* didn't see any grammatical problem in it, and *Chris* explained that *Holy Ghost liberty* was the kind of liberty *Chris* was asking the spirit for! Actually, to use pronouns, Chris replied that *he* didn't see any grammatical problem in it, and *he* explained that *Holy Ghost liberty* was the kind of liberty *he* was asking the ghost for.

[144] This includes the egodirectional, for example inner reflection.

[145] Compare Ps.68:4 in the KJV, to the NKJV. Some prefer *halleluyah* to *hallelujah*, for instance the ethnic Jewish CJB/TLV. NB: *Imma(n)* (with) *–u* (us) *–el* (God).

Proseuchological Problems

youngsters ever crossing it. Why did the chicken cross the road? Because it understood you. Incessant *hallelujahs* can actually prevent the exploration of praise, tripping us up if we begin to actually explore *hallel*. Let's cross the road. To those who roll out Incessant *hallelujahs*, I wish to say, "Please stop and let me obey!" Like an order to troops to get into battle, just one call to *hallelujah* should lead to a brainstorming of Yahweh's praiseworthiness, a going into praise.

Let's then ask ourselves what is actually praiseworthy (for example, his character), about how *benevolently,* and how *well,* he's worked, etc. Then meditate on such, and share with others. *Hallelujah* is positive. Brueggemann taught that praise should be specific, and that "when praise gets flattened out and generalized...decline is setting in" Though Brueggemann has been rightly knocked for knocking Ps.150—what I'd call a rousing let-it-rip call to symphonise praise—in general his observation here is valid.

However, exploration does not mean that the praiseworthiness we have already discovered is yesterday's news, *passé*, history! The wonderful remains wonderful, even if we are now at home with it. Each year, Ethnic Israel was told to recollect the wonderful way Yahweh had delivered them from Egypt (Ex.12:26-7). In salvation history terms, yesterday's news is life to us. Old and new insights should be itemised, and often pondered. Count your many blessings, and consider them one by one. Christmas, Easter, and Pentecost, should be daily events, melded together as one. I would honour Christmas in my heart, and try to keep it all the year, living in its past, present, and future, spirit.

Hallelujah, mishandled, is meaningless, disempowered. Over excitedly, Mick Ray cried "hallelujah, lord", while Robin Mark was also busy urging Yahweh to praise Yahweh, and while I was wondering why Yahweh should obediently praise himself.[146] Objectively Mick and Robin were mistaken, but so what, lots of folk sprinkle *hallelujah* over whatever is on the table, so why shouldn't our

---

[146] *I'm Forgiven* (1978): www.higherpraise.com/lyrics/love/love853113.htm; *Garments of Praise* (2007): *Hallelujah / sing hallelujah / we give all honour and praise / to your name.*

songwriters? And doing so seems to make fine sense if you don't know hallelujah's sense: ignorance can be bliss.

Some simply take the line that like Humpty Dumpty's "glory for you," *hallelujah* should mean what they say, and God be praised, "it is the blessed sun: But sun it is not, when you say it is not; and the moon changes even as your mind. What you will have it named, even that it is; and so it shall be so for Katharina" (Shakespeare 4.5). No, *hallelujah* has its biblical meaning, and so it should be for us. Clichés like *hallelujah*, should be avoided in songs, and avoiding them also helps in avoiding polydirectionalism, an even worse form of misvisualisation.

Many, feeling God, pray *hallelujah*, unaware of what it means, simply because it feels right. But heh, I'm not planning on asking Mary to pray for me a sinner, either now or at the hour of death, even if it feels right to those acclimatised to praying to her. To me, knowing right is truer than feelings. Paul grieved that his kinfolk's enthusiasm trumped understanding (Rm.10:2). He himself harnessed Jewish enthusiasm to messianic understanding. Yes, ignorance can be bliss, but let's ave appy earts hunder heducated eads.

Unique Sonship

"God did not keep back his own son, but he gave him for us..." (CEV: Rm.8:32). If I pretend to overcome the deity barrier, replacing Jesus as God's son by myself, I'm not getting the true picture. There's an added gender barrier for the fair sex, who have to do, may I say, the trans-visualisation twist. Having spoken of being *a son* among *his sons*, in *Now Are We* (1990), Kayla Parker crossed both gender and deity boundaries, and sung that she was chosen *to be his son*. Adding confusion, though specifying the father, she called him both *lord* and *prince of peace*, perhaps thinking him to be his own son, which turns out to be, herself. So a lot of misvisualising, Kayla, biblical terms thrown willy-nilly into the pot.

Let's focus here on the singular expression, *his son*. Is any Christian, *God's* son, *his* son? Firstly, let's look at how we often talk. I've watched many a *Bonanza*, and Hoss could say he was his father's son, though Adam and Little Joe were also sons of Ben Cartwright. Many of us have related thus to parents. Had Hoss said that he was *a* son of his father, he would have sounded pedantic, though being pedantic in a good cause works well. In common language, an exclusive term can sometimes allow inclusivism, even as once upon a time *fishers of men* could include women and children, and a girl could happily confess to being *a sinful man*.

However, the Cartwrights' common sonship was purely within similarity, whereas Jesus combined similarity within dissimilarity: *my father and your father* (not *our* father); *even God, who is mine and yours* (not *our* god)—Jhn.20:17. That is, he specified that we'd never be God's children, in the way he was God's child. As regards our relationship with God, though varying their approaches, the biblical writers likewise kept clear blue water between Christians and Christ. I am anointed but I am not *the* anointed; a child of God, but not *the* child of God. If truly Christians, we are children of God, say sons of God if you insist,[147] but never is any individual Christian God's son/child. We have group identity, but never individual identity in that way. *God's son* is a unique title for a unique man, and there ain't no competition.

So, we have God as our father, and he does not have any of us down as *his son*. I really do feel that talking otherwise talks down the biblical teaching of God's one-of-a-kind son.[148] Am I Jesus? No. Am I a bit like him? Yes, Christlike, but not Christ. Even "I am your child", is not as clear as, "I am *a* child of yours". God has *many* children, though, as shaper and shaker David du Plessis said, no grandchildren.[149] It can pay safety dividends to be annoyingly

---

[147] The relevant texts are: Rm.8:14,19; Gal.3:26 (the Greek *huioi*) & Php.2:15; 1 Jhn.3:1-2 (*tekna*). *Huioi* more readily translates as *sons*, or *sons & daughters*, but may be put as *children*. *Tekna* more readily translates as *children*, but may be put as *sons/daughters/sons and daughters*, as *per* context. Curiously, for *huioi* the KJV has *sons* in Rm.8:14,19 and *children* in Gal.3:26, and for *tekna* *sons* in Php.2:15 & (very badly) in 1 Jhn.3:1-2. For formal but misguided consistency of *huioi* always as *sons*, and *tekna* always as *children*, see the NKJV. Justifiably for function, the ERV/NCV/NIV/NLT/NOG/NRSV consistently translate *children*, for both. The NET is inconsistent on the wrong side. Despite any explanations, saying 'literally' *sons* (NLT) misreads the Greek: *sons and daughters*, or *children*, will do.

[148] For translation for the Gk. *monogenēs*, see the NET comment on Jhn.3:16.

[149] Ie, children born to Christian parents aren't Christians though potentially, as any human being, may become so. Christianity is a belief about Christ entered by welcome of him. I could not be a Christian before being able to believe

pedantic. Paul and John used different approaches. John's was to keep *son* (*huios*) exclusively for Jesus' relationship to God, and *children* (*tekna*) for Christians' relationship to God, so he never called Christians God's *huioi*. Christians who insist that 'son' alone highlights inheritance, arguably downgrade John for downgrading that theme. Did John miss the inheritance theme? They also overlook that even Jesus used *tekna* to speak of heirs (Lk.15:31), as did Luke (Lk.1:7), Stephen (Ac.7:5), and Paul (Rm.8:17). Paul used *son*, to be more precise, *huios*, for both the one-of-a-kind son, and for Christians in general, but his contexts made the distinction between the one-of-a-kind son, and us, very clear: Mormonism need not apply.

I2: Medium Misvisualisation

For this, I deduct 20 points. This is where a song is theodirectional, but jumps blindly between persons. At its simplest, it might say, "lord, we love the lord".

I3: Hard Misvisualisation

For this, I deduct 25 points. This is where there is a simple misvisualising between deity and humanity, a lack of direction that disempowers prayer. Like the punishment of Tantalus, these songs switch between looking up to the sweet fruit of prayer, to snatching it away as we look to the mortal flow of human fellowship, itself snatched away as we again look above. These songs are polydirectional. Henry, driving two children, drove straight into a hedge. Why? Because coming to the T-junction, the boy said 'left', the girl said 'right', and they didn't make up his mind quick enough. Understanding direction is important.

Polydirectionalism

Let's recap some terms below.

Christianity, and would arguably cease to be a *Christian* if I ceased to believe it and closed to Christ.

Proseuchological Problems

Anthrodirectional[150]	Unidirectional to man (yourself, and/or others)	God is praiseworthy, isn't **he**?
Theodirectional	Unidirectional to deity	God, **you** are praiseworthy.
Polydirectional	Part to deity, part to man	God, **you** are praiseworthy, isn't **he**?

What is prayer toggling? Song leaders sometimes toggle between a theodirectional song (for example, Jesus How Lovely You Are), then an anthrodirectional song (for example, Majesty, Worship His Majesty), then a theodirectional song (for example, Reign in Me), without any apparent awareness of changing the direction of our focus. And if the offering bag passes under the nose while we are singing—that is, *praying*—to deity, why then we'll simply interrupt *prayer*. After all, deity's not really listening, and we're not *really praying*, right? Hopefully, wrong! Strictly speaking, politeness to deity would require the worshipper to stop singing, ask him to whom they were singing, to excuse them a moment, then put something into the bag, then perhaps resume their pray-song where they left off. Didn't Jesus face a situation when finances were put above prayer?

But *prayer*-song isn't actually *prayer*—and of course we all know that, don't we? Hum. After all, after prayer-songs end, we're sometimes invited to begin to pray, as if we're to switch from mere song (therefore not prayer) to prayer. Sadly, song leaders and church leaders can be equally oblivious to the obvious fact that some songs are actually prayer—prayer without an Amen is still prayer. Some lyricists share this blindness, and by mixing two or more directions within songs, produce polydirectional songs. We should see that "when singing is spiritual, it is as important an exercise as prayer—and for the most part it is prayer, only sung rather than spoken" (Prime and Begg 209). Theodirectional songs gems; good songs add value to worship.

Of course, polydirectionalism can be creative. Many of the psalms— Hebrew songs—were in fact *polydirectional*, as antiphonal/ responsory. That is, they were sung or chanted between, or by, two

---

[150] This includes the egodirectional, for example inner reflection.

Problems and Christian Songs

groups, a kind of a dance, between leadership and people. Ps.136 is a good example. Yet biblical polydirectionalism doesn't transfer well into our culture. Using functional equivalence,[151] some translate polydirectional psalms into our culture, even changing them into unidirectional psalms. Isaac Watts perhaps started this ball rolling by enculturating *Psalms*, dressing Sinai in Christian garb.[152]

Comparing the NIV and the CEV shows some interesting ways in which functionalism makes for better English. Starting easy, compare Ps.43:5's "why, my soul, are you downcast?" (NIV), with, "why am I discouraged?" (CEV).[153] Does the CEV lose my soul, or simply get to the heart of what it means? Why, O my mind, does it matter? When we think reflectively, what is our natural style? At a more radical level, let's compare Ps.23:1-2,5-6's "Yahweh is my shepherd...he leads me...You prepare a table before me...in the house of Yahweh" (NIV), compared with "You, Yahweh, are my shepherd...you lead me...you treat me to a feast...in your house" (CEV: both retetragrammatised).

Should our songs switch between the third person (he), and second person (you)? Sure, Christians can acclimatise to the original speech style, but it's likely this'll seem silly to outsiders. True, there are some gains in reading the dialogue, the drama, as it was initially structured. However, the elegance of the CEV's innovation should serve as a lesson to lyricists. They should not throw in needless complication. New songs should usually conform from the outset to the principle of directional consistency. How about this lively little song?[154]

---

[151] Functional equivalence is an accepted method of translation that seeks to translate textual meaning above textual words.

[152] There is scope for this: *Israel's Gone Global*, ch.2

[153] The CEV's wider context may suggest that the psalmist was speaking to God. The Amplified Bible has the expression, *O my inner self*, to highlight that *soul* (*nefesh*), sometimes carried the idea of how we are deep down inside, core. On this the CEV can be handy, but can also be conceptually wrong, as in Ps.93:1, where it suggests that some have *their* different Yahweh: "Our LORD, you are king". There is only one Yahweh (Dt.6:4), wherever you go.

[154] Patricia Morgan's *Come on and Celebrate* (1984). Grimace: the king is a *thing*!

Proseuchological Problems

Inconsistent			Consistent
Anthrodirectional: I'm singing to *you*	Come on and celebrate *his* gift of love	Come on and celebrate *his* gift of love	Anthrodirectional: I'm singing to *you*
Theodirectional: I'm now singing to *deity*	We'll shout *your* praise O king	We'll shout and praise *the* king	Anthrodirectional: I'm still singing to *you*
Theodirectional: I'm still singing to *deity*	*you* give us joy *nothing* else can bring	*who* gives us joy *no one* else can bring	Anthrodirectional: I'm still singing to *you*

If this song had been written consistently anthrodirectional, would it have been sensible to change it into inconsistent style? If not, was it sensible to write it inconsistently in the first place? Take another example, *Blessed Be the Name of the Lord*. Outstandingly, it urges lament in a Christian land where lament seems scarce. It nevertheless suffers from gaffes, boasts, and undermining God's name. As polydirectional, it presumably intends we sing to others that Yahweh—or Yeshua—should be praised (though it says blessed), switching to Yahweh—*you give and take away*.[155]

Even commendable songs can be ill-conceived in polydirectionalism. If you had to close your eyes at the prayer bits, and had to open your

---

[155] I've heard someone say they felt blessed at having discovered that the words are really *you give and make a way*! The blessings of exodus? But no, the words are from Job 1:21 (see NKJV). Ancient Near East Yahwism often spoke in terms of Ultimacy. Yahweh might not have directly stepped in and blessed or spoilt whatever, but *ultimately* he had allowed it. This included *the problem of pain* (see C S Lewis), yet Job would praise him. In western terms, we might cram in (as if) *you give and take away*, and follow it, perhaps, *but my heart does choose to say, Yah prais-ed be your name / praised be your name, Yahweh*: how about *whatever comes my way*, instead?

Problems and Christian Songs

eyes at the congregational bits, you might call them blinking songs. Follow your eyes, for eyes, and eyelids, tell a story. Sometimes a very bad one, such as a solo artist singing a worship song to their audience—and their audience sure isn't with the king of kings, even if their hands are in the air. If I didn't know better (which I don't) I'd suspect that they had an oversized ego, an undersized idea of worship, strength in entertaining but not in enlightening, and good performance fees and CD sales. Worship songs should be sung with the people, not to the people.

Do we look around us? Anthrodirectionally, you can sing to yourself. "Why are you cast down, O my soul, and why are you in turmoil within me? Hope in God; for I shall again praise him, my salvation" (Ps.42:5; ESV). Quite a few of the psalms were about inner reflection, egodirectional. For visualisation, I like to look at human faces if singing anthrodirectionally, and avoid them if singing theodirectionally or egodirectionally. From what I've seen, most usually consciously pray with their eyes closed.

OK, that's fine. Each to their own. Indeed, at least in early Christian years, closed eyes even to God might be best to block out distracting noise, but once our minds get used to spiritual focus, I've found it's nice to usually pray with eyes open. But if closed eyes help for theodirectional songs, why not at least open eyes for anthrodirectional songs, even making eye contact with those to whom you sing? I love that bit in *Wall·E* when for people on the good ship Axiom, overlooking turns into looking at each other.

Looking *at* each other when we are singing *to* each other, makes sense. Sometimes a song leader encourages the congregation to do so, which for some adds the fun of novelty. Otherwise it might freak folk out, not because the logic is faulty, but because western conventionality is below the logic. We don't do because we haven't learnt. We haven't learnt because we haven't been taught.

Unlike in *Phantastes* (George MacDonald: ch.16), where the White Lady cries, "you should have sung to me," we usually say "you're not supposed to sing to me!" What's the difference between saying to you and singing to you the words, be bold, be strong? Easy, I look at you when I speak to you but not when I sing to you. Perhaps the KJV is right to call us a peculiar people (1 Pt.2:9). Does it make sense to see

Proseuchological Problems

people with their eyes shut singing *to you*, "be bold"? Bring back King Arthur's Round Table, please. Circular seating can help folk unabashedly sing to each other, though bowing to our wish for personal space. More intense face to face singing may be more appropriate at a fair distance between singer and sung to (singee), whereas talk prefers closeness.

Do you sing with your eyes open, looking at the congregation or above the congregation, depending on whether a song is to them or to deity? Or do you close your eyes to heaven, and open them to church? Either way will increase your empathy with songs, and lead to, and maintain, spiritual crescendos through visualisation. Ideally, don't look to church when you sing to deity, and don't shut your eyes when you sing to church.

Put the latter this way. Imagine I visit your local church as guest speaker—perhaps less likely if you read this book! I invite you to close your eyes (and of course to bow your heads) in prayer. A hush descends. Reverently standing at the front, I close my eyes and bow my head. "God, please bless us this day. Pastor, I noticed that your building project is getting along well. God, please meet our needs. It is good to see that your flower bed is blooming. Who looks after it? You are Jehovah Jirah. We'll sing a song I've written, after we've taken up the collection. Lord, thank you for your blood. I've some books for sale, which I've put at the back of the church. And please anoint my words. Amen."

All the time, my head is bowed, my eyes tightly shut.[156] Perhaps you opened your eyes to stare at me, ever since I started talking in prayer to *you*, and you've been wondering when on earth I'd look at you as if I were now talking *to* you, and not *to* God. Of course, we all know that eyes need closing and heads bowing when it's Godward (do we?), but when it's manward, it's certainly awkward. But please feel free to invite me soon to be a guest speaker, since my doctor assures me that I've almost gotten over my bad case of polydirectionalism, and believes there's every chance of my full recovery. I rest my case.

To really sing a song's meaning means to be in tune with the song's language. To do that we must visualise it, caress it in our mind's eye.

---

[156] I have witnessed with amazement folk close eyes for prayer, and soon, keeping their eyes shut, talk to the church. "Look at us!", I silently plead.

And then we must decide whether we agree with its message, whether to marry up with it, letting it come into our life. Have you developed the art of analysis and understanding while singing? If so, you have learnt to visualise to whom you sing. If not, you're only dreaming, at best your spiritual Reticular Activating System is beginning to awaken your spiritual brain. If a polydirectional song forces you to switch faces willy-nilly, it's a shoddy song.

I4: Hyper Misvisualisation

It can get worse. For hypermisvisualisation, I deduct 30 points, where it adds misvisualising the members of deity to a hard polydirectional song. This can be mid misvisualisation plus soft misvisualisation, for example, through the ambiguous *you*. Hypermisvisualisation songs fall short, not by denying the trinity, but by merely confusing the three persons in the mind's eye. They are neither Jesus alone does, nor Jesus alone is God, songs. Just foolishly confused. But that rubs off on us, and that's the rub.

If I sang *The lord on high, we love him true / I love you father, yes Jesus, I do*, that'd be such a song. It'd verge on the deeper problem of unitarianism, but might be no worse than not really focusing on the father, his son, and ourselves, as we sing. It does not predicate actions of the one to the other, as patripassian songs do. It does not proclaim a doctrinal error, simply a visual error, and makes an already polydirectional song worse.

Chapter 9   Miscellaneous Problems

"Speak...to one another in psalms and hymns and spiritual songs, singing...making melody in your heart to the lord, giving thanks always for all things to God the father in the name of our lord Jesus Christ, submitting to one another in the fear of God.... Christ...loved the church and gave himself for her, that he might sanctify and cleanse her with the washing of water by the word, that he might present her to himself a glorious church, not having spot or wrinkle or any such thing, but that she should be holy and without blemish" (NKJV: Eph.5:19-21,25-7).

J: Boasting

For this, I deduct 10 points.

J1: Can Do, Will Do

In 1895, aged 23, Edith Cherry, described as a "simple little cripple girl", wrote that *we go in faith our own great weakness feeling / and needing more each day your grace to know*. Two years later she had died. About 60 years later, Jim Elliot and four fellow missionaries would sing this before going as martyrs through the gates of [pearly] splendour at the hands of the Waorani Indians (Ecuador). They felt their own weakness. Proper humility is a virtue.

Boasting can flood the world with good intentions, and comes in many shapes and sizes. There is a generational boast, in which we feel proud to be in such fine company. I see a near revival in boasting, perhaps few on their knees in prayer, but many singing about their selfless praise. Or so 'tis sung.

Have you notified how certain songs exalt "our generation" to eschatological level? All other generations might have betrayed messiah, but Simeon's eyes may now close in peace, for we have come, and Jesus may return for the church triumphant—that's us. My generation is rising up to get the job done. Well, Jeremiah would have hoped for no less (Jr.28:6), though later in that story we see that Hananiah's optimism was ill judged. Perhaps a generation must mature first, before it can truly see if Yahweh has had a special message to it. I don't like to preach disillusionment, but if we build a house of cards, please God knock it down.

Problems and Christian Songs

May I not believe that I am included in "my set", and that me and my set are special? Funny, now I think about it. I can't think of any songs that say "your generation" shall be key. Me songs, egocentric songs, tend to concentrate on each singer as an outstanding individual.[157] They are often either about what I will do, or about God having acted for special me. Jesus died, but I was well worth it. Boastful songs are about how great we are, how confident, how loyal. God should take heart. Indeed, deity has my heart; it's God's (or the lord's) heart that's a little harder to pin down, according to Martin Smith's *Lord You Have My Heart* (1994)! Boots on the wrong feet can foster egotism.

A humbler, perhaps more biblical approach, is to replace terms such as *I will*, with *I wish, I would* (the subjunctive), *I desire*. Statements of fact, not of pledge: *I believe, help thou mine unbelief*![158] Let me backtrack a moment. The psalmists often boasted that they would greatly praise Yahweh. Does that make our boasting safe? I suspect that their meaning was not prediction, but intentionality, however the translations read. That is, not that it was going to happen, but that they reasonably hoped it would be so.

Whatever the case, as C S Lewis noted in *Reflections on the Psalms* (*Imprecatory Psalms*), *Psalms* contains salutatory warnings of unredeemed passions: the righteous, capable of great heights and great depths, can feel quite justified in calling down fire to revenge insults. Righteousness denounces the unrighteousness of the righteous (Lk.9:54-5). Might the psalmists' confidence in their commitment to praise, not be questionable? Paul's team member Demas, featured earlier with honour (Col.4:14/Phm.1:24), finally let down the team by misdirected *agapē* (love: 2 Tm.4:10). I neither preclude bitterness, nor boastfulness, from the psalms: they are an uncertain pattern for us of the new creation. Sometimes we should know better.

Anyway, I'm safe. Frankly, *I* wouldn't waste time boasting about other people anyway, for unlike me they might well abandon the way. Ring

---

[157] http://lestyouforget.wordpress.com/2008/04/11/bad-worship, covers this well and suggests that non-Christians might not be impressed by our god.

[158] Mk.9:24 has a plea to overcome unbelief (NIV), to have more faith (CEV): strength with weakness.

Miscellaneous Problems

any bells? When Jesus spoke about being deserted, Peter protested: "not by me you won't!" (Mk.14:29). Who was right? After a good long talk with Peter, Paul later wrote that "...if you think you are standing firm, be careful that you don't fall" (NIV: 1 Cor.10:12). Peter's reinstatement shows this well: "we should soundly distrust self-serving pledges of loyalty today that [portray] self-reliance rather than a humble awareness of one's own limitations in acting on one's best intentions" (Köstenberger 598).

What then of Matt and Beth Redman's *Blessed Be Your Name* (2002)? It clearly promises deity that singers he blesses will in turn pay him back in praise, even under severe trial.[159] However, in my world, many blessing escape my notice, and many painful lessons can be blessings in disguise. If any Christian *turns back* (transforms?) every single blessing in praise, or even every blessing they recognise as blessing, they would be a most incredible exception to the rule, and, probably be about the least likely to boast in advance.

The spiritually mature know that they ought to thank deity for as many of his blessings that they manage to identify, even if through gritted teeth.[160] And speaking of teeth, Page recounted Sunday School days in which the children sang their commitment to being eaten by large wild animals—Daniel in the Lions' Den? One might ask what

---

[159] This song also fails to turn back into the first person the third person line blessed be the name of *the* Lord, *even* when immediately followed by *blessed be your name*! Besides removing God's name from the plot—probably they meant the LORD, Yahweh, to whom the biblical words referred, rather than Jesus the lord—they should have changed *the name*, to *your name*, since the song is *to deity*, and not to one deity about another deity. We cannot *bless* God, and incidentally *the name of*, was an ancient way of indicating the person. Fairly current English would be *praised be you* (better, *praise to you*) instead of *blessed be your name*. Imagine someone saying to their spouse "darling your name is wonderful" instead of "darling, you're wonderful": counselling should follow. Finally, it can sound as if we're tempting God to bless us by pandering to his supposed vanity: "you want flattery? I'll give you plenty if you bless me." In reality, God's commands to praise him are for our blessing, since praising the most praiseworthy is good focus for our souls (Php.4:8). Yet the Redmans got a song that speaks of Christians suffering onto the market: a commendable achievement in spite of the problems noted above.

[160] God seeks an attitude of grateful awareness, not verbal response each time.

all the other Jews had done wrong *not* to be in the same den, and whether under pressure we'd be with the majority people of God, or with the minority Daniel. Page quipped, "If you ask someone, 'Would you mind being eaten alive by a large hairy animal as part of your faith?' I wonder how they'd reply" (Page 26). Many Christians were ripped to shreds in Rome's arenas, and the attitude in which some died impressed their pagan compatriots.

But let those not vow to walk in the dark, who have not seen the nightfall. How would we fare? We're taught to thoughtlessly pledge deity, in song, what we would not pledge without the group seduction of a silly song. John lost his head, because Antipas lost his because the dancing Salome sizzled (Mt.14:6-7/Mk.6:22-3). Heads still tumble through sizzling songs.

Heedless if not headless, I'm singing, what a lucky god has me, I'm faithful in all my ways. We frequently assure God that we'll give him *all* the praise and *all* the glory. Absolutely! Yet this imaginary god is not God, and our words' cash value is far far less than their face value. We can't give deity all that there is. We don't have it all (Ps.50:12), and even if I had it all, I doubt I'd give it all. Are we not really like a little boy commending Einstein for being able to work out 2 + 2? Are we saying that God is no more praiseworthy than our puny minds perceive? We shouldn't overplay (nor underplay) our own penneth of praise. Does the whole universe, let alone our tiny little planet and our little self, know how praiseworthy he is?

Also, only pride or fantasy believes that if we had all to give, we would give all. Jesus taught that, unredeemed, the greater the earthly riches, the greater the earthly enslavement.[161] Are we so very proud, and deity so very small, that we imagine that he has needs *we* can fulfil? It is he who bestows blessing, and we who should humbly receive. I hear prayers conclude that they ask what they ask for Jesus' sake. C'mon, Jesus gave himself for *our* sakes, and has no need of us. We ask for our sakes (in Jesus' name), and rightly so. For our sakes, God would

---

[161] Even C19 Christina Rossetti's *Bleak Midwinter*, with its humble *if I were a shepherd I would give a lamb*, assumes we would have been on the side of the angels. How many Jewish shepherds would have sided with Herod?

rather us see that what we have to offer him, including our praise, is at best a widow's mite.

Rash assertions seldom enrich. Of course, some folk are careful to promise deity everything, not because they boast or bargain, but because they fear that otherwise he'll be angry. When David Wilkerson wrote, *I'm Not Mad At God*, he was recovering from years of misplaced fearful obedience. The fear of Yahweh can still be the beginning of wisdom, but some unwisely read too much into bad death in *Acts*, such as Agrippa 1's (12:23). They picture themselves as cringing servants of an intolerant sovereign. Such misinformation is sadly in the Christian domain, underplaying God's love. Pride and fear, *hubris* and *phobos*, are follies. Having shaken my head over one Redman number, I give a nod of commendation to his *Heart of Worship* (1999). Yes, I know it claims that, whatever *it* is, *it's* all about *Jesus*, not God, and that we can bless him, but I for one maintain that its challenge to self-aggrandisement is a very real good.

Temptation invites our pride to boast. Even if we do not run into temptation's arms as a lover, we sometimes crawl away hoping it will overtake us. We love to speak about our praise, and some Christian songs can be gratefully sung by Narcissus himself. One song sings that deity is worthy of *our* praise.[162] Wow, he made the grade. Are we praising our praise? Should we not first ask whether our praise is worthy of deity?

Paul encouraged us to use sober judgement about our missional roles (Rm.12:3), not to let egotism get the upper hand. We should be serious about what we should, and should not, do, and at what level. Sorry folks, not everyone's an apostle! But then again, Paul implied that underrating our missional call is wrong in the opposite direction. Please don't get me wrong. We are not spiritual worms, whatever our

---

[162] It is better, with Nathan Fellingham, to sing that he *is worthy of praise*. Sadly, Fellingham's song descends into patripassianism, misidentifying Jesus with the lord God, almighty (Rv.4:8). Ironically, after misidentifying the name, it invites us to lift up the wrong name. Rv.5 puts Jesus, as Apocalyptic Lamb, into the picture. He is then proclaimed worthy to open a new history, and the summary (13) pictures him at joint level *with* the lord, God Almighty, but he is not the same person.

Problems and Christian Songs

diet. We *are* praiseworthy, and our humble praise of deity does please him. In tandem with the spirit, we can do great good in God's will, as we yield to him.

What I'm saying is that even our humble yielding to God is imperfect, and that we should be daily aware of this. And also, thankfully, that deity can do a lot from even our imperfect surrender—our two fishes can feed a multitude. To be content that though he does not value us (all would be unequal), he loves us equally—so far as we let him. But if you feel you really must tell him he makes the grade in your books—as the disreputable beggar (or frog) tells the princess she's worthy of him—he won't take the huff. He is humility itself.

Why should I boast of me instead of deity? Theocentric boasting, perhaps *bragging* (CEB), is good for us (1 Cor.1:31). So far as we know, Paul only cited Jr.9:24 twice—to the same church (2 Cor.10:17). Did that church need a double dose of medicine seldom needed? Do we? "The current trend in praise, which begins with our thoughts and feelings, needs to be challenged for the good of the congregation and for the sake of God's glory" (Prime and Begg 207). Let's highlight songs that hit us with God's glory. The more we sing of ourselves, the more likely to highlight songs that have either a direct or indirect egocentric boast. "Predominance of the first person singular pronoun [(I)] in so so much recent writing, has concerned many people" (Reform).

Boasting about God should be biblically sensible. The Jews who boasted that he *could* save them, did not boast that he *would* save them (Dan.3:17-8). We may as well thank God that we live in cloud cuckoo land, as thank him that all is sweetness and light. James encouraged us to rejoice when troubles trouble us (Jas.1:2). Indeed, he used the word often translated as *temptation*—temptations test us. As Australia's Leo Harris used to say, we only have what we can keep under pressure. Difficulties and opposition can both be used positively and can show us our state of play. They can be a useful health check.

Some songs, like John Gibson's (1987) *Jesus, We Celebrate Your Victory*,[163] feed a dualism between real and idyllic life: "Pentecostal

---

[163] A good song, but to say that, *in his presence our problems disappear*, is debateable: at the Burning Bush Moses' problems became international.

theology and worship does not easily respond to the times of doubt and the seeming absence of God" (Warrington 196). This weakness isn't just in Pentecostalism. Warrington's point was about automatic removal of problems. Those who stand up, stand up, for Jesus, might be crucified. And even the bravest can deny him thrice rather than face death. Confronting the world is a very significant problem, and increasingly threatens careers in the public sector which seeks either avid agreement (homogeneity), or shameful silence.

Boasting in God should be realistic. On God's side, some knew victory, some knew defeat (Heb.11). Praising him, thanking him, trusting him, should be based on a good dollop of biblical realism, not on treating him as a genie at our disposal. How absolute is our self-assurance and self-adulation?

J2: Just One Cornetto?

Another absolute claim is one of absolute limitation—*only*, rather than *all*.[164] We seem to sing about how easily we are satisfied, or how fully focused we are. How virtuous. C S Lewis' *Screwtape Letters* (ch.17), shows how smug and vexatious our fussiness can be (gluttony of limitation). Such songs, of course, may simply be grammatical blunders, a dichotomy between feeling and words, what some call poetic licence, rather than real reflections of thinking. But what we think goes into words, and words go into what we think. Words are worth thinking about, and getting right.

In 1984, Arthur Tannous *just* wanted *to praise you*—whoever *you* is, or was.[165] I *just* want this, I *just* want to do that, I *just* want to see the other, I *just* want everything. Many actually pray like this: "we *just* thank you for this, and *just* thank you for that, and *just*...as well"! Meaningless padding, perhaps as they were taught to pray. But imagine saying the same to a mortal person—I just A, I just B, I just

---

[164] On the social level, some, by asking others for just so and so, can be boastful. We can feel so virtuous, that *all* we ask for is so, so little, ignoring that the particularity of what we ask for can seriously inconvenience others to the point of tyranny. It can be a form of gluttony, not of excess but of exactness (Lewis 1975:87).

[165] *I just want to praise you / Lift my hands and say I love you / You are everything to me / (And) I exalt your holy name on high.*

Problems and Christian Songs

C.... *Just* really means A *or* B *or* C, not the whole job lot. If your shopping list says ice-cream, and spuds, and washing powder, you don't tell the shopping assistant that you *just* want ice-cream, and *just* want spuds, and *just* want washing powder, though you might say you *just* want apples, potatoes, and washing powder. But then that would be speaking in real world terms, where we're more likely to engage brain before opening mouth, and where we visualise—we see an actual shopping assistant, so talk sense.

When I pray, have I really tuned in to deity as if he were if anything *more* real than a mere mortal, or have I a fuzzy vision hovering above my head? It's easy to try to impress him, myself, and others listening in, by the idea that I *only* desire him. As a Christian I married. Wasn't deity all I needed? Biblically, I should desire much more than deity. Deity is not everything—that's Hinduism—but he created everything. God is creator, and creatures should desire creation, as well as its creator. God himself said that he himself was not all that Adam the man needed, hence Eve. Nor should I implicitly seek praise by the moderation of my requests—will just one Cornetto do me? No, it won't, so why say it will? Let's avoid even the appearance of boastfulness, except about God, of whom we should boast.

K: Decontextualising

For this, I deduct 10 points. Decontextualising can be lifting scripture from its context (for example, its grammatical, cultural, and theological, contexts). Craig Terndrup's *Blow the Trumpet* (1983) was very upbeat.[166] In one church I visited, young adults locked arms in circles, and danced in the aisles. Fair dinkum. The unreflective rejoiced in victory; the reflective and the shy hesitated. Church victory, or repentance? Joel and Jeremiah spoke of Yahweh's people being attacked, because of their sin, by Yahweh's foreign army, Babylon (Jl.2:1-12; Jr.6:1ff.). The

---

[166] *They rush on the city / they run on the wall / Great is the army that carries out his word / The lord utters his voice before his army / Blow the trumpet in Zion, Zion / Sound the alarm on my holy mountain.* Incidentally the Lord is never mentioned in *Joel*, though the LORD is. We might also call the song bivocal: we sing as reporter and as Yahweh.

Miscellaneous Problems

unreflective, triumphalism's fans, felt that the church was Zion and that it was Yahweh's army trampling the Enemy—what a blast!

Whether *Blow* died off because folk eventually realised it was about Israel's defeat, not her triumph, simply because it aged (and old ain't cool), or the church wave of triumphalism wavered, is moot. Potentially, it was a useful song, if humbly sung in the spirit of repentance (Jl.1:13), with a more mournful tune as befits psalmic laments. As it stood, its meaning was immediately inaccessible, and the melody misrepresented the lyrics. Joel's context, along with a background study of Israel's silver trumpets, clearly shows the real theme. When in Leeds, my once upon a time local song leader, told me that another church member had at seminary level argued against his class that Israel *had* been the army—so putting me in my place: the minority must be right. When I later asked that other church member to explain how he had arrived at that idea, he seemed to have forgotten. He might remember, but I remain sceptical.

Another decontextualisation is being tardisial, anachronistic. Christmas songs in particular like to time warp our imagination, whisking us back to the C1 to witness the pivotal birth. We might even be asked to sing to ancient Bethlehem, and pray to the baby stage of one would mature into glorification. Why call a butterfly a caterpillar? Why pray to what doesn't exist? There is no longer a baby Jesus. And wasn't prayer to inanimate objects something that Isaiah rubbished? Decontextualising songs can remove us from Scripture.

There's a more serious kind of decontextualisation. I once read a Cliff Richard book entitled, *New Singer, New Song*. At the time I suspect it truly spoke of one who had come to sing the Christian song and walk the Christian walk. We Christians should be new singers, with new songs, within the new creation. How many of us sing the songs but don't walk the walk? After Sunday worship hour, do we exit from Christian context—decontextualisation of lifestyle? It is true that the primary meaning of holiness is dedication to God (conversion). It is also true that its secondary meaning applies to how we live a godly lifestyle, obedient to God, maturing through discipleship.

Arguably not enough songs draw attention to ethical 24/7 life. Pliny noted how Christians had the early morning habit of singing of their pledges to the Christian walk. He even tortured some to check if they were serious for God—UK 'equality' laws do likewise. So, there are different types of decontextualisation. It is best to decontextualise neither song nor singer from Scripture. I can downgrade for the one; God downgrades for the other.

L: Hermit's Harakiri

For this, I deduct 15 points. This anthropology basically pretends that deity alone is all we desire, so that without him we might as well be dead. The first part is summed up in the word, hermitism. Forget creation, humanity, etc. God—or Jesus if we forget the trinity—is all we need.[167] A reasonable example of this unreasonable idea is Darlene Zschech's *Jesus, You're All I Need* (1998).[168] This little number blithely ignores the father, spirit,[169] and creation, while Darlene tells Jesus that he's all she needs and only he gets her life. Strange to hear that she married—wasn't Jesus *all* she needed?—and possibly now 'lives,' in some sense, for her children as well. Actually, Jesus needs her not, and she's always needed more than him.

Genesis pictures God as saying he wasn't all that Adam the man, needed. Hence *Ish* has *Ishah*, and Eve has Adam. Humanity was created as a social creature.[170] God always seeks to share us, never to hog us. He created us shareable. On what basis do we now dismiss fellow humanity, especially the redeemed who are eternally our brothers and sisters, and to whom we are to do good (Gal.6:10)? What now of food for our body, air for our lungs, gravity for our feet, church for our maturation? Jesus is all I need? In fact, forget him, Darlene, the spirit is all *I* need! Huh? But why compete for folly?

---

[167] www.joshhunt.com/mail48.htm, is sensible.

[168] *Jesus, you're all I need / Now I give my life to you alone / Lord, you gave yourself / So I could live / Oh, you purchased my salvation / And wiped away my tears / Now I drink your living water / And I'll never thirst again / For you alone are holy / I'll worship at your throne / And you will reign forever / Holy is the lord.* The last phrase either means that the *lord* is other than Jesus to whom she is singing, or should be, *Holy are you, lord*.

[169] Does *Drink your living water*, hint at the spirit as being symbolised by water?

[170] Incidentally the emphasis (unique to man) was not on society for procreation but for companionship. Yahweh, in whose image we are, is the eternal society.

Miscellaneous Problems

Against our fantasy that we live for deity alone, is the reality that deity does not need us. From the outflow of his utter completeness, the source of creativeness created a material universe, his work of art painted in atoms, bundles of energy created by the uncreated source. Perhaps it is to be our playground, once we're released from mortality. Be that as it may, so far as we know, only our planet has been given any creatures who have sufficient personality level (*Imago Dei* level) to fellowship with him: each of us is unique, and together we are united as human family.

But perhaps beyond Earth, millions of planets have such species, with Earth being the only sheep lost in rebellion, as *Out of the Silent Planet* imagined. Will we sheep join a larger flock? What we do know is that *Genesis* pictured a single human as needing companionship other than God. Come in Eve. OK, Christians have entered a new phase, what C S Lewis said might be called the next step in evolution, a spiritual birth into a kingdom unknown to Adam, and a new relationship, pictured as God's spirit indwelling us (Steve Hakes' *Israel's Gone Global*, 2013:chs.4-5).

Paul is sometimes misread as a lone bachelor, best placed for spiritual life! He's sadly misread. My take is that had his mission been much less risky, he would have loved to have been married, as Peter was. He certainly enjoyed working with women, whether they were apostles, teachers, whatever, and encouraged them to be active in church. He was a team leader and a key player. The corporate relationship of Christians together, is a biblical picture. God may be all I need to exist as a spirit, but he's never intended to be all I need to enjoy as a spirit.

Who dares dismiss their fellow humanity, and say that deity is all we need? It sounds so spiritual, so sapient, so silly, so unspiritual. John's *Revelation* pictures redeemed humanity as still having a corporate voice. True, postmortal relationships will be different. As John Bunyan understood, all marriages will be off[171] (sorry Mr. Mormon), and family trees won't be seen for the true wood. Though some gravestones often preach heresy, thinking that blessed unions here and now, will be picked up after death, simply isn't biblical. Couples

---

[171] Great Heart's dialogue with Valiant for Truth (*The Pilgrim's Progress*, Pt. 2).

here won't reunite the other side. Death ends the blest ties that bind (Rm.7:2). The woman who had had seven husbands does not return to any or all (Mk.12:23).

As C S Lewis said, the wonder of chocolates will give way to the wonders of deepest love. Fellowship with each other will far exceed the deepest of loving bonds possible here, as universal joy replaces parochial touch. Deity will infuse all fellowship, all beauty. We definitely won't have a God-only mentality. For fullness of immortal life, we will need others, since that's how God's made us, a symphony, not mere soloists. God shares.

Jesus maintained his physicality, and we will have physicality. In the life to come, our bodies will be invulnerable, useful for containment, for differentiation from others, and for sensory contact with others. Others then; others now. Human fellowship was designed by God. Church fellowship is needed for present spiritual wellbeing, even as food is for our physical wellbeing. Those cut off from church can survive on starvation rations, but at best it's on the them-and-God life of hermitude. And alas, some wither in spiritual winter.

However, suitable qualifications to "all I need" expressions, can justify them. All I need to satisfy my hunger, is food; all I need to wash my hands, is water; all I need to do for eternal life now, is to accept God's offer of it. But many "all I need" claims are erroneous, because they're incomplete statements. Do "all I need" songs answer the question, "all I need for what?" Like "he is worthy", for what?

Songs that say that Jesus *only* lives to do a job, miss the point as much as singing that we live *only* for some purpose. "Jesus lives to save", is foolish, as is, "I live to serve." Of course, Jesus' living does save and unite, and my mortal life serves. But that's not a general reason why God chooses us to live, nor why we choose to live—I don't think that we need a general reason to justify living mortal life. More anon. Incidentally, the directional word *unto* is handy: we live *unto* Jesus, but not *for* him—he doesn't need us in any absolute, ontological, sense. Individualism is downplayed by Hinduism, not Christianity.

True, in war many individuals' deaths for the many, can be needed by the many, but this isn't a pattern of persons being lava lamp blobs, which by losing individuality enrich the underlying blob. Creator and creation eternally remain distinct. That is the creator's will.

Miscellaneous Problems

Individual personalities, yielded, desirous, are eternally incorporated into the One's life. That is the creator's grace. In *Antz* (1998), Z4195's psychiatrist taught that realising the insignificance of individualism meant finding meaning in the collective, a real breakthrough.

French existentialist Albert Camus, argued that the Greek myth of Sisyphus showed what life was about: absurd Sisyphus lived fully; hated death totally; existed meaninglessly. We go on without hope. Protesting hopelessness was as good as life gets. Life is meaningless, but even this doesn't warrant suicide. He taught that we should live in the enjoyment of the ridiculous, rejecting the idea *God*, without rejecting life (suicide). Is solitaire the only game in town? I weep for Camus and for Sisyphus, precisely because they missed God's light, and so never lived life to the full (Jhn.10:10).

What do Christian lyricists say, when asked why we should live? Some reply that we should live in order to work for and/or worship deity. So *apart* from such a reason, does suicide, harakiri, seem logical, since *only* the spiritual reason warrants human life? It is possible that some lyricists have been tempted to suicide (I know that feeling), and have smuggled a spiritual reason to live into their lyrics. In the black hole, the abnormal, only one ray of light might seem to offer hope. *The Dawn Treader*, suffocating in nightmare, followed the albatross into light.

But the majority, who live in the normal, even in the humdrum of life, do not need a reason to live—they simply lack a sufficient reason to die. Here, is the presumption of good philosophy *what justifies dying, not what justifies living*? Here, *live* and *die* relates simply to mortal life. On the secular scene, Liz Anderson's (1967) *Excuse Me for Living*, was a boyfriend thing: "excuse me for living my whole life for you".[172] A depraved girl/guy romance. Some Christians make it a deity thing. We ought to never live *for* God, but ought to obediently live *unto* him. Direction, not purpose.

---

[172] Many secular songs fail miserably and lead to misery if swallowed, in proclaiming meaning as existing only in another human being: the romance of the Void, Nightmare Island.

Problems and Christian Songs

Did Wayne and Cathy Perrin live in order to worship deity,[173] Ronnie Wilson to see God's kingdom come,[174] and Reuben Morgan for the lord alone?[175] Incidentally did he mean obeying or having the *lord* (I presume Jesus)? Had the Perrins a better reason to live, and did they really need to justify the fact? Have non-Christians insufficient reason to live, since they don't have Christ? Why should we boast of what God doesn't want? I don't want to be an eternal hermit, simply myself and God. God's created far more to life—why knock it? Must we buy into existentialism, to the extent that mortality is merely meaningless mockery, and outside Christ the only reason to live being defiance against absurdity? No.

Life remains a wonderful thing in the natural world. Life without God is meaningless, true, no matter how purposeful, but it can still be enjoyable. And for Christians it is still a wonderful universe. I for one don't need a reason to keep on living. Being alive I simply see no overwhelming reason to end my mortality. God is not the one being that keeps my soul content, even though he is the ground of my being. The abnormal is different.

Imprisoned, wracked perhaps by pain, Paul was given the option to be with the lord though death, which would be better. He said his reason to postpone, rather than welcome death, was in fact to mature God's people, who still needed him. An altruist, not a mercenary, he had reached that abnormal point where things are so wretched, that it seems as if the only thing that keeps us going is.... The point where, if we can't have that missing factor, we at least wish to seek death. But normally, we sing within the normal, not the abnormal. If we sing that God is the only reason that justifies mortal life, will not unbelievers say that we have lost connectivity with the joy of life? In the normal, to sing the abnormal is abnormal, not spiritual.

---

[173] *When I Look Into Your Holiness* (1980) reaches into the awesome. *Awesome* is an adjective I seldom use of songs, so feel my deep grief as I lament its alien idea that suicide has lost the vote to its rival, worship—there should be no vote, no either/or.

[174] *The Time We Have Is Precious* (1981)

[175] For example, *I Give You My Heart* (1995).

Miscellaneous Problems

Summary

Some issues for me probably aren't issues for you. OK that's fine. I respect your freedom to be wrong; I respect your freedom to be right. I mistrust my judgements. If they're correct, I'd hope you'll accept them. If they're wrong, I'd hope you'd correct me. If you write songs, well it's at least good for shepherds to know what some sheep are bleating. If you have affirmed at least a couple of these issues, it helps validate entitling this Part, *Problems*.

Ironically, I often feel a problem part of any church, because I really do think that a least some of my bleats are of genuine problems infecting God's flock. The state of play is such that issues are largely unseen, illusive, probably because we have given too much glory to Christian lyrics. In short, we have been seduced by the seductive power of song, and the assumption that what comes from the front of a church must be good to back. Yet as Anthony Flew put it, "a person can be persuaded by an abominable argument and remain unconvinced by one that ought to be accepted" (Flew 41).

It's easy to be persuaded by a handsome/pretty face, and/or by the majority flow. Sherlock Holmes noted that Sunday School mannered Bert Stevens had been a mass murderer (*The Norwood Builder*), and that a charming woman had poisoned three children for their insurance money, and that a brutal looking man was an outstanding London philanthropist (*The Sign of Four*, ch.2). If charm is deceptive, let us judge by reason. I'd encourage dissatisfaction in the hope that it will lead to better songs from better song writers, especially when it comes to handling biblical teaching about God and our fellowship with him.

Part 4   Particulars and Christian Songs
Chapter 10   Selected Song Books

I once analysed three songbooks, 40 songs from each, every 22nd, 5th, or 9th, respectively, to reach that target. I chose intentionally dated songbooks—dead toes don't kick back. Some definitions had to be judgement calls. For instance, one person's *garment* is another person's archaism. One may be puzzled by *the fairest of ten thousand*; another will assume it means Jesus, in line with traditional Christian exposition of *Songs/Canticles*. Is *the lily of the valley* (also from *Songs*) too girl/guy romantic? He says yes, she says no, I say, I don't know.

There are subjective issues—a carnivore's meat is a vegetarian's poison. I sought to judge gently, by assuming that singers would know at least a bit of Scripture and evangelical church tradition. But it would be interesting to quiz new converts from non-theist backgrounds, having them record they're initial attempts to interpret alien songs. Or maybe just get the marketing research team into play. But then, whenever we join new things, we usually assume there'll be learning curves. That's life. So, I've made some allowances.

My *Elim Choruses* (1966) analysis covered under 5% of the songs from the Elim Choruses: Books 1-18. This book was compiled by William George Hathaway, a main player in the early days of Elim UK. It began with one book, then expanded over many years, before stopping when 18 books were published under the one roof. A lot of its songs probably originated in Elim circles. Hathaway's perspective would have shaped his chorus books, which were widely used in Pentecostal and non-Pentecostal circles, even in some officially anti-Pentecostal networks, showing his broad appeal.

It has been a global resource of great blessing, and one I have happily sung from, initially no doubt happier to sing from the same hymn sheet, than to analyse it. An iced cake with a midge or two can be better than a midge free plain cake, but a midge free iced cake is best. So a better job could have been done, and a better blessing obtained. Many of its songs are little more than ditties, yet even a ditty can be a small yet powerful applet for life and for good. And so it was, for which many of us give thanks.

Selected Song Books

My analysis showed that, compared to *Songs of Praise*, Elim's compilation had slightly more archaism, but slightly less misvisualisation. Perhaps the older generation, or at least the older pentecostal one, was more prone to the outgoing style, yet more theologically alert. Very few other issues were in this selection.

My *Songs of Fellowship* analysis covered 20% of the songs from Section 1, Book 3 (1985). The publishers, Kingsway, of course had made their own selection from songs on the market, a selection which would have reflected their judgements. Perhaps a number of problems I've elsewhere flagged up, were simply not in fashion at the time. After all, fashions can rise and fall, even as there can be bulls (confidence) or bears (nervousness) in stock markets. An intensely rational Christianity can be superseded by an intensely experiential Christianity. A militant Christianity can supersede a defensive Christianity. Going to sleep with Athanasius doesn't preclude waking up with Arius...and a subsequent morning with Athanasius *contra mundum*, till Sabellius takes our fancy. Unbaptised infants, damned by Augustine, are blessed by Leibnitz. Lewis boarded a bus with Hegel, and left with God.

Fashions are reversible. Some are biblical, at least in part. Chronological snobbery assumes that whatever happens to be in fashion is right, and conversely that whatever is out of fashion is wrong. No song issues should be accepted simply because they are in, or rejected simply because they are out. But perhaps Kingsway were wise to those absent problems, excluding them as unwelcome guests?

My analysis showed that almost half of these songs jumped between audiences as if mentally asleep, oblivious to the difference: misvisualisation. These errors include toggling between deity and humanity, as well as some toggling between different persons of trinity or at least being ambiguous about the difference. The next biggest issue was over archaisms, with about a quarter of these songs failing this test.

My *Carol Praise* (1987) analysis covered about 11% of its songs. This was a compilation by Michael Perry and David Peacock. Where I marked down for decontextualising, it was solely or usually because of poetically picturing ourselves back at the birth, a common complaint of annualism, the church calendar. Overall, I tried to use the same analytical rules for these songs, but I added an extra column to indicate some extra issues.

This looked at Christmas gaffes, whether historical or theological. I marked down for anything denying that Joseph and Mary were married before she conceived; mention of an inn/manger/stable as birthplace; shepherds and magi meeting together; magi as kings, and/or assumed to be three; praying to a baby or to a donkey, etc; docetism—an unrealistic baby (eg the cryless Mothers Union type), a cuckoo in the manger, so to speak. I overlooked such as wintry imagery, whether cattle were present, and whether Mary rode a rent-a-donkey.

For decontextualisation, *Carol Praise*, at almost 60%, was extremely high, mainly due to tardisizing singers into the C1. Misvisualisation was as big a problem as in *Songs of Praise*. Over a quarter of these songs show Christmassy errors, often based on traditional assumptions. We should challenge these errors, especially where they misrepresent biblical teaching on marriage and on God's son. It showed far less archaism that the other two works, contained many then recent songs, and showed updating of language.

Summary

As it stands, every Christian who hasn't written a song, might agree with every song suggestion I have made. I'd be amazed if they did! In life, perceptions vary, and there is latitude in theology. My best hope is that some will with some things agree enough to stir things up to the good of all. Me in my small corner, and they in theirs, together reshaping song writing for the common good.

But if this alone is the change, there would still remain the enslaving shackles of copyright law, and therefore self-censorship—the fear of improving. Individuals might sing their own words, even in church, rather than affirm, and internally lodge, what they disagree with—that's often my coping mechanism. However, singing from differing hymn sheets isn't ideal, but then what is?

Changing the hymn sheet isn't easy. Our system even has feedback checks built in to ensure conformity. Conformity is fine if the songs are perfect, but what if they're not? Are we who ought to strive for impeccable holiness, to settle down to peccable songs? Songs are artistic property. Fine, though perhaps, as in Jerusalem, we should hold all properties for the common good. Perfecting the art, being at home in the property, isn't always easy.

Each church or Christian wishing to amend the words, even by a jot or tittle (Wycliffe: Mt.5:18), seemingly must ask permission. In practice, how many churches are going to bother, even to improve the lyrical teaching their folk are getting? This is the curse of copyright.

Some Christians simply curse copyright, assuming that if the songs, as all good gifts (even if imperfect!), come from the father of lights—rather than from the father of lies—then the writers should not be paid any more than were the prophets of old for prophesying. I wonder if they deny their *own* pay-packets. I don't buy their argument, nor would I sell it to you. I guess that some who argue it simply don't wish to buy the right to use the songs. The fact is that a professional writer of Christian songs might have their pay-packet limited to the songs they sell, which can include CDs and royalties. This is the blessing of copyright.

Honest workers deserve their pay (Lk.10:7), and we should not be pirates, ripping off revenues to the worthy. In short, the claim that the songs are all from God, therefore public domain, can be a disingenuous guise for theft from the needy. OK, God makes it grow, but humans provide skilled labour (1 Cor.3:8). I affirm copyright and royalties. I disaffirm the idea that we must simple endure what is on the plate, rather than talking with the chefs. I seek perestroika and glasnost, not deregulation. Here is my proposal for good change.

Firstly, that we reject the silly notion that writers write as divine scribes, what some call *mechanical inspiration,* or in occult circles, *automatic writing.* As regards the Bible, we may truly hold that its original text is canonical, and that additions have been at most subcanonical, inspired by church but not by God.[176] Our songs are not canonical. To say otherwise is to degrade the idea of canonicity and

---

[176] Craig Blomberg's *Can We Still Believe the Bible* (2014) is an A+ investigation that concludes that the Bible's manuscript record is amazingly accurate, that God, not man, decided what writings to include, that every version has every basic that God inspired, that, sensibly understanding the Bible's genres, we can accept the Tanak & New Testament as God breathed & inerrant, and that miracles (supernature stepping in) did & do happen.

Particulars and Christian Songs

to foster the degradation of ethics. Even where Christian prophets operate,[177] their prophecies are not canonical. I say again, songs are not Scripture, no matter how *in the spirit* the writer was. Like any student, they should be prepared to defend each choice of word and nuance. Global change—for fallible songs.[178]

Secondly, that every song be placed on a global not-for-profit database, with administration paid for from royalties, and given sole right to authorise the use of its material. This would *per force* have to be an open host, uncritical to all reasonably claiming a Christian base for their songs. There could be free initial hosting, afterwards an annual fee. Uncopyrighted material could be freely hosted. For copyrighted material, remuneration could be made annually through the global administration site, or through regional administration, divided pro-rata according to licensee feedback of songs that the licensees around the world have used within the calendar year. A fair price; a fair service; global for convenience and uniformity.

Thirdly, all songs should be open to global amendments. For all its potential to encourage professional songs to bless the church, the copyright system as stands is a mess stacked against the church, and too close to Pilate's *ho gegrapha gegrapha* for comfort (Jhn.19:22). Christ's body gets a raw deal. Songwriters' jobs should not end with producing the songs. Ongoing accountability should require open commitment to global improvement. Enhancements and corrections should be doable at a global, public, level. Each song should be accessible by each singer and have a section for suggestions along with reasoning: a what should be changed, and a why it should be changed. Suggestions would be permanent, not repeatable, and start with a tentative status, permitting licensed users full immediate use

---

[177] Some think prophecy is merely preaching, as if Agabus merely preached that that great famine would happen (Ac. 11:28), as if Jesus was asked to preach who had hit him (Mt. 26:68). Yahwistic prophets could & can preach (proclaim/forthtell) God's message. Plus, they could & can prophesy (predict/foretell). Rebel prophets were failed for their preaching, not for their prophesying (Dt.13:2).

[178] I would assume that music variations would be disallowed, that music royalties would be sorted as a percentage of gross royalties *per* song, and that some form of picnmix could operate between lyrics & music.

without affecting royalties or infringing copyright. Suggestions should be instantly passed to the songwriter, who would have perhaps 6 months in which to respond.

Songwriters would be obliged to examine all suggestions made, and, giving their reasoning for their decisions, adopt them, permit them, or reject them. If no response is given, the suggestion, as if tacitly approved, would automatically gain the stability of official Variant status, giving global licensees a little more confidence to use the alternative version. Both default, tentative, and variant, versions, would be visible side by side. Rejected suggestions would remain off page but accessible. Songwriters could authorise representation to step in should illness or death prevent them from responding directly. Permission should be granted when suggestions improve, equal, or at least do not substantially spoil, the lyricists' aims. Since an open forum, the sanity of the songwriters could be publicly assessed by how they respond to suggestions, and their popularity perhaps upgraded or downgraded accordingly. Such openness might also profit their learning curves. Finally, the suggestees should have no stake in the copyright, so will have helped on a not-for-financial-profit basis. They could be acknowledged within the global site and even gain credibility points. Global obligations—to the church.

Let's illustrate the amendment process. OK, my next song says that "Jesus came to earth from heaven." That has **A** (Default) status. Someone objects that God's son was not Jesus before the incarnation but became Jesus by the incarnation, so strictly it was God's son the logos, not at that stage Jesus, who came to earth: "God's son came to earth from heaven." Someone else objects that God, not just his son, came to earth from heaven (Emmanuel, God with us): "God then came to earth from heaven." Both suggestions start with a **C** (Tentative) status and I (or my representative) would have 6 months to consider them.

Meanwhile, licensing law would permit churches everywhere to use A or C, noting that they are using a copyright variation. After a month I might decide that singing "God's son", instead of "Jesus", is true but unnecessary, but "God then" isn't true because my song is about the incarnation, and God's son alone was incarnated and he alone (not God) died on the cross—did God turn away from himself or from his son? I therefore upgrade the first suggestion to a **B** (Variant) status, and downgrade the second suggestion to a **D** (Rejected) status, giving my reasons for both decisions.

Churches would then have either A or B to choose, but not D. Of course, folk could still publicly put forward reasons to allow D, or to disallow B, but I wouldn't have to respond—I'd have done my job. Next year, I might revisit B ("God's son came to earth from heaven"), and decide that it's both true and important. So, I make it A, making my original A ("Jesus came to earth from heaven"), either a B or a D.

Chapter 11   Selected Songs

As said, songs have a number of factors, such as catching the prophetic moment, and musical relevancy (eg insider entertainment, and outsider evangelism). As a Christian lyricologist and song rewriter, my areas of interest are theology, logic, and grammar. Though it may help to grade songs I've highlighted, I can only grade by my own perspective. You might grade very differently, but grade you should, whether formally or informally, and hopefully without the music washing you down.

One of the follies of much secular politics, is the idea that one mustn't *discriminate*, until that is the Parties seek your vote and beg you to discriminate *in their favour*! Generalised, moral discrimination is not immoral; moral non-discrimination is immoral. We ought to discriminate right from wrong, good from evil, sin from justice. Judgement calls about people is one thing, but about principles it is quite another. To judge that murder is evil is one thing; to judge that so and so is a murderer, is quite another. Judgement is good. Discrimination is good. How often the pc world shouts down a Christian, because they are judged to have discriminated, instead of asking whether they have discriminated rightly or wrongly, as distinct from legally or illegally. That folly is the path to tyranny and to nihilism.

Discrimination between songs is a virtue, but can be done well or badly. There are songs on the market that cause me to momentarily wince, or might so upset my theological bladder that I rush to the nearest Gents[179] (toilet songs). There was an ancient joke about John the apostle running out of a public house because he feared that, an arch-heretic entering, the building might be demolished by God! There are times to leave. I offer a Problem Avoidance Grade, which shall be limited to my grading of Part 3 issues. The issues are fairly objective, but determining marks *per* issue is more subjective.

KEY TO PROBLEMS: **A** = **Incompletism** (-5): since/worthy dotdotdot; **B** = **Archaism** (-10): verily, ye, sageism; **C** = **Blessing God**

---

[179]   More and more toilets are called *male* or *female*—will they bear children? Or *disabled*, as if they're out of commission. Worse ideas have been mooted.

Particulars and Christian Songs

(-5): a problem with praise; **D = Boyfriend Buddy** (-5): gushy gabba; **E = Polytheism** (-10): my good god; **F = Voxdeism**: Soft (-25)/Hard (-50): I the lord will build my church/I the lord will dance to your tune; **G = Unitarianism**: Soft (-65)/Hard (-75): Jesus alone saves/Jesus alone is God; **H = Misdirection** (-15): please lord; **I = Prayer Misvisualisation**: Soft (-15)/Medium (-20)/Hard (-25)/Hyper (-30): for example God I love you, don't we, ever since Jesus sent the father in the spirit's name, so bless me Jesus, hallelujah, in Jesus' name;[180] **J = Boasting** (-10): me will do; **K = Decontextualising** (-10): for example, back to Sinai; **L = Hermit Harakiri** (-15): only deity meaningfully matters to me for life.

My method is simple. Each song begins with 100 points, and is subject to demerits. Those I think slightly silly I slightly downgrade, although in some contexts they might be enough to encourage a young believer to exit, or a nonbeliever not to enter, a church. These are (**A**), Blessing God (**C**), Buddy or Boyfriend (**D**): minus 5 points. A bit worse, I think, are Archaism (**B**), Polytheism (**E**), Boasting (**J**), and Decontextualising (**K**): minus 10 points. Of moderate seriousness, I would list Misdirection (**H**), Soft and Medium Prayer Misvisualisation (**I1-2**), Hermit Harakiri (**L**): minus 15 points. Of high seriousness, Voxdeism (**F**), and High and Hyper Prayer Misvisualisation (**I3-4**): minus 25-50 points. And of extreme seriousness, Soft Unitarianism (**G1**) at minus 65 points, Hard Unitarianism (**G2**) at minus 75 points, and Hyper Unitarianism (**G3**) at 90 points.

Percent	100-95	94-90	89-85	84-80	79-75	74-70	69-65	64-60	59-55	54-50	49-45	44-40	39-27	26-14	13-00
Grade	A+	A	A-	B+	B	B-	C+	C	C-	D+	D	D-	U+	U	U-
Grade Point	4.3	4	3.7	3.3	3	2.7	2.3	2	1.7	1.3	1	0.7	0	0	0

---

[180] I have demerited songs where we aren't told who is meant (ambivalent *lord*, or ambivalent pronoun in first lines), and/or where request is clearly to Jesus (and/or the spirit). For mere ambivalence, nondirective leaving to the discretion of each singer, when at least a uniformity of addressee seems to me likely, I'd merely deduct 15 points.

My Problem Avoidance Grade must inevitably be wooden, for it simply deducts from a nominal perfection (100 points). And high cringe can mix with sparks of genius. Sometimes one phrase in a maelstrom of nonsense raises a song well above the norm of a generally good song: a glimmer of gold among the rubble; a diamond set in pig iron—though it should be set in finest gold. Sometimes a work of deep significance can be let down by a unitarian phrase by an ostensibly trinitarian writer: a Mona Lisa spoilt by a mo. Also, the longer the song, the more scope for penalties: in a china shop, a careful bull visiting for an hour might cause more damage than a careless bull in one minute. Also, a song may say nothing of formal demerit, yet say nothing of merit, so pass with 100% as a trite time-filler, too insipid for virtue or vice.

This grading is only a Problem Avoidance Grade. The girl I love may have many issues that cause me pain, yet be better to have than a girl lacking all problems except the blemish of blandness. Christ sees his bride's blemishes, yet shall raise her to perfection (Eph.5). Song interest; song redemption. Let's heal the broken. I'll examine some songs below to touch on most of these problems.

We Declare Your Majesty: Malcolm Du Plessis[181]

Visualisation: Polydirectional worship

Analysis: The stanza is theodirectional, probably to God, not to Christ. The chorus has several problems. We interrupt this singing to deity about *our god* (polytheism), for a quick announcement to *sing it again* (misvisualisation). *Lifting up a name* is archaism, less suitable for non~ and neo~Christians than for mature Christians, especially when a *name* isn't given. *All honour and glory*, while not boastful, seems an orphan, an incompletism: "what about *all honour and glory*?" we ask. Some keywords are good (for example might/holy/honour/adoration/bow/throne) but aren't connected well.

---

[181]   www.weareworship.com/uk/songs/song-library/showsong/565 (1984): *We declare your majesty / We proclaim that your name is exalted / For you reign magnificently / Rule victoriously / And your power is shown throughout the earth / And we exclaim, our god is mighty / Lift up your name, for you are holy / Sing it again, all honour and glory / In adoration, we bow before your throne.*

Suggestions: The chorus should be changed from PD (polydirectional) to TD (theodirectional), and synchronised to the stanza. With further tweaking, perhaps "we do exclaim, O God, you're mighty / Sing of your fame, for you are holy / You will retain, all honour and glory / In adoration, we bow before your throne".

A	B	C	D	E	F[1,2]	G[1-3]	H	I[1-3]	J	K	L	Total	Grade
5	10	-	-	10	-	-	-	25	-	-	-	50	D+

Will You Come And Follow Me?: John Bell and Graham Maule[182]

Visualisation: Polydirectional

Analysis: I don't say that the challenge isn't good; I do say both that Jesus doesn't sing it, and that I am not Jesus. It is hard voxdeism. Some phrases are not simply a challenge to do right, they challenge as to what is right. For example, is kissing the lepers (they prefer 'the leprous') the way forward? To show the milk of human kindness is good, and to touch is safe. But Jesus possibly never met what we medically call *lepers*. He could touch, against taboo, in healing some from skin diseases that had made them, through no fault of their own, culturally outcasts (Mk.1:41). True leprosy (Hanson's Disease) is today curable by medication, and even prosthetic limbs can be used. If the song is about *social* lepers, outcasts, it should say so.

Personally I don't think we need, or should ask, the lord (to me, Jesus seems strongly implied) to *let*/allow us to *follow* him—he's laid that road for us, not put up a barrier, and anyway asking the lord, rather than God, is misdirection.

Besides implying a barrier, the song seems to me to imply that we're ready and willing, just awaiting access—*in your company I'll go*: thus boast. The boot's on the other foot! Incidentally, I prefer "walking with Jesus" to be put as walking with the spirit as guide. It also implies that we're not already on the discipleship road—some are, some are not. To *turn* may needlessly, or needfully, invoke the concept of repentance (*metanoia*)—depends on the Christian. It is a one-size fits all approach.

---

[182] www.whatdidjesussay.com/follow-me (1987)

Selected Songs

The stanzas all keep the rhyme, *name/same* for lines 1&2, always rhyme for lines 3&4, and always keep the end words *you/me*, for lines 5&6. A lively song, it has much to offer, encouraging socio-spiritual engagement in line with Christification.

Suggestions: Thoroughly replace the voxdeistic approach, for example, *will you let my name be known*, by *we should let your name be known*. In addition, replace *let me turn and follow*, by *I desire to follow; in your company I'll go*, by *with the/your spirit I would go*.

A	B	C	D	E	$F^{1,2}$	G^{1-3}	H	I^{1-3}	J	K	L	Total	Grade
-	-	-	-	-	50	-	15	-	10	-	-	25	U

<u>The Lord's My Shepherd: Stuart Townend</u>[183]

Visualisation: Polydirectional

Analysis: In favour of this being polydirectional, we may cite the original psalm. Yet the original setting may have been antiphonal, and anyway its pattern of speech is not ours. Whether or not the CEV is justified in its approach to the psalms, it at least shows the way that our lyricists should go—unidirectionalism. Thus, visualisation is faulty, confusing prayer. Stuart has modified a traditional song, removing the more obvious archaisms. Yet newbies will doubtless wonder what head is 'anointed' (der?) with oil, and what overflowing cups, as well as *feasting on his delights*, actually mean.[184] Stuart could have done a little more modernising: how does the original setting translate into our words, and into our covenant setting? It took me years to understand that the "shepherd I shalt not *want*" didn't mean that I didn't want the shepherd! I note without deduction.

Even on the lyricist's site, it is *Lord*, not *LORD*, so implies a Jesus song: Jesus is lord. In 1650 Francis Rous got it right; in 1996 Stuart Townend got it wrong—theologically the West is now on a Sabellian slide.[185]

---

[183] www.stuarttownend.co.uk/song/the-lords-my-shepherd (1996)

[184] I heard about a beautiful young woman who, in combining prophesying as if from God's perspective with a touch of sageism, said "come unto me, all you young men, and I will give you the delights of your hearts". It caused a stir!

[185] "To tie the spirit too closely to the person and work of Christ is to underestimate that differentiation within the one [deific] life and thus to

Soft unitarianism excludes the trinity. The new covenant upgraded our knowledge of God, and to downgrade to trusting in *Jesus* alone, from the Sinaitic covenant's more secure trusting in *Yahweh* alone, fails the grade (if anyone, Yahweh is the father, not the lord). Nor, for that matter, did Sinai teach even that: *trust alone* should always add context. I can trust my wife alone to cook my next meal (granting some basic givens, such as the food, availability of heat, her physical wellbeing and closeness), and God alone to grant me physical immortality. To the extent that by singing it we promise never to trust—though may still desire—another human being, it falls at least into soft hermitude. However, if we disengage brain when singing, all should be well.

Unlike Rous and the psalmist, Stuart sandwiched a theme of God's house (stanza 2), within two pastoral slices (stanzas 1&3), mixing themes instead of progression from first to next. Even so, it might be better to keep a song to only one of these themes.

Finally, there is an implied boast. Stuart has spiritualised the psalmist's setting of human enemies, to the diabolical enemy. Fine, but there is a difference between not *needing* to fear, and boasting that I *won't* fear.[186]

Suggestions: Replace *the Lord's*, by *you are*; *want*, by *lack*; *he/his* (throughout), by *you/your* (and any following word changes as needed); swap positions of stanzas 2&3; *trust in you alone*, by *trust in you, Yahweh/father*; *will not fear*, by *need not fear*; *on your pure delights*, by *as a special guest*.

A	B	C	D	E	F[1,2]	G[1-3]	H	I[1-3]	J	K	L	Total	Grade
-	-	-	-	-	-	65	-	25	10	-	15	-15	U-

<u>Holy Spirit, Rain Down: Russell Fragar</u>[187]

Visualisation: Theodirectional 3 request

---

encourage the slow drift into modalism which is so common in western Trinitarian theology" (John Webster, *Themelios* 1983:9.1).

[186] Yet *I will trust* does not carry this boast, since it is of reliance, even though we cannot know (unless elected to Calvinism) whether we *will* rely on God.

[187] http://higherpraise.com/lyrics/love/love202317.htm (1997)

Selected Songs

Analysis: As request to the spirit, this is misdirected. There is no biblical reference to the spirit (nor for that matter of the father or Jesus) as our *friend*. *Comforter* is archaism and mistranslation nowadays. Arguably, *rain* can convey the ideas of power and voice. *Come and change* overlooks the facts that he has come with the covenant, remains, and has changed our hearts (Rm.5:5), though we can certainly profit from continuing upgrade. Yahweh's words will stand, but I don't see that the Bible speaks of *us* standing on his words— mystification? Will you stand on my words or stamp out my message?

The chorus throws in 1 Cor.2:9.[188] Paul's meaning is probably that what had been hidden had been revealed to be the new covenant, God's wisdom (v6-7). Fragar seems to have thought it was perhaps blessing *for* the church, rather than the church *being* the blessing— existentialism rather than eschatology, so to speak. Thus decontextualising. *Open up heaven*? There is an 'open heaven' teaching on the market. Roughly, this idea is that 1 Jesus didn't perform miracles until after his baptism; 2 his baptism was the point of full submission; 3 therefore, we need to arrive at full submission in order to work miracles; and 4 even as heaven opened to Jesus, so it will for us.

In my opinion it 1 likens Jesus' boyhood to imperfect submission; 2 fails to see that Jesus' miracles began sometime after his baptism; 3 puts too much weight on water baptism as symbolising submission; and 4 puts too little weight on Eph.2:18 which speaks of the 'open heaven' for all Christians.[189] Immersion marked a new phase linked to John's mission, not the crucial point of submission. Jesus' miracles began afterwards. Only then did his mission require them. On the plus side, the song can help remind us of the spirit, even to the extent of the church being *his* church, which I think is justified and useful. By mention of God as distinct from the spirit, it avoids Oneness, but is guilty of tritheism, where the persons are all playing the same parts the same way.

Suggestions: Too much change is needed to suggest a simple rewrite. If keeping request, it could be redirected to the father (TD1

---

[188] This in turn links an OT theme of hidden plans, with phrases from Is.64:4.

[189] They might say that all Paul addressed in *Ephesians* had been water-baptised.

request). If keeping as prayer to the spirit, it could be rewritten, removing the requests by transformation into statements (you are, we are, we need) and appreciation (TD3 appreciation). Either way, terms such as *comforter*, and *friend*, need removal. *No eye/ear had seen/heard...what you had*, would work. Similarly, *open up heaven* should be rewritten that having being opened, heaven remains open—we are more closed to it than it is to us.

A	B	C	D	E	F[1,2]	G[1-3]	H	I[1-3]	J	K	L	Total	Grade
	10	-	5	-	-	-	15	-	-	10	-	60	C

Chapter 12   Selected Carols

When New England was under Puritan rule, there were no problems with carols, since Christmas was banned and celebrants fined, along the lines that Peter and Paul would not have celebrated it, and that celebrants were often into other spirits than a godly spirit. Their idea did not win the global battle, so let's look at carols.

Do we wrap history as a myth? Have carols a sense of reality or of unreality? C S Lewis vividly portrayed the tension between Historical Event and Annual Re-enactment Myth (liturgical year), between historian and storyteller. Whereas Queen Orual wished to know when the next *historical* stage of her sister Istra's life would occur, the Essurian priest believed Istra was a *mythic* annual cycle of events: "In spring, and all summer, she is a goddess. Then when harvest comes we bring a lamp into the temple in the night and the god flies away. Then we veil her. And all winter she is wandering and suffering; weeping, always weeping…" (Lewis 1980:255-6).

Likewise each Christmas, baby Jesus is tucked into his little crib, and animals mill around. Each Easter Jesus rises. Each Whitsuntide, the spirit comes. Was 'Christmas' for Peter and Paul an annual, or a daily, celebration? I prefer to sing carols from the distance of time, looking back to the historical event, rather than imagining myself in Bethlehem's maternity unit awaiting the annual news of new birth, an annual Corn King cycle. But siding with the queen, not with the priest, and moving from singing a myth to singing of facticity, often requires changing carols.

Appropriate changes aren't always simple, and for global use must gain enough respect to fit in with folk who already like the song, as well as with folk who don't know it. It's a bit like pruning, cutting off deadness to encourage new life, and training the plant in the way it should grow. One should wish to preserve, where theologically permissible, the original point of view—authorial intent: Calvin should not have to sing with the voice of Wesley. The first part involves looking into the song's history, and trying to squeeze into the mindset of the writer and their wider culture. The latter, quite frankly, should involve many years of theological study, cross-

Particulars and Christian Songs

fertilised by theologians across denominational divides, in order to avoid mere sectarianism.

Having other versions of the song can help, allowing a survival of the fittest. Some mistakes will have already been spotted by others. A particular dilemma is about changing first lines. If I change, *We Three Kings*, to *Persian Magi*,[190] will you quickly find it in your hymnbook? Making the familiar unfamiliar, can kill the song. Keeping rhyme is another issue. If an end rhyming word needs to be changed, does the word it rhymed with also need changing? Can such be done within the timing of the music? Would the change be true to the previous meaning, theme, emphasis? I have tried, not my best, but at least I have tried. You might find it useful to get hold of the earliest English form available. And then its standard form. And then my tweak. Compare them with an inquisitive mind. Can you see why changes along the way have been made? Only then ask yourself if you think the reason for each change was merited.

Hark! The Herald Angels Sing[191]

The background to this hymn might have been the joyous sounds of London's church bells, thrilling Charles Wesley as he walked to church one Christmas morn. Perhaps to his ears it sounded as if the heavens, the *welkins*, were ringing the bells as for a coronation of the king of kings. It was published in 1739, and various people have tweaked it. People who did such somewhat annoyed the Wesleys, who thought that mucking around with their songs could only cheapen them. Yet I believe that Charles would now happily admit the need of updating, though might well smile with a head shake at my feeble efforts. I am well aware that though the Wesleys made their own changes to songs written by Isaac Watts, that nevertheless the strap of their shoes I am not worthy to stoop down and unloose. Their blessings to the church have been astronomical. In composing my version, I have compared a few versions to Wesley's original. I don't wish change for change's sake, nor to overlook improvements already

---

[190] They were at least two magi, probably representing their king.
[191] www.hymnsandcarolsofchristmas.com/Hymns_and_Carols/hark_how_all_the_welkin_rings.htm

made. I keep *hark*, as in "hark hark the lark", since it is not too archaic and keeps the title. Wesley's 10 stanzas of 4 lines, became 5 stanzas of 8 lines. The last 16 lines, being less common, I have ignored.[192]

Rhyming is a simple ABABABAB pattern, though nowadays *come/ womb* seldom rhyme. A number of archaisms exist, not least *welkin*, *men*, and *sons*. A tardisial element is built in, yet Christ wasn't born last Christmas, nor will he be born again this Christmas. The historical reality of the incarnation predates the Christian celebration, Christmas, which seems to merely have converted a pagan festivity, Saturnalia, upgrading its prophecy of the risen sun (effectively a then winter solstice day) to the true rising of God's light: Christ was myth incarnate. It is unlikely that Jesus was actually born on our Dec.25th. My main concern, however, is the imagining of an annual rebirth day, as if it's an annual myth. I dismiss the argument that Wesley implied that God needed to be reconciled, since I dismiss the assumption that a breach between two parties always stems from both parties being at fault. The mediator, Christ, brought the flawed party, man (in part), back to the flawless party, God. Since a little mystery stretches the mind, I have maintained the idea of deathlessness. The mystery is solved quite simply by realising that it is spiritual deathlessness (which will include bodily resurrection, or perhaps, more precisely, re-embodiment).

---

[192] *Come, Desire of Nations, come / Fix in Us thy humble Home / Rise, the Woman's Conqu'ring Seed / Bruise in Us the Serpent's Head. / Now display thy saving Pow'r / Ruin'd Nature now restore / Now in Mystic Union join / Thine to Ours, and Ours to Thine. // Adam's likeness, Lord, efface / Stamp thy Image in its Place / Second Adam from above / Reinstate us in thy Love / Let us Thee, tho' lost, regain / Thee, the Life, the Heav'nly Man: / Oh to All Thyself impart / Form'd in each Believing Heart.* It features terms from *Genesis*, John, and Adam Christology. On the negative side, if sung by Christians, it asks Jesus (bad) to come where he already is (foolish) in order to convert the converted. Moreover, it seems that redemption is getting back to *Genesis*, rather than getting into *Revelation*: Jesus has not restored me what I had, or to what sinless Adam had, but gives me what neither Adam nor I ever had. On the positive side, the gospel is about Jesus offering mystic union to all, a 'vertical' link, and us letting God replace the fallen likeness by the new (Eph.5:26-7).

Particulars and Christian Songs

From	To
Hark how all the Welkin rings / Glory to the King of Kings / Peace on Earth and Mercy mild / GOD and Sinners reconcil'd / Joyful all ye Nations rise / Join the Triumph of the Skies / Universal Nature say / Christ the Lord is born to Day.	'Hark!' the heralds loud did sing glory to the one born king / Peace on earth and mercy mild / God and sinners reconciled! / Joyful now our hearts arise / join the triumph of the skies / With angelic ones we say / Christ was born, momentous day. *Hark, the heralds loud did sing glory to the one born king.*
Christ by highest Heav'n ador'd / Christ the Everlasting Lord / Late in Time behold him come / Offspring of a Virgin's Womb. / Veil'd in Flesh the Godhead see / Hail th' Incarnate Deity! / Pleas'd as Man with Men t'appear / Jesus our Immanuel here!	Christ by highest heaven adored / Christ the everlasting lord / Let all hearts prepare him room / firstborn of the virgin's womb / One with us God's son we see / come to show us deity / Pleased as one with us to dwell / Jesus our Immanuel. *Hark, the heralds loud did sing glory to the one born king.*
Hail the Heav'nly Prince of Peace! / Hail the Sun of Righteousness! / Light and Life to All he brings / Ris'n with Healing in his Wings. / Mild he lays his Glory by / Born that Man no more may die / Born to raise the Sons of Earth / Born to give them Second Birth.	Greet the heaven born Prince of Peace / in his name all war shall cease / Light and life to all he brings / and frees us from evil things / Selfless left his home on high / born that death itself shall die / Born to raise us from the earth / born to give us heavenly birth. *Hark, the heralds loud did sing glory to the one born king.*

Joy to the World[193]

This was written by Isaac Watts (Nonconformist) in 1719, and loosely based on parts of Ps.98. There, Yahweh's people were urged to a mega celebration over his decisive kingly victory and justice, shining particularly through his covenant people, and in which nature, even

---

[193] www.hymnary.org/text/joy_to_the_world_the_lord_is_come/fulltexts

the mountains, will delight, and other positive results will be seen by others. If war is the aggravation of the normal human situation, it shows the abnormality of man. Watts looked for the still soon to be return of King Jesus, which will end the cause of wars, bringing man into normality. God's son, the true king, had made his decisive victory through incarnation and crucifixion, and his return will complete the two-stage plan of global redemption and shalom (Lk.2:10). Nature shall fully rejoice when Gen.3:17's curse (separation) ends (Rm.8:19-22), but even now we see glimmers of that light.

I have changed wording from the see it happening, to the see it happened, viewpoint. I have removed the sageism, *men*, and the dubious, *floods*—had Watts thought about a devastating flood, and would he have spoken of a typhoon, or of a tornado, of joy? I have presumed that, though in the present tense, *he comes to make* refers to the incarnation, not the parousia (second coming), contrasting the new creation blessing to the old creation curse. Finally, Christ's rulership of the present world (*kosmos*) is moot. Is *he* responsible for its lawlessness, or is it the ruler of this present evil, Satan? The facts that deity has ultimate oversight (ultimacy), and as love allows the fruits of rebellion to be significant, are another matter. But a new age is to dawn, when Christ shall rule unopposed, under the ultimate king.

From	To
Joy to the world! the Lord is come[194] / Let earth receive her King / Let every heart / prepare him room / And heaven and nature sing, / And heaven and nature sing, / And heaven, and heaven and nature sing.	Joy to the world, messiah came / The earth received her king / Now we with joyful hearts / can bear his family name / And heaven and nature sing / And heaven and nature sing / And heaven, and heaven, and nature sing.

---

[194] It doesn't quite rhyme. A Wesley song had *Late in time behold him* come, *Offspring of a virgin's* Womb. Watts here had *Joy to the world, the lord is* come! *Let every heart prepare him* room. Possibly their dialect once had *come* share the same *oom* sound as *womb* and *room*. Keeping 'come', something ending in 'not shun' would be perfect rhyme, but would turn a positive *accept*, to a negative *don't refuse*. Watts' rhyming fails with his *He rules the world*, stanza (grace/righteousness; prove/love).

Particulars and Christian Songs

From	To
Joy to the earth! the Saviour reigns / let men their songs employ / while fields and floods / rocks, hills, and plains / repeat the sounding joy, / repeat the sounding joy, / repeat, repeat the sounding joy.	Joy to the earth, the saviour reigns! / Let us our songs employ / While fields and forest woods / rocks, hills, and peaceful plains / Repeat the sounding joy / Repeat the sounding joy / Repeat, repeat, the sounding joy.
No more let sins and sorrows grow / nor thorns infest the ground / he comes to make / his blessings flow / far as the curse is found / far as the curse is found / far as, far as the curse is found.	No more need sin and sorrow grow / Nor thorns infest our ground / He came in joy to make / God's wondrous blessings flow / Far as the curse was found / Far as the curse was found / Far as, far as, the curse was found.
He rules the world with truth and grace / and makes the nations prove / the glories of / his righteousness / and wonders of his love, / and wonders of his love, / and wonders, wonders of his love.	Soon all the world, shall see his face / The nations look above / We'll see heavenly his glory / the fullness of his grace / And wonders of his love / And wonders of his love / And wonders, wonders of his love.

Oh Come All Ye Faithful[195]

John Wade, a 32 y.o. Roman Catholic Lancastrian, probably wrote the first four stanzas (1740-4), Abbé Étienne Jean François Borderies (1822) added three more, and someone added an eighth sometime before 1886. Wade was a fervent Roman Catholic, who moved from Lancaster to escape religious persecution, when with some cause commitment to Rome was still feared to endanger English monarchy. In Continental Europe, he acted as a scribe and taught church music. Over a millennium earlier, it is said that Pope Gregory the Great had seen some angelic looking English slave children. Told that they were Angles/English, he responded, *"Non Angli sed Angeli"* (not Angles, but Angels). This encounter inspired his Romanisation of Angland/ England, which he begun through monks in 597. They were led by Augustine [of Canterbury], later to become the first archbishop of

---

[195] www.hymnary.org/text/o_come_all_ye_faithful_joyful_and_triump

Canterbury. Augustine's mission was to suffer a setback of repaganisation. After King Henry 8, when Rome thought Anglicanism pagan, there is some reason to think that Wade's song, its Latin title *Adeste Fideles*, at least doubled as a coded signal for re-Romanisation of the English Angles. Truth be told, there were true Christians in Rome and in Canterbury, and both sides shed blood for religious freedom.

Fideles could have meant *faithful* Roman Catholic Jacobites. *Bethlehem* might have been a code for *Britain*. *Angeli* had long had the word-play with *angli* (English). In effect, faithful Romanists should rally behind Bonnie Prince Charlie, born to be *the king of Angles*, and the exiled return to Britain. However, whatever code, if any, is written into a song, its face value can often conceal that hidden value. Simon and Garfunkel's *Bridge Over Troubled Water*, probably referred to Peggy Harper, Simon's wife, having discovered her first silver hair (or had "sail on, silver girl," a drug connection?), but how many have enjoyed the silver sail, riding the wind of hope through the storm of life? Likewise, whatever Anglicans might think about re-Romanisation, they are happy to sing of the faithful arriving in Bethlehem to join the *angeli*. Let us not be too quick to assume hidden meanings. And to accuse the Roman Bath attendant of arson, simply because, when a user had complained hours earlier about it being too cold, he had replied that it would soon be "hot enough," was taking an unintended truth too far (see C S Lewis' *Reflections on the Psalms: Second Meanings*). Besides, while Wade might have doodled sketches of the prince alongside the lyrics, would he have called any mortal *Jesus*, or attributed incarnate birth to another? A later Roman Catholic, J R R Tolkien, cautioned that applicability need not mean intentionality.

Translating into English has been done many times. Rev. Frederick Oakeley, who later switched from Canterbury to Rome, translated Wade. William T Brooke, who moved from the Baptistism to Canterbury, translated Abbé Borderies and the untraced stanza, sandwiching them within *Adeste Fideles*. For simplicity, I have discounted the additions by Abbé Étienne Jean François Borderies. They invite us to prioritise meeting Jesus, in line with the shepherds, to tell Jesus the saviour (in his infancy!) of our love, and to muse over the incarnation. I have also discounted the untraced addition which contrasts the magi's gift to our hearts' gift. While I look to retain Wade's Nicene terms, his use of *begotten* I discount. Let's briefly look at this.

Talk about God's son being *begotten* can mislead. Theologians speak rather of God's son *per se* being eternally generated, and Jesus as born within time. In short, Jesus is the permanent time (temporal) mode of the uncreated second person of the eternal tripersonal society. Yep, that came from me. Was *begotten* brought in as a reaction to some early controversies? Against Arius, orthodoxy said that God's son was more like what one *births*, rather than what one *makes*. Against Valentinus, that only *one* was birthed/*emanated* (within eternity), not multitudes. When asked to produce the definitive Latin Bible translation, perhaps Jerome of Stridon felt he should introduce the stronger idea of 'only begotten' into the text, which many translations have kept. Indeed "'only begotten' probably originated from Jerome's Latin translation [the Vulgate,] when Jerome changed unicus (unique) to unigenitus (only begotten). Prior to Jerome's translation, the old Latin Codex Vercellenis (AD 365) had translated monogenous, as unicus" (Comfort 128). Sure, we may ask whether Vulgate corrected Vercellenis, but in Heb.11:17 *only begotten/born*, or *one and only*, does not fit, since Abraham had had another son, Ishmael: *special/unique/beloved son* was meant. For Jhn.1:18, something like *the one-of-a-kind [son], himself deity*, for the matrix of deity and humanity, is perhaps the better translation.

From	To
O come, all ye faithful, joyful and triumphant! / O come ye, O come ye to Bethlehem! / Come and behold him, born the King of angels.	O come all you faithful, joyful, and triumphant O come now remember, humble Bethlehem Come and behold Christ, born the king of angels.
God of God, Light of Light eternal, / lo, he abhors not the virgin's womb / Son of the Father, begotten, not created.	He came, God's true word, light from light eternal God's son incarnated to dispel all our gloom Truly eternal, he was not created.

Selected Carols

From	To
Sing, choirs of angels, sing in exultation, / sing, all ye citizens, of heaven above / "Glory to God, all glory in the highest!"	Then choirs of angels, sang in celebration rejoiced all the citizens of heaven above "Glory to God, all, glory in the highest."
Yea, Lord, we greet thee, born this happy morning; Jesus, to thee be all [the] glory given / Word of the Father, now in flesh appearing.	We sing and praise him, born that happy morning To Jesus now be the sovereign glory given Word of the father, Christ the Second Adam.
O come, let us adore him, O come, let us adore him, O come, let us adore him, Christ the Lord!	O come, let us adore him x 3 / Christ the lord (venite adoremus Dominum!)

<u>O Come, O Come, Emmanuel</u>[196]

The substructure, as *Veni, Veni Emmanuel*, seems to date from the C12 or earlier, and was translated into English in the C19. It was written as a pre-Christmas Advent reflection, sung in the persona of Ethnic Israel awaiting her messiah, yet doubling for Christians, True Israel,[197] awaiting the Parousia. It asks Jesus about Jesus [and himself!] returning, specifically, returning to save his lost people. Visualisation is patchy, and if unexplained, some might sing with the idea that it's to encourage pre-messianic Ethnic Israel to await the Second Advent, as a shared hope with Christians. It confuses singers about vision. If we are singing as pre-incarnation Israel, then it's not [Rod of Jesse...give *them* victory], but [Rod of Jesse...give *us* victory]: let *their* shoes become *ours*—we are *thy* people, bless *them*? Unless we are singing *to* Jesus *about* another Jesus, then not [come, Emmanuel... Israel...mourns...Until *the* Son of God appear], but [come,

---

[196] http://traditionalcatholic.net/Tradition/Prayer, augmented by http://songsandhymns.org/hymns/lyrics/o-come-o-come-emmanuel *for Sapientia and Rex*. I suggest *Venisti, Venisti, Emmanuel*.

[197] I use *true*, in John's sense of *alēthinos*, not as true *vs* false, but as fulfilled *vs* foreshadowed, spiritual *vs* ethnic.

Particulars and Christian Songs

Emmanuel...Israel...mourns...Until *you* Son of God [do] appear]. The song misvisualises.

In my *Israel's Gone Global*, I have argued that *Israel* is a term with many layers, including the messianic community as the NT church, and that at least some terms analogous to Ethnic Israel may be applied to it. For example, we are the true diaspora, the true church of the wilderness, as well as in another sense being the true church in the Promised Land. In Christ, we have entered this Promised Land *vis-à-vis* our prior captivity and wanderings. Yet *vis-à-vis* the ultimate dimension of eternal life, we are but wanderers still awaiting the Promised Land. In other words, *Wilderness* and *Promised Land* have layers of reality. This is likely to have been the original approach behind the song, which seems to have been a later paraphrase of earlier advent antiphonies.[198] In its Latin original, there were 7 stanzas, one for each successive day from Dec.17 through Dec.23. Each had a supposed Isaianic title of Christ, and when you arrived at the stanza for Dec.23, you could take the first letter from each of the titles of Christ reading backwards to the 17th, and see that they were ERO CRAS, which is a Latin phrase for "I will come tomorrow." I have reordered the stanzas to reflect this earlier monastic SARCORE order. If, as I suspect, it was by monastic design, then it was a touch of genius lost in translation and the mist of time.[199] I would however change the song's tardisial[200] nature, and sing it as *fait acompli*—after all he has come, though may well return tomorrow. The term *Adonai* is dangerously close to the idea that it means only Jesus. Yet, in the context of the incarnation of God's son, I think it may stand as a Hebraic reminder of ancient covenant times, though a title (not the name) that God's son and spirit share with the father.

---

[198] http://songsandhymns.org/hymns/detail/o-come-o-come-emmanuel

[199] Against, it is argued that that is not today's pattern, and that the order varied in different communities. This does not dismiss the idea that one ancient community arranged the stanzas to have added meaning.

[200] By which I mean it can travel in time, whether to the Birth or 10,000 years forward when "we've no less days to sing God's praise, than when we first begun".

Selected Carols

	From	To
Dec. 17.1 Sapientia: Wisdom	O come Thou Wisdom from on high / Who orderest all things mightily / To us the path of knowledge show / And teach us in her ways to go.	You came God's loving wisdom from on high / with him you did make earth and sea and sky / creating man from just dust and clay / now you have made a new and living way.
	Rejoice! Rejoice! Emmanuel / Shall come to thee, O Israel.	We now rejoice, our lord Emmanuel you came to save your heavenly Israel.
18.2 Adonai: Lord	O come, Adonai, Thou Lord of might, / Who to Thy tribes, on Sinai's height, / In ancient times didst give the law / In cloud and majesty and awe.	You came in truth to save us adon-ai / who to the tribes on height of stark Sin-ai / in ancient times gave Mo-ses your law / in cloud and majesty and holy awe.
19.3 Radix: Root	O come, Thou Rod of Jesse, free, / Thine own from Satan's tyranny; / From depths of hell Thy people save, / And give them victory over the grave.	You came of ancient royal line to free / the slaves from Satan's pitch black tyranny / from depth of hell lost peo-ple to save / and give them vic-tory beyond the grave.
20.4 Clavis: Key	O come, Thou Key of David, come / And open wide our heavenly home; / Make safe the way that leads on high / And close the path to misery.	You came to give us all a royal throne / to open up your heavens for our home / to make the way that has set us free / and close the path to death's dark misery.
21.5 Oriens: Dawn	O come, Thou Dayspring, from on high, / And cheer us by Thy drawing nigh; / Disperse the gloomy clouds of night, / And death's dark shadow put to flight.	You came as radiance to replace our night / and cheered us by the bright dawn of your light / dispersed the gloom and clouds of our night / our futile shadows you have put to flight.
22.6 Rex:	O come Desire of nations bind / In one the hearts of all mankind; /	You came O glorious prince of peace in you / man's hopes of peace were by

Particulars and Christian Songs

	From	To
Ruler	Bid Thou our sad divisions cease / And be Thyself our King of Peace.	death born anew / and we who have bowed down to your call / are better than we were before the Fall.
23.7 Emmanuel: God with us	O come, O come, Emmanuel, / And ransom captive Israel, / That mourns in lonely exile here / Until the Son of God appear.	You came you came, our lord Emmanu-el / to ransom once bound captive Israel / that mourned alone in dark exile here / until to set us free you did appear.
	Rejoice! Rejoice! Emmanuel / Shall come to thee, O Israel.	**Final**: We now rejoice, our lord Emmanuel Oh come oh come to save your Israel.

Oh Holy Night[201]

Around 1847, a Roman Catholic parish priest living near Avignon, France, thought it would be nice to have a new poem for Christmas Midnight Mass, particularly after getting a new organ. Perhaps he also thought it nice to covertly evangelise a gifted parishioner, Placide Cappeau (wine merchant and poet). Two birds with one stone?

With the priest's request for a poem on his mind, Cappeau went on a business trip to Paris. He read the birth narrative in *Luke*, and probably in *Matthew*, imagining himself being present, and wrote *Minuit, Chrétiens* (Midnight, Christians), which later became known as *Cantique de Noël* (O Holy Night).[202] He then asked an acclaimed Parisian friend, Adolphe Adams, to write a tune, and hopefully it drew Cappeau and Adams towards messiah.

---

[201] www.hymnsandcarolsofchristmas.com/Hymns_and_Carols/o_holy_night.htm. Some great renditions, too, such as Jul3ia Richard's https://www.youtube.com/watch?v=R5xBIHA-Dsc&list=RDR5xBIHA-Dsc&start_radio=1&t=0

[202] Luke and Matthew wrote as redactors, selecting material that fitted their main interests. Matthew thus picked up the royalty theme, while Luke picked up the humility theme. Their accounts complement and tie into each other. My tweak has used *Luke* for stanza 1, and (not the same night) *Matthew* for stanza 2.

Selected Carols

Anyway, the song was on the priest's desk in time for that midnight mass, and it became a firm favourite in France. When word came out that Cappeau and Adams had written, respectively, as backslider and as Judaic, it lost Rome's vote and was officially blacklisted. But, judged on its merit, not its authors', the song got the people's vote.

It certainly had some good insights. For instance, it picked up that Jesus was against blind slavery (see Lk.4:18; Gal.3:28; Phm.16). John Sullivan Dwight's version (1855?) might have been blind to *spiritual* emancipation (Jhn.8:34), though I think that Cappeau saw that the deliverance was for all—that is, that all were born *spiritually* enslaved.[203] Overlooking *that* kind of slavery is common enough, as well as, sadly, overlooking vocational slavery to Christ. Messiah's own people had largely limited their sight to freedom from slavery to Rome, blind to their enslavement to sin and death.

And Dwight may have been blind to the fact that though human slaves were part of the human family (brothers and sisters, Imagoes Dei), from a new creation perspective not all in Adam are in the Second Adam, ie *spiritual* family (Imagoes Christi, slaves in Christ). Dwight, a transcendentalist post-Unitarian and Abolitionist, of Boston, Massachusetts, gave us our first and favourite English version, which speaks of Jesus as our brother and social reformer abolishing slavery.[204] Upto and within the American Civil War, it was given star status by Dwight's fellow Americans in the north. The song was destined to achieve a special global accolade, too, when, on Christmas Eve, 1906, the first ever radio transmission of a human voice (and human tune) was made. To some that seemed a Christmas miracle, as Prof. Reginald Fessenden read from Lk.2, and then played on his violin, *Oh Holy Night*.

That *day* (possibly *night*) was holy in the sense of set aside by God. Probably in all of cosmic history, there has only been one actual incarnation, though by grace some prophetical myths had done the rounds in the Gentile world, and been prophesied too unto the Israelites and Jews. The song's poetic licence draws a parallel between sin and nature's night, and the stars illuminating the fact that the true

---

[203] ..*attends ta deliverance / Noël! Noël! Voici le Rédempteur!*
[204] Further assessment is based on Dwight's version.

Particulars and Christian Songs

light had come to mankind, and it deserves some slack. Likewise, the bit about Jesus being our friend. While the context doesn't require us to assume more than that he was a friend in the sense of an ally "in all our trials" (I doubt that Dwight would have meant more), it can nowadays reinforce buddy theology, so is safer dropped. Another issue for me is the puzzle over what on earth "the soul/spirit/Spirit [feeling] its worth", should mean. Did the human soul feel its own worth; did the Holy Spirit feel the worth of the incarnation; did each Christian *person* feel the incarnation's worth? Dwight set the puzzle, perhaps from Transcendentalist mindset of a world soul. Cappeau's *Et de son Père arrêter le courroux*, carried the plain picture of messiah's mission likened to protecting sinners from his father's anger, which probably sounded anathema in a post-religions ideology.[205]

From	To
O holy night! The stars are brightly shining / It is the night of our dear saviour's birth / Long lay the world—in sin and error pining / 'Til he appear'd and the soul felt its worth. / A thrill of hope the weary world rejoices / For yonder breaks—a new and glorious morn / Fall on your knees! O hear the angel voices! / O night divine, O night when Christ was born / O night, o holy night, O night divine.	Oh holy night, the stars were shining brightly / It was the night of—our dear saviour's birth / Long weary lay—the world in sin so tightly / Then he appeared and we sang with true mirth / A thrill of hope—for now the earth rejoices / For then did break—the new and glorious morn / Fall on your knees, Oh hear the angel voices / Oh night divine—oh night when Christ was born / Oh night divine—oh night, when Christ was born.
Led by the light of faith serenely beaming / With glowing hearts by	Then led by light—of star especial gleaming / There came the magi—from

---

[205] It is a just picture, and the term *expiation* is sometimes used. God's wrath at the cancer of sin, and those who harbour it, is well justified (righteous). Getting away from objective truth, we have gotten away from objective redemption, and are in danger of being blind to the fact that evil, even for its own sake, should be rejected. God's wrath is primarily rejection of sin, a walking out on fallen humanity, but he provided his son, his very 'heart', as the only one who could beyond our comprehension cosmically absorb that wrath, allowing humanity to walk back to him and individuals to walk unto him. Other biblical pictures, such as it allowing transformation akin to being adopted, even being spiritually born into God's family, help paint redemption's true landscape.

Selected Carols

From	To
his cradle we stand / So led by light—of a star sweetly gleaming / Here come the wise men from Orient land / The king of kings lay thus in lowly manger / In all our trials born to be our friend / He knows our need, our weakness is no stranger / Behold your king! Before him lowly bend! / Behold your king, Before him lowly bend!	eastern far land / They worshipped Christ—but Herod was not heeding / He was enraged—and God's own son was banned / The king of kings—he then was in grave danger / Against our pride—our guilt and our discord / He knows our need—our weakness is no stranger / Worship your king!—And bow, he is the lord / Worship your king!—and bow, he is the lord.
Truly he taught—us to love one another / His law is love and—his gospel is peace / Chains shall he break—for the slave is our brother / And in his name all oppression shall cease / Sweet hymns of joy in grateful chorus raise we / Let all within—us praise his holy name / Christ is the Lord! O praise his name forever / His power and glory evermore proclaim / His power and glory evermore proclaim.	He came in love—to free us from our slavery / Emancipated—oppression shall cease / Christians unite—and live and love as family / His law is love and his gospel is peace / Sweet hymns of joy—in grateful chorus raise we / May all within us—praise his holy name / Christ is the lord! From earth into eternity / God's love—is now and evermore the same / God's love—is now and evermore the same.

Oh Little Town of Bethlehem[206]

In 1865, Rev. Phillips Brooks (Episcopalian) went to Bethlehem, and three years later wrote a Sunday School Christmas song, for which a friend (Lewis Redner) wrote its tune. Brook's biographer, Rev. Louis Benson, reckoned that the tune sold the lyric. For construction, each stanza has the same weight. Each stanza has 8 lines. Looking at stanza three, typical of all, we can see that Lines 1 & 5 lack rhyme, that L2 & L4 rhyme (given/heaven), that L3 rhymes in itself (imparts/hearts), that L6 & L8 rhyme (sin/in), and that L7 rhymes in itself (will/still). That's a

---

[206]   https://www.carols.org.uk/o_little_town_of_bethlehem.htm. Composed & dropped by Brooks: [*Where children pure and happy / Pray to the blessed Child / Where misery cries out to Thee / Son of the [Undefiled/Mother mild] / Where Charity stands watching / And Faith holds wide the door / The dark night wakes, the glory breaks / And Christmas comes once more.*]

Particulars and Christian Songs

double ABCB¹ sequence in each stanza. Yet for content, the stanzas have different weight.

One stanza (which, incidentally, urged children to pray to a baby Jesus) was challenged. Consequently, Brooks changed a line from [*the Undefiled*] to [*the Mother mild*], to avoid sounding Romanish, then wisely dropped the whole stanza. A far better stanza, *How Silently*, possibly had a young friend, the deaf and blind Helen Keller who had 'always' close to felt God, in mind. A 1903 song book transposed the two halves of stanza 2, an error long righted. Benson was uncertain about whether the carol should be called a hymn, because until the last stanza the singer sings to *Bethlehem*—but carol or hymn, tweaking could make me happy.

Firstly, I'm not happy to sing to a town, especially to a ghost town of history. Obviously, some are. There was this guy, Ernst Anschutz, who wouldn't talk to daisies, yet he affectionately sung to Christmas trees destined for the fire (Is.44:14-7)—much pleasure they didst give him.[207] Call Anschutz a nutter, if you like, but Christmas trees, Christmas towns, is there really much difference between singing to Bethlehem and singing to its trees? Ask no favours of your firs.

Secondly, Phillips Brooks' song has picked up archaism. Of course, the new becomes old, but from the word Go this has had an annualism, whereby the past is imaginatively presented as the present: it's what I call a tardisial song.[208] I would rather sing the lyrics historically, as if looking back on an event, than watch it unfold. Thirdly, its line, *peace to men on earth*, besides showing sageism, is based on a scribal error with Lk.2:14.[209] Fourthly, I jib at asking Jesus himself for anything. True, there are rare critical circumstances

---

[207] I think of a Germany C16 firtree song that picked up the idea of human relationships not staying ever true, ever green. That song eventually became a dubious custom stateside.

[208] A Tardis is sometimes a blue box, bigger inside than out, an acrostic for Time And Relative Dimensions In *Space*, and a fun way to visit the Manger.

[209] Luke wrote *eudokias*, the genitive form, meaning not that it was God giving peace & goodwill, but God giving peace/shalom to those *of* goodwill towards him, the faithful such as Simeon (Lk.2:29-30). My, *The Word's Gone Global*, covers this text more.

Selected Carols

permitted, such as *maranatha*.[210] But to actually ask him *as if he is an infant*, is probably something that even the Blessed Virgin would not have done. Jesus is no baby, though he has been one.

If we ask Jesus, it should at least be asking one who has been a baby, not one who still is. Is it the cute and cuddly fantasy we seek, or the nail printed lord? It gets worse, since the request, if by Christians, is asking him to convert the converted. Ask him no folly. Have we not even the sense of Nicodemus, who gaily joked about his mother rebirthing him (Jhn.3:4)?

On a positive note, as Benson noted, is the line about hopes and fears converging, which is a powerful take on salvation history: at last, God has come when we feared he'd given up on us, though to some it's "the dreadful smell of death and doom" (NLT: 2 Cor.2:16)! Those who loved God hoped he would visit, and feared he would not. Those who hated God hoped he would not visit, and feared he would. In *The Lord of the Rings* (Tolkien 2.3.6.505), "hope and fear bore their thoughts still on, beyond dark mountains to the Land of Shadow", as the pivotal place of world history.

From	To
O little town of Bethlehem / How still we see thee lie! / Above thy deep and dreamless sleep / The silent stars go by. / Yet in thy dark streets shineth / The everlasting Light; / The hopes and fears of all the years / Are met in thee to-night.	Oh little town of Bethlehem / how silently it lay / Above its deep and dreamless sleep / the special light did stay / And in its dark streets God did shine / the everlasting light / the hopes and fears of all the years / were met in it that night.
For Christ is born of Mary / And gathered all above / While mortals sleep, the angels keep / Their watch of wondering love. / O morning stars, together / Proclaim the holy birth; / And praises sing to God the King / And peace to men on earth	For Christ was born of Mary / And gathered all above / While mortals slept, the angels kept / Their watch of wondering love / the heavenly choir together / Proclaimed the holy birth / And they did sing to God the king / and of his peace to earth.

---

[210] If from *marana tha* (invocation), rather than *maran atha* (declaration). In any case, see Rv.22:20.

Particulars and Christian Songs

From	To
How silently, how silently / The wondrous gift is given; / So God imparts to human hearts / The blessings of his heaven. / No ear may hear his coming / But in this world of sin / Where meek souls will receive him still / The dear christ enters in.	How silently, how silently / the wondrous gift was given / So God imparts to human hearts / the blessings of his heaven / No ear can hear his coming / But in this world of sin / Where needy will receive him still / the dear christ enters in.
O holy Child of Bethlehem / Descend to us, we pray! / Cast out our sin and enter in / Be born in us to-day. / We hear the Christmas angels / The great glad tidings tell; / O come to us, abide with us / Our Lord Emmanuel!	The holy one of Bethlehem / is with us to this day / He's cast out sin and entered in / was born in us his way / We can hear the Christmas angels / who glad tidings did tell / He's come to us, to live with us / our lord Emmanuel!

Silent Night[211]

As legend has it, in 1818, Roman Catholic Father Joseph Mohr, an Austrian, wrote the lyrics and a friend (Franz Xaver Gruber) set them to guitar music for Christmas Eve. Why not the organ? Well, that was awaiting repairs. Some say it was sabotaged in order to stop an incoming traditionalist priest from converting the local congregation back into Latin-only mass. Perhaps someone hoped to give more time for an experiment in German-Latin masses to become established? But when the organ repairman arrived, he left with a copy of the song, passed on copies, and it went on a world tour, attributed to an anonymous history within the Austrian state of Tyrol.

This identity, as a "Tyrolean folk carol," was held until the original manuscript was found and identified in 1995. It seems that Mohr, a guitarist, wrote the poem in 1816, and had Gruber give it a guitar tune two years later. Gruber's tune was soon slightly changed, and the song was first published in 1832, and translated several times into English in the C19. The standard English translation (a creative translation) is

---

[211] www.carols.org.uk/silent_night.htm

Selected Carols

John Freeman Young's (1859?). Perhaps the first was J F Warner's, 10 years earlier. Another translation was by Emily Elliot (1858).

Silent Night united English and German sides during the trenches' Christmas Truce of 1914, when many guns were indeed quiet. Most English versions[212] include just three of Mohr's six verses, stanzas 1, 6 and 2, in that order. I have focused on these three. The missing stanzas include reference to Jesus as our curly haired brother. I've switched the historical present to the historical past. I prefer the past indicative (he slept) to an imperative (you sleep). I back away from the idea of visual radiance coming from Jesus in his babyhood.

From	To
Silent night, holy night / All is calm, all is bright / Round yon virgin mother and child / Holy infant so tender and mild / Sleep in heavenly peace / Sleep in heavenly peace.	Silent night, holy night / In the dark—shone God's light / Shining where that mother so mild / Looked upon her holy child / Christ the light of the world—Jesus the light of the world.
Silent night, holy night! / Shepherds quake at the sight / Glories stream from heaven afar / Heavenly hosts sing Alleluia! / Christ, the Saviour is born / Christ, the Saviour is born.	Silent night, holy night / Shepherds quaked—at the sight / Glory streamed from heaven afar / Heavenly angels sang Hallelujah / Christ our saviour was born—Jesus our saviour was born.
Silent night, holy night / Son of God, love's pure light / Radiant beams from thy holy face / With the dawn of redeeming grace / Jesus, Lord, at thy birth / Jesus, Lord, at thy birth.	Silent night, holy night / Gift of heaven—oh how bright / Shone God's love through that pure infant's face / With the dawn of redeeming grace / Christ was lord at his birth—Jesus was lord at his birth.

---

[212] I looked at over 24 on http://silentnight.web.za/translate/eng.htm. All had tardisial elements.

Book Conclusion

It should be clear that some songs I love, some I loathe, with a great many more in-between. Even some non-Christian, nontheistic, secular songs, speak to my heart and offer me wisdom. Songs are part of human history, sometimes reflecting something beyond space and time. At the right time, intervening in history, one from beyond the stars became one with us: "no one has ever gone to heaven and returned. But the Son of Man has come down from heaven" (NLT: Jhn.3:13).[213] Thus, best insights of transcendence are christologically based, though not christologically limited: deity is more than Christ, who is the truth about it. Christianity is key, God's key to us.

Yet even the best of songs are not in essence worship, though they can work alongside biblical worship. The worst of songs work against biblical worship: heresies within the church have been aided by heretical songs, and pagans have sung to idols. The best songs will see Christ, not as the End, but as the Way to the father, whom he died to make known. To the extent that the father is not known, Jesus has failed. If we sing that Jesus alone is God, it is his failure we see, not his glory.

Father and son go together in defining eternal life now (Jhn.17:3), the steak on the plate while we wait. They who would worship God the father, must know God the son, and must be able not to confuse the two: biblical worship has a learning curve. They must be able to worship the father at the deep level of their spirit, and at the level of reality—in fact of transreality, transcendency, beyondness, the revelation of God in Christ. Jesus used the word *alēthinos* (Jhn.4:24) to indicate the reality of the new covenant, the new reality that had dawned with his arrival—his light. He was and is the *alēthinos*.

Truth is powerful, and extends into the Transreal.[214] Truth is important, and I have sought to highlight that songs are powerful, and potentially rich in spiritual value. This is why we ought to invest

---

[213] A unique reading, uniquely right.

[214] I picture the space-time continuum as reality, that which is above as transreality, and that which is below (fantasy) as subreality. As J R R Tolkien said, man is a subcreator under the creator.

Book Conclusion

time and effort into their wellbeing, so that they will be a rich blessing to us, not a dark curse. Even at a social level, songs such as the Beatles' *Hey Jude* can help the shy to open up to a richer world, and (less commonly) a few like Abba's *Angel Eyes* are warning songs of the selfish advantages some will take to our disadvantage, of the dangers of being too trusting in a too faithless world: they can teach us prudence, self-protection, not to open up to the big bad wolf, yet to open to the good. But songs neither please God nor petrify the devil.

That said, spiritual warfare will be better if we are built up by good songs (Jude 1:20). And spiritual worship can be enhanced by songs. They can also be useful in evangelism, and what some call pre-evangelism. On the other hand, singing folly about the saviour will not make one wise unto salvation. And singing a false gospel will not profit our spirits. Against a multimillion-dollar industry, there should be many voices attacking the un-attackable, the mûmakil. I have tried to be one such voice, one small step for the church.

Prayer is a general given for Christians, indeed for most theists. Many songs are either prayer songs or have prayer splattered in them to the point of negation. Therefore I have looked at types of prayer, as well as the persons to whom we should pray. As a trinitarian, I have tried to fit prayer type to deity person, to cultivate a Christian instinct in line with the better part of the Athanasian Creed. In particular I have stressed the idea of Father First, as right in itself and as an antidote to the Jesus Only mentality increasingly in songs. Even songs from high places can mislead: as Charles Spurgeon put it, "salvation comes not from the hills" (www.spurgeongems.org/vols61-63/chs3546.pdf).

There are a lot of silly, downright bad things all too common in Christian (and non-Christian) songs. Over decades I have evolved my own private list of problems. Feeling that it might be high time to share them, I began this book, and consequently for a few years, ran www.lyricology.eu. Here, I have tried to point out a number of lesser and greater dangers, putting a number of songs (including Christmas carols) under my microscope. My lens has its problems. No system can be definitive, but they can be suggestive, and hopefully helpful. If only one warning is heeded, and I substantially help even one person as a Christian should, then my writing has not been in vain.

But that has not been my main aim. Rather, by flagging up objections to a good many songs that have done, or are doing, the rounds, I would to God that the whole process of managing songs would move to being more consensus than copyright. Why on earth must we only pass on the *paradosis*, the tradition, which has simply been penned by an errant believer? Their words are fallible—yes, so too are mine (let the prophets judge). They have not jotted down new additions for the Bible, which are too holy to be challenged and changed.

We should not face a straight dichotomy of love us or leave us. A Christian approach to copyright should allow us an easy, free, and open way to be critical allies of the songsmiths. My book, offered as wonder and critical education, might produce better informed allies for them. I don't wish to leave Christian songs; I wish to love them. Christ loves the church as his bride, in spite of her blemishes which he aims to sort out.

At the end of the day, songsmiths are our servants, not our masters. Let us help them help us, thus fulfilling the command to help each another. *When I was younger, so much younger than today, I never thought I needed anybody's help in any way. But now those days are gone, I'm not so self-assured, now I find I've changed my mind and opened up the doors. So won't you please, please help me?*[215] We can all do with a little bit of help from our friends. Feedback on this book can help me to improve my idea for the common good, and that is what I seek.

Gloria in excelsis Deo

---

[215] It seems that John Lennon really meant these words back in '65.

Books cited:

Tokunboh Adeyemo's *Africa Bible Commentary*: 2006
David Allen's *There is a River*: 2004
Jane Austen's *Pride and Prejudice*: 1980
Karl Barth's *Fragments Grave and Gay*: 1976
R D Blackmore's *Lorna Doone*: 1995
Leonardo Boff and Clodovis Boff's *Introducing Liberation Theology*: 2000
Henry Bett's *The Hymns of Methodism*: 1954
D A Carson's *Jesus and His Friends*: 1986
D A Carson's *A Call to Spiritual Reformation*: 1992
D A Carson's *The Gagging of God*: 1996
D A Carson's *The Inclusive Language Debate*: 1998
Owen Chadwick's *History of Christianity*: 1995
Chant and Pratney's *The Return*: 1988
Philip Comfort's *Complete Guide to Bible Versions*: 1991
Brenda Cox' *Fashionable Goodness*: 2022
Howard Ervin's *These Are Not Drunken*: 1968
Gordon Fee's *Listening to the Spirit in the Text*: 2000
Anthony Flew's *There is a God*: 2007
W H C Frend's *The Early Church*: 1998
Getty and Getty's *Sing!*: 2017
Wayne Grudem's *Systematic Theology*: 1994
Craig Hawkins' *Witchcraft*: 2000
Christopher Idle's *Hymns in Today's Language*: 1982
R T Kendall's *Meekness and Majesty*: 1992
Kenneth Kitchen's *On the Reliability of the OT*: 2003
Andreas Köstenberger's *John* (BECNT): 2004
Robert Letham's *The Holy Trinity*: 2004
C S Lewis' *Voyage to Venus*: 1971
C S Lewis' *The Screwtape Letters*: 1975

C S Lewis' *Till We Have Faces*: 1980
C S Lewis' *Christian Reflections*: 1981
C S Lewis' *The Silver Chair*: 1985
C S Lewis' *Mere Christianity*: 2002
Alister McGrath's *In the Beginning*: 2001
Elmer Martens' *God's Design*: 1994
Richard J Mouw and Mark A Noll's *Wonderful Words of Life*: 2004
Nick Page's *And Now Let's Move into a Time of Nonsense*: 2004
Geoffrey Parrinder's *Africa's Three Religions*: 1969
R S Pine-Coffin's *Augustine's Confessions*: 1973
Prime and Begg's *On Being a Pastor*: 2004
Alan Richardson's *An Introduction to the Theology of the NT*: 1958
Gail Riplinger's *New Age Bible Versions*: 1994:
William Shakespeare's *The Taming of the Shrew*
Stevenson and Frend's *A New Eusebius*: 1999
J R R Tolkien's *The Lord of the Rings*: 1997
George Tyrrell's *Lex Orandi*: 1903
Geoffrey W Bromiley's *Kittel and Friedrich's Theological Dictionary of the NT (abridged)*: 1985
Willem VanGemeren's *New International Dictionary of OT Theology and Exegesis*: 2001
Keith Warrington's *Pentecostal Perspectives*: 1998
Mark Yarhouse's *Understanding Gender Dysphoria*: 2015
Frances Young's *The Making Of The Creeds*: 1991

Selective Index

A

Abraham, 11, 72, 100, 101, 166
Ambrose of Milan, 17
anthrodirectionalism, 118, 123, 125, 126
Arius, 39, 145, 166
Athanasian Creed, 51, 59, 60, 61, 64, 112, 114, 179
Athanasius, 17, 145
Augustine of Hippo, 17, 36, 41, 63, 81, 145

B

Booth, William, 21, 82
Bowater, Chris, 58, 71, 117
Brewster, Lincoln, 50, 99

C

Calvin, John, 20, 159
Cho, Yonggi, 65, 66, 72
Christmas, 91, 92, 119, 137, 146, 159, 160, 161, 167, 170, 171, 173, 174, 176, 177, 179
Clement of Alexandria, 17, 19
copyright, 37, 146, 147, 148, 149, 180
correctivism (political), 36, 44, 151

D

decontextualism, 106, 136, 137, 138, 145, 146, 152, 157
demons, 28, 33, 93, 107, 111
Dominus Factor, 114, 115

E

egodirectionalism, 33, 118, 123, 126, 130, 134
Erasmus, 20
eschatology, 10, 35, 65, 69, 83, 85, 87, 105, 129, 157
Ethnic Israel/Jew(s), 11, 12, 13, 14, 15, 19, 26, 29, 30, 106, 108, 119, 137, 167, 168, 171
evangelism, 21, 23, 35, 41, 43, 44, 62, 74, 82, 83, 86, 89, 92, 106, 144, 151, 170, 179

G

Global Israel, 15, 19, 30, 76, 167
glossolalia, 13, 23, 82
God the father, 19, 22, 30, 33, 34, 37, 39, 47, 48, 49, 50, 52, 53, 55, 56, 57, 58, 59, 60, 61, 62, 63, 64, 65, 66, 67, 68, 69, 71, 72, 73, 74, 75, 76, 77, 82, 83, 85, 86, 87, 88, 90, 95, 100, 101, 102, 103, 108, 112, 113, 114, 115, 116, 117, 120, 121, 128, 133, 138,

148, 152, 153, 154, 156, 157, 161, 162, 164, 167, 168, 172, 174, 175, 177, 178, 179
God the son, 15, 16, 17, 22, 28, 29, 30, 32, 33, 34, 35, 37, 39, 42, 47, 48, 49, 50, 52, 53, 56, 57, 58, 59, 60, 61, 62, 63, 64, 65, 66, 67, 68, 69, 71, 72, 73, 74, 75, 76, 77, 83, 85, 86, 87, 88, 89, 91, 92, 94, 96, 99, 100, 102, 103, 104, 105, 106, 108, 109, 112, 113, 115, 116, 120, 121, 128, 133, 138, 146, 152, 153, 154, 168
God the spirit, 13, 15, 23, 25, 30, 33, 34, 38, 41, 42, 48, 49, 50, 52, 53, 54, 58, 59, 60, 61, 62, 63, 64, 65, 66, 67, 68, 69, 70, 71, 72, 73, 74, 75, 76, 77, 78, 82, 83, 88, 101, 102, 103, 112, 113, 114, 115, 116, 117, 118, 134, 138, 139, 152, 154, 155, 156, 157, 158, 159, 168, 172, 178
God's name, 47, 48, 60, 86, 87, 131
Gregory the Great (pope), 17, 18, 164

H

Hewitt, Garth, 12
Hillsong, 26, 60, 86, 88
   Morgan, Reuben, 86, 142
   Zschech, Darlene, 40, 88, 138
holiness, 12, 20, 27, 42, 137, 146
Hugo, Victor, 80

I

Idle, Chris/Reform, 10, 26, 34, 48, 52, 81, 102, 103, 134
Islam/Muslims, 91, 101, 107, 110, 112

J

Jerome, 17, 166

K

Kay, William K, 38
Kendrick, Graham, 22, 32, 33, 45, 79, 81, 82, 83, 111

L

Levites, 26, 27
Luther, Martin, 20, 21, 24, 41, 54, 106

M

MacDonald, George, 33, 126
Mark, Robin, 85, 119
millennialism, 35
misdirectionism, 71, 114, 152, 154, 157
misvisualisationism, 112, 114, 115, 116, 117, 120, 128, 145, 146, 152
   hard, 111, 153
   hyper, 128
   soft, 110, 116, 117, 120, 122, 128
Moody & Sankey, 21

N

Nicea, 51, 63, 166

P

patripassianism, 64, 72, 116, 128, 133

Paul (Apostle), 13, 14, 15, 22, 23, 25, 27, 29, 31, 39, 44, 57, 58, 59, 60, 65, 66, 68, 82, 113, 114, 116, 120, 122, 130, 131, 133, 134, 139, 142, 157, 159

Pliny the Younger, 16, 29, 43, 137

polydirectionalism, 49, 85, 88, 118, 120, 122, 123, 124, 125, 127, 128, 153, 154, 155

polytheism, 106, 107, 152, 153

praise, 12, 14, 15, 17, 22, 27, 29, 31, 34, 44, 50, 69, 70, 71, 77, 83, 87, 88, 89, 98, 115, 118, 119, 125, 126, 129, 130, 131, 132, 133, 134, 135, 136, 145, 146, 152, 168, 173

prayer, 12, 26, 37, 45, 46, 47, 51, 53, 54, 55, 56, 57, 58, 68, 69, 71, 77, 83, 89, 92, 95, 112, 114, 115, 116, 117, 120, 122, 123, 125, 126, 127, 129, 135, 136, 137, 146, 152, 155, 158, 167, 174, 176, 179

R

Redman, Matt & Beth, 104, 133
relativism/subjectivism, 23
ritual, 26, 27, 28

S

Sabellius/Sabellianism, 60, 145, 155

Satan, 29, 30, 32, 57, 94, 163, 169

Simon & Garfunkel, 36, 165

Sinai/Sinaitic, 13, 18, 19, 26, 28, 30

Smith, Martin, 27, 50, 130

Spener, Philip, 20, 21

spiritual warfare, 32, 34, 179

Spurgeon, Charles H, 37, 179

T

Tertullian of Carthage, 16, 50, 64, 83

thanks, 29, 68, 69, 70, 71, 77, 88, 144

The Promised Land, 76, 168

The Salvation Army, 19, 21

theodirectionalism, 51, 54, 118, 123, 125, 126, 153

Townend, Stuart, 155, 156

trinity/trinitarianism, 26, 47, 48, 50, 51, 52, 53, 54, 58, 59, 60, 61, 62, 63, 64, 65, 69, 71, 77, 83, 84, 86, 88, 112, 113, 114, 128, 138, 145, 153, 156, 179

U

unidirectionalism, 54, 85, 118, 123, 124

unitarianism, 49, 51, 52, 53, 54, 59, 60, 74, 95, 112, 128, 152, 153, 179
  hard, 16, 50, 52, 64, 86, 104, 112, 113, 128, 152, 157
  soft, 50, 60, 62, 112, 113, 152, 156

W

Watts, Isaac, 15, 21, 35, 91, 124, 160, 162, 163
Wesley, John & Charles, 21, 22, 35, 36, 65, 92, 93, 102, 159, 160, 161, 163
westernism, 40, 58, 63, 102, 103, 109, 110
worship, 10, 13, 14, 15, 17, 19, 25, 26, 27, 28, 29, 30, 33, 36, 38, 40, 46, 48, 51, 52, 59, 64, 65, 71, 73, 77, 81, 89, 94, 103, 104, 110, 123, 126, 130, 133, 135, 136, 137, 138, 141, 142, 153, 178, 179
worship leaders, 25, 26
Wycliffe, John, 20, 114, 147

Y

Yahweh, 11, 12, 13, 19, 26, 28, 29, 37, 40, 45, 48, 49, 52, 60, 72, 75, 76, 86, 87, 90, 92, 99, 101, 106, 109, 111, 112, 118, 119, 124, 125, 129, 130, 131, 133, 136, 137, 138, 148, 156, 157, 162

Z

Zwingli, Ulrich, 20, 21

Like or loathe any of my books? Please feedback to Amazon.

Books by this Author
Theology

Israel's Gone Global

Israel's Gone Global traces salvation through the term, Israel. Was the covenant with the people-nation of Yakob-Yisrael, crossed out? How eternal is covenant? To examine that, we examine marriage. Can a covenant partner be truly divorced? Has Yeshua-Yisrael mediated a spiritual covenant with a spiritual Israel? Is evangelism of ethnic Jews needless, a priority, or neither?

No one could have everlasting life but for the cross, but has it always been globally accessible? Might any who die as Atheists, Hindus, or Islamists, make heaven? And is eternal life joyful? Is everlasting life fun?

Tackling the question of people who die in infancy (or as adults who never heard the gospel), we consider whether it is fair if only those who don't die in infancy get a chance of eternal damnation (if infant universalism), or alone get a chance of eternal heaven (if infant damnation). Does predilectionism make best sense of biblical revelation?

Opportunities to enjoy eternal life spring from the new covenant—reasons to rejoice. But what about salvation history before that covenant?

∞

Singing's Gone Global

Singing's Gone Global, briefly explores the background of singing, before and into ancient Israel. It examines the impact songs have on those who sing, and on those who listen, touching on spiritual warfare. It looks at how nonsense songs neither make sense to evangelism, nor to the evangelised, and asks, "Is there a mûmak in the room?"

Oddly some songwriters simply misunderstand prayer. Part two covers the basics of the trinity, focusing on the spirit in order to understand types of prayer (eg request, gratitude, adoration, chat), leading in turn to a better understanding of our heavenly father, our brother, our helper, and ourselves in Christ's likeness.

Next we look at some common problems. Part three focuses on problems such as buddyism, decontextualising, misvisualisation, and unitarianism. Diagnosis can help Christ's 'bride' to recover from suboptimal and unbiblical songs (Eph.5:18-30).

Giving a Problem Avoidance Grade (PAG)—an A+ to Unsatisfactory scale—in part four we examine specific songs. Weapons forged (Part three), the mûmakil can be attacked, seeking to save and be saved.

Subsequently the book concludes by showing how Christmas carols may be tweaked to better serve our weary world, rejoicing that joy to the world has come.

∞

The Word's Gone Global

The Word's Gone Global, examines Bible text (trusted by early Islam) and introduces textual critique. It looks at the Eastern Orthodox Bible and the Latin Vulgate. Did the Reformation improve text and translation? Were Wycliffe, Tyndale, and Martin, helpful?

Why did the New International Version begin, and why does it enrage? Why did complementarians Don Carson and Wayne Grudem, clash? Is marketing hype between formal and functional equivalence, meaningless? Which version or versions should you regularly read?

In English-speaking circles, Broughton wished to burn Bancroft's King James Version, yet many KJV proponents—think Gail Riplinger and Peter Ruckman—wish to burn all alternatives. More heat than light?

Grade Charts cover 30+ English versions on issues such as God's name, God's son's deity, marriage, gender terms, anti-polytheism, and various issues in John's Gospel. No, Tyndale was not 'born again'. No, John was not antisemitic. No, he did not disagree with the other Gospels.

∞

Books by this Author

Prayer's Gone Global

Prayer's Gone Global, begins with ancient civilisations and prayer (the Common Level). Then it narrows into Ancient Israel and prayer (the Sinai Level). Then it deepens and widens into Global Israel and prayer (the Christian Level). Deity is revealed as trinity: Sabellians mislead.

Relating to the trinity includes the Holy Spirit. We should of course work with him, but should we worship him, complain to him, chat with him? Above the spirit stands the often forgotten father—oh let Jesusism retire.

Authority is another issue. Are we authorised to decree and declare? Is binding and loosing actually prayer, or is it evangelism? Is it biblical never to command miracles? Do we miss out on the supernatural which Jesus modelled for us, too fearful of strange fire to offer holy fire?

You can freshen up your prayer life—ride the blessed camel, not the gnats. Listen to Saint Anselm pray, and C S Lewis and 'Malcolm' discuss prayer, and be blessed.

∞

Revelation's Gone Global

Revelation's Gone Global, is a telling of John's future, as if by a then contemporary named Sonafets speaking to his church about how John's apocalyptic scroll related to their days, and about what was still future to John.

Encouragement is a big theme. Roman persecution was an unpredictable beast which ferociously lashed out here and there—what church or Christian was safe? But God stood behind the scenes, allowing but limiting their enemy, and messiah walked among the churches, lights to the world.

Victory lay neither with Rome nor demons, but with God, and with the warrior lamb who had been slain. Victory was guaranteed, and would finally be enjoyed.

Exhortation was given to believers, to play their part while on the mortal stage. They were to walk in the light, and not to let the show down by straying.

Angels of power, actively working out God's will, far exceed the puny forces against God and his church. His wrath was not pleasant, but could be redemptive until the new age begins.

C S Lewis' essay, The World's Last Night, is briefly examined to enjoin a calm awareness of the ongoing battle we are in, and the brightness to come when the king returns.

∞

The Father's Gone Global

Focusing from God as father, to the specific person of God the father, The Father's Gone Global looks at the biblical parent/child pattern from Genesis, through Sinai, and into the Church.

Abba as a new covenant word expresses deep filial affection even under deep anguish in our Gethsemane battles. Coming through God's belovèd son, it speaks into the church and into our lives.

Though to many the 'forgotten father', human parents/fathers should 'put on' God the father, and his children should 'put on' his son. We forget him to our cost.

Human applications aside, what is the Eternal Society? Is filial relationship modelled by God the son incarnate? Are we to be always obedient to our father and guided by the spirit?

Eschatologically the father will be supreme, but even now he is the one to whom the son points. Christian life should relate to God our father, God our brother, and God our helper, prioritising the father.

Renewal of the church is vital for our confused world, but renewal which downplays the father falls short of the good news which Christ created and the spirit circulates. May this book play its part.

Books by this Author

∞

Salvation Now and Life Beyond

Salvation Now, divides the doctrine of salvation into the four main levels of common humanity, the old covenant, the new covenant, and life beyond.

A big weight is put on the term, Israel, as God's master plan. This too has four levels, meaning a man, a people, a new man, and a new people, respectively.

Various ideas of what Christianity, the new covenant for the new people, is good for, and how we get into it and best enjoy it, are examined, and a faith-based inexclusivism is suggested.

Everlasting life is seen as the ultimate goal of salvation, universal meaningfulness and love beyond all fears and pains.

∞

Revisiting The Challenging Counterfeit

Revisiting The Challenging Counterfeit, is an extended review of Raphael Gasson's 'The Challenging Counterfeit' (1966). Raphael was an ethnic Jew whose spiritual journey included many years as a Christian Spiritualist minister.

Today, when psychic phenomena captures the imagination and the bank accounts of popular media, it is useful to unearth the witness of one who had well worn the T-shirt of a medium with pride, only to bury it in unholy ground as a thing of shame and of sorrow and of wasted time.

Challengingly, his book exposes what true Spiritualism is. He had nothing but high praise for Spiritualists, and deep condemnation for Spiritualism. For he had discovered true Spiritualism to be itself a fake of true Spirituality, a mere Counterfeit that, in deposing death in the mind, enthroned it in the soul.

Counterfeit phenomena covered include apparitions, Rescue Work and haunted houses, materialisation of pets, psychic healing, Lyceums, clairvoyance, and OOBEs—to name but a few. This book surveys his exposé of Spiritualism's offer of fascinating fish bait, false food falling short of real food for the soul. Though it takes issue with

Books by this Author

Raphael on a number of points, his core insights are powerful and timely, helping us to avoid—or escape from—a Challenging Counterfeit, and to discover true spiritual currency.

∞

Revisiting The Pilgrim's Progress

Revisiting The Pilgrim's Progress, is a re-dreaming of John Bunyan's most famous dream. An ex-serviceman and ex-jailbird, he found fortune, freedom, and fans worldwide.

This dream journey is substantially Bunyan's from this world, and into that which is to come. It is not a fun story, but it has lots of danger, and joy, and reflection on some big life themes.

Profoundly, sinners who become pilgrims become saints. But that can make life more difficult. One big question is, Is it worth it? One big temptation is, Turn back or turn aside. And if you see others do so, that makes it harder not to. Bunyan was tempted. And he discovered that not deserting, can lead to despair. But he also discovered a key to liberty.

Pre-eminently, it is a story of grace which many follow. Grace begins the journey, helps along the way, and brings the story to a happily ever after. Are all fairy stories based on heaven?

∞

Fantasy

The Simbolinian Files

From Simboliniad, a crystal planet long gone, came the vampire race, the wapierze, thelodynamic shapeshifters seeking blood. Most oppose Usen, King of the Light, so side with the Necros. Seldom do the Guardians intervene. These files, secretly secured from various insider sources, reveal something of what they have done, and will do.

∞

Vampire Redemption

Artificial intelligence, created by superpowers to save man, questions man's worth, and becomes The Beast. Escaping into the wild, many discover a wilderness infested by zombies and diabolical spirits. Who will help? Father Doyle? He's tied up with the mysterious Lilith.

Tariq? He's tied up with Wilma. Can the bigoted old exorcist deliver him from evil?

Radical problems can require radical solutions. But does man really need hobs, elves, and the more ancient of days? In the surrounding shadows, vampires and demons form an alliance, raising the stakes against Whitby and Tyneside. Powerful vampires live shrouded within Whitby, speaking of life beyond this galaxy. Is salvation in the stars? Is Sunniva, the despised woman of Alban, worth dying for? Big questions, needing big answers. Not even Guardian Odin can foretell man's fate and, as silent stars go by, one little town must awake from its dreams.

Though The Beast slumbers purposeless and undisturbed, in the far west a global giant slowly opens its yellow eyes and threatens to smother the earth in fire and ice. There is one chance only.

∞

Vampire Extraction

Bitterly long their imprisoned spirits lay, fast bound to Earth's drowsy decay. To the Simbolinian race, there was no hell on Earth, for Earth was hell, and Usen the cosmic jailer. Was it so surprising that as vampires they stalked Usen's children for blood? Most chose the Kingdom of Night, wary of both the Kingdom of Necros and the Kingdom of Dawn.

As queen of the Night, Lilith's story streams through the summer sands of Sumer, and through the green woods of Sherwood. It flags up both dishonour and joy, and cuts across the paths of Ulrica the Saxon and Robin the Hood, as tyrannies rise and fall in merry England. Bigotry seldom has a good word to say about Usen, nor about mercy. Reluctantly, Lilith examines what it means to show mercy, to show weakness. Wulfgar had enslaved Ulrica: is it mercy to let her burn; should mercy have spared Lona? Could Hamashiach turn daughter into sister? Could Count Dracula be turned from his madness? Has Draven really betrayed his mother? Life has many questions.

Tales picture ideas, letting us walk through the eyes of others to better see ourselves. This story exposes subplots behind common history. How these chronicles came to be written up is, in the spirit confidentiality, not for the public eye. What truth is within you must judge. Discrimination is a gift from Beyond, from which the words still echo: mercy is better than sacrifice. Indeed, mercy can be sacrifice. Judge well.

∞

Vampire Count

Vampires were not always earthbound, nor are all evil, but being victims of Usen's Eighth Law, his Children became their fair game. Yet the Night Kingdom was divided: some veered to the Necros; some to the Dawn. Who was wrong; who was right?

Long ago one incited his people to racial violence against elven and human kinds. Ever he strove to be king of the Night, and unto Necuratu the Dark Lord he gave the dragon shape. He made war upon the ancient Middle East, even the Nephilim War. Against him the Light raised flood and division.

At last his own people, paying the price of his rampage, bound him in deep sleep. Yet the millennia seemed meaningless to him: even the rising of Hamashiach hardly disturbed his dreams. At last awoken, he and his brides stalked the hills of Transylvania. Only the fear of Lilith—and after her unforgivable sin, Queen Rangda—chained their bloodlust.

Dracula sought escape and autonomy. By cunning and devious means, he immigrated to London via Whitby. Pursuit followed swiftly, with a shadowminder helping a circle of human headhunters, though they sought the death of all vampires.

∞

Vampire Grail

Wulfgar is a vampire, a thelodynamic creature from another galaxy, now locked into our world by one called the Cosmic Jailer. He hides a tormenting secret from his queen, Lilith, which the Necros use as blackmail. She will only go so far with the Necros against Hamashiach—Wulfgar must go further.

Unknown to the Darkness, to bury Hamashiach is to plant the Light. From the buried seed springs life, and humanity must reimagine itself. Longinus turns to The Way, the nexus of the Seventh Age. His spear goes on a special mission to the island of Briton, where Wulfgar lives again.

Logres is centred on Avalon, but raises up Arthur, a man of mixed race, to carry its flag and to protect against the Saxons. But its main enemy is the Darkness, which ever seeks to extinguish the Light it hates and fears.

Finally, it seems as if the Darkness has won, and the dark ages descend. But does the Light not shine in the Darkness? Must Wulfgar remain in the Night?

∞

Vampire Shadows

Dark vampires, hidden within the ancient empire of Khem, fall out with the king who, stirred up by the Necros, enslaves the Sheep People. But Iahveh, the shepherd-divinity, is stirred up, and stirs up a hidden hero to force a way out.

Apprehensively the two vampire-magicians join the Sheep of Iahveh, on their long and deadly trek in search of a promised land. Can any survive?

Warily they ask deep questions. Is Usen evil, as prejudice says? Is he possibly a good jailer? Are his unusual regulations, meaningful? They risk ending up in death.

Neverendingly the Sheep's sorry story drags out in interminable peregrination. Weary of wandering, most would settle for some green pastures and untroubled waters. But as they well know, that would take a miracle.

www.ingramcontent.com/pod-product-compliance
Lightning Source LLC
Chambersburg PA
CBHW071500040426
42444CB00008B/1426